D1011050

QUALITY
PROCESS
MANAGEMENT

QUALITY
PROCESS
MANAGEMENT

GABRIEL A. PALL

PRENTICE-HALL, INC., *Englewood Cliffs, New Jersey 07632*

Library of Congress Cataloging-in-Publication Data

Pall, Gabriel A.
    Quality process management.

    Bibliography: p.
    Includes index.
        1. Process control.   2. Quality control.
3. Factory management.   I. Title.
TS157.P35   1988   658.5   86-25552
ISBN 0-13-745027-3

Editorial/production supervision and
    interior design: TKM Productions
Cover design: 20/20 Services, Inc.
Manufacturing buyer: Rhett Conklin

Material on pages 158-160 is adapted from *General System Theory* by L. von Bertalanffy
by permission of George Braziller, Inc., New York.
Material on pages 12-16, 19-40, 48-50, 60, 66-67, 80-83, 91-92 is adapted
by permission from *Process Control, Capability and Improvement* by W. J. Schultz
© by International Business Machines Corporation.

Printed in the United States of America

10 9 8 7 6 5 4 3

ISBN 0-13-745027-3 025

Prentice-Hall International (UK) Limited, *London*
Prentice-Hall of Australia Pty. Limited, *Sydney*
Prentice-Hall of Canada Inc., *Toronto*
Prentice-Hall Hispanoamericana, S.A., *Mexico*
Prentice-Hall of India Private Limited, *New Delhi*
Prentice-Hall of Japan, Inc., *Tokyo*
Prentice-Hall of Southeast Asia Pte. Ltd., *Singapore*
Editora Prentice-Hall do Brasil, Ltda., *Rio de Janeiro*

CONTENTS

2 Prevention: Managing Intent   48

3 Control: Managing the Outcome   84

Part II MANAGEMENT FUNDAMENTALS   145

4 The Process   145

5 The Management System for Quality   171

Part III EXCELLENCE THROUGH PROCESS MANAGEMENT   195

6 Process Management Implementation   195

7 Case Study in Quality Management   228

FOREWORD

Today, our nation's number-one policy issue is the economic competitiveness of our industry and society. We have seen over the years a deterioration of our productivity increases compared to that of our trading partners, and a worsening of our already negative trade balance, even in high-technology industries. Moreover, high quality is too many times no longer associated with U.S. products, even in the perception of U.S. consumers. One can only question what effect this has on the profitability of our industry sectors and on their survival. In contrast, Japan, which before World War II had a poor reputation for quality, has used it as the single-most important criteria in its drive to become one of the foremost industrial countries of the free world.

Quality, like productivity, did not suddenly get worse in the United States. Quality has not necessarily been on the decline; in most sectors of our industry, it has continued to improve. But the rate of improvement has not been sufficient to satisfy increasingly demanding requirements of products and expectations of customer demands, nor has it kept abreast of significant gains made by foreign competitors.

One major reason for this state of affairs is a heritage of the past: American industry in its heyday took the approach of dissecting its operation into elements, each one finely tuned and optimized. What has been lost in the process is the concern for and the management of the total operation. Suboptimization at the component level has jeopardized the total performance. In this process, quality became a component part, with its own rationale, its own purveyors and promoters, and subject to its own justification and profit contribution. This, coupled with the drive for short-term results and a concern for the quarterly report, made us neglect long-term goals and strategies. When labor cost increased in the United States, companies went overseas without regard to quality, responsiveness, or the impact on the total enterprise, its product line, and service.

Fortunately, these are not universal truths, and all is not bleak. More and more businesses in all industries are rethinking their practices and approaches. There is certainly no single issue more important than the quality of our nation's products.

Gabriel Pall's book, *Quality Process Management*, is timely and focuses on quality and quality management from a process viewpoint. It considers quality as a management tool, a financial tool, and a motivator for the whole enterprise. Through examples, Pall clearly shows that quality can contribute to competitiveness and profitability—rather than being an incurred cost, as has been erroneously asserted. *Quality Process Management* is primarily intended for managers who can avail themselves of quality as an overarching motivator and management tool. It is hoped that it is also a treatise that can profitably be used in university and college curricula.

Historically, quality has not been viewed as a subject worthy of academic research or teaching. Just as manufacturing has not been a topic of great academic concern, quality topics—which include statistical methods, probability distributions, sampling techniques, and inspection procedures—were only sparingly discussed and never effectively integrated in our scientific and engineering curricula.

These concepts and tools must certainly be taught to every engineering graduate. Equally important is their inclusion in the business administration courses and management schools, and in all studies that bear on engineering, manufacturing, and management of organizations in general, because the concepts, tools, and techniques described are equally applicable to the service sector, offices, government operations, banks, insurance companies, and other suppliers of services.

ERICH BLOCH
Director, National Science Foundation

PREFACE

This book is about the successful management of quality.

Social and economic progress increasingly depend on the quality of products and services provided by business and government. These products and services, in turn, are the result of a variety of organized work *processes*. Such processes, whether they occur in manufacturing plants, engineering laboratories, hospitals, restaurants, or gas stations, always comprise some combination of inanimate resources and, most importantly, people. People are the key to performing the work process and, therefore, to its ability to meet quality expectations and objectives. If there is a quality problem, it is ultimately a people problem; thus, the management of quality must, above all, focus on the motivation and commitment of people.

Survival in the business world and the viability of any enterprise have two fundamental prerequisites: *competitiveness* and *profitability*. The two go together; no one can stay in business too long without being both competitive and profitable. The purpose of this work is to show that, if well managed, quality can contribute to both. Quality is not only free; it pays handsome dividends to those who prudently invest in it.

Initiating and implementing change and the prudent investment of resources — human, financial, and material—for a stated objective is what management is all about. Management is a beginning-to-end, cradle-to-grave process. So is the management of quality—from objective setting to the final outcome.

Therefore, I reject the narrower view that treats quality management primarily as a control problem. Traditional quality improvement and quality control approaches have always focused on outcome, that is, the end result of a process. This approach has long been used in technology-related areas, such as product development and manufacturing. My view is that in managing quality the entire work process must be focused on; that is, both *intent* and *outcome* must be within the scope of quality management.

Managing intent involves the requirements phase, planning and design for quality, as well as planning and managing investments in such quality-related areas as prevention and error avoidance. Managing the outcome comprises the traditional quality assurance and control methodologies, but it also includes recently developed techniques of defect detection and removal, as well as the continued management of the process through the cost of quality and the return on investments made in prevention at the outset of the process.

The idea of compiling a book on quality management originated during a series of presentations and lectures I prepared based on the real-life management experience of planning and implementing the quality improvement program at IBM Sterling Forest (which I shared with management and professional audiences, both in and outside IBM, in the years 1982–1985). During these sessions, it became clear to me that, while considerable material is available on theory and abstract approaches to quality improvement, managers are still confused and apprehensive as to (1) what is the definition of quality best suited for management purposes, (2) how to manage quality in practical terms, and (3) what to expect in the end. Too many lectures ended with the question from the audience: "What do I do when I get back to the office?"

A number of outstanding texts and presentations on the subject of quality are presently available—books for professionals in quality control; manuals for designers of experiments or statistical control systems; texts for educators who need a comprehensive coverage of theory, or for administrators and managers who only want an "executive level" introduction to the subject. However, there is a clear need for material to help practicing professionals and managers who are responsible for the implementation and success of quality improvement and who want to understand the consequences and implications—even possible pitfalls—of their actions.

From this perspective, *Quality Process Management* should fill a gap in the available literature. It aims to take the management approach to assuring both quality and profitability. I believe that managers or executives of any organization or function can take practical and consistent measures not only to improve their quality but also their competitiveness and profitability. Not only can they prevent errors, whether these be in the information systems area or in such practical concerns as misplaced luggage at airports, erroneous customer bills, or stale food in vending machines; they can also increase the satisfaction of their customers, the productivity of the users of their products and services, and the cost effectiveness of their own business.

The key concepts and means of making quality management a success are laid out in this book. It is, then, prepared primarily for executives and line managers who face the practical task of introducing and implementing an effective quality improvement program in their own organizations. It is not an educational text but rather a basic guide to the management of quality through the continuing application of process management techniques. Since we are also concerned with the management of outcome, it also addresses certain basic concepts related to the theory of quality control. Thus it should also help educators structure a course on the fundamentals of process management and related statistical methods—and hopefully to stimulate their students' thinking! Readers of this book are not expected to have any mathematical knowledge beyond that acquired in high school; college algebra is helpful but not a prerequisite.

The material is structured to lead the practitioner directly through all the key management steps required in a proper quality improvement effort. To accomplish this, the book is divided into three major parts.

Part I introduces the fundamental concepts, tools, and techniques related to quality management. Also, because there still is considerable confusion and disagreement over the most appropriate definition of quality itself, we will present a set of rigorous definitions. It seems to us that too many experts in too many articles and books have presented their own version of these definitions. Yet, for the successful management of quality, the fundamentals as well as the requirements and objectives must and can be clearly and simply presented.

Next, we focus on the requirements process and the completion of specifications as key ingredients of managing intent—that is, *prevention*. This section also includes fundamental management techniques in the design and planning for quality. As a further key concept, the *cost of quality* is introduced as a process management tool—both for control and investment decision making—and the relationship between quality, productivity, and profitability is explored in terms of cost. The fundamentals of *quality control* are also included, and such key aspects of outcome as reliability, availability, and serviceability are addressed.

Part II applies the concepts of prevention and control, described in Part I, in a systematic and organized way to the management of quality through *total process management*. This, then, is a structured approach to quality management that has as its objective not only improving the present quality level but also to ensuring continual improvement toward zero defects. Total process management also places primary focus on people management—the human component within the process. This part describes the systematic, disciplined approach of establishing the requirements, plans, and controls that make the elimination and prevention of defects not only possible but certain. The process management approach is used because in our sophisticated and increasingly complex business world, nothing is simple anymore and almost everything—from an interoffice memo to a space vehicle—is the result of a process rather than an individual act. Part II also expands on the overall management system for quality that includes policies and objectives, as well as organizational and communications mechanisms.

Part III is concerned with the *implementation* of a successful quality management program, based primarily on my own professional experience. The material here also includes a case study that deals with the introduction and implementation of one of the earliest planned quality management programs in IBM, and traces its continuing progress toward "zero defects." Since quality management is a never-ending process, this part of the book also presents the practicing manager and executive with some observations and challenges for the future.

Acknowledgments

My views on quality have been shaped over the years by three factors: first, my life experiences from early childhood that the only way to do things is to do them right and to one's own satisfaction, through my years as an IBM executive when I managed one of the company's first successful quality efforts. Second, observing and learning about the work of, and especially through direct and indirect contacts with, those who have provided leadership, through their examples and writings in key areas of quality management: Crosby, Deming, Juran, Shewhart, and many others. Third, my association, first as a guest lecturer and more recently as its director, with the IBM Quality Institute over the past five years.

It is very difficult to give proper credit to all the people who have assisted me in the preparation of the manuscript or who helped in one way or another make this book a reality. To thank everyone in the manner properly deserved would require at least an additional chapter. However, I do want to take this opportunity to acknowledge the efforts of those who contributed the most: Karl Karlstrom of Prentice-Hall for his initial encouragement; Bob DeSio, Jim Hewitt, Al Pietrasanta, and Ed Van Schaik of IBM who made valuable comments and suggestions regarding the contents and structure of the book; and Erich Bloch of the National Science Foundation for his timely foreword. I also give special acknowledgment to my associates at the IBM Quality Institute for the stimulating exchange of ideas that in turn helped me stay in touch with progress during the preparation of the manuscript. Also, I owe special thanks to the IBM Corporation for its generosity in providing copyrighted materials and administrative support to my efforts. To all of these people and many others, I wish to express my personal gratitude.

ABOUT THE AUTHOR

Gabriel A. Pall has had many years of first-hand experience in quality management. As a line executive, he was directly responsible for the planning and operational implementation of one of the early quality improvement efforts in the IBM Corporation. He joined IBM in 1960, where his areas of activity encompassed applied science and systems engineering, operations research and management science, software development, product line management, and information systems management. The author of *Introduction to Scientific Computing*, he is also known as a lecturer on subjects related to information technology management and quality. He has most recently held the position of Director of the IBM Quality Institute in Thornwood, New York. He and his family live in Stamford, Connecticut.

INTRODUCTION

Product quality has become American industry's most important competitive issue in the 1980s. In a recent study[1] of the business units of major North American companies, managers ranked "producing to high quality standards" as their chief current concern. In addition, a number of market surveys have revealed consumer dissatisfaction, and even frustration with the lack of quality in the products and services they buy.

The essence of the successful management of quality is to: (1) understand that quality means conformance to requirements, (2) establish and communicate the requirements that are to be met, (3) produce and deliver products and services which will meet those requirements without error or defect, and (4) maintain error-free performance over time in the face of changing requirements. Causing this to happen is what this book is all about.

> "We are in favor of quality and we believe in zero defects. But that is perfection and, realistically, it just cannot be done. And even if we knew how to build error-free products, we could never afford the cost—perfection is just too expensive."

> "Today's products are so complicated, today's services are so sophisticated, that they cannot be provided without errors. Humans are still part of the process and humans are known to make errors."

---

[1]See J. G. Miller, *The 1983 Manufacturing Futures Project: Summary of North American Survey Responses and Preliminary Report* (Boston, MA: School of Management, Boston University, 1983), p. 14.

"Quality improvement is the hobby horse of the quality staff—it only adds to the overhead."

"Zero defects is Oriental sloganeering and regimentation—it cannot be implemented in our culture."

"The economics of quality require trade-offs; beyond a certain point, it is just not profitable."

These are the views of many businesspeople and practicing managers about quality. Unfortunately, it is a perspective still held by executives as well, because this is what they hear from their financial advisors and engineering professionals. But they are being proven wrong. The evidence is mounting—and unhappily at the expense of American business and American industry—that low-defect, low-maintenance television sets, cars, data processing equipment, and cameras can be built and that, in the long run, these products cost less to produce and operate than did their counterparts in the past. Error-free administration of services, courteous and helpful telephone operators, and knowledgeable, attentive salespeople are all within the realm of possibilities. And, in the final analysis, they contribute to customer satisfaction and the reputation and profitability of their business.

The late 1970s and early 1980s saw a tremendous increase in management attention to quality in American business and industry. Certain areas of technology and industry have traditionally been known for their emphasis on quality (data processing, airlines, telecommunications, and industries related to the space program), but the marked increase in interest across the board is a new and, we might add, welcome development.

Why this sudden interest and concurrent investment in quality? Why the focus on managing quality and searching out successful ways of doing it? The plain and simple truth is that management in American business and industry has, for the first time, realized that quality—the quality of products and services provided in a world full of economic and competitive pressures—may be the necessary ingredient for *business survival*.

American Business and the Focus on Quality

The lack of attention to quality characteristic of many executives seems to be changing toward an appreciation of quality improvement. And the change is likely to accelerate in the years to come. In fact, time is running out for our leaders in business, industry, and government to understand the significance of quality and recognize the need for its successful management. Fortunately, at this point there are several factors that will compel a change in management attitude toward quality.

The first and probably most pressing factor is *competition:* the sudden realization that the United States is beginning to lag seriously behind its chief foreign competitors, notably Japan and West Germany, in the quality of products and, partially as a result of this, is developing an international trade deficit of alarming magnitude. This may come as a great shock to many Americans who still remember Germany's and Japan's defeat in World War II and the latter's reputation as the producer of primitive toys and cheap appliances.

In the two decades following World War II, with Western Europe, Japan, and the Soviet Union still recovering from the ravages of war, American industry enjoyed a position of unprecedented advantage. It produced its goods and services from a well financed and recently modernized base, and the free flow of its products to markets around the world was assured by the most ambitious and far-reaching mechanism of free trade in the world's history—the General Agreement on Trade and Tariffs (GATT), fashioned in 1947. No wonder that such phenomenal commercial and financial success made American management complacent: The glow of military victory, resulting in uncontested technological, industrial, and financial leadership, permeated American political and business thinking up to the 1960s. In retrospect it is clear what went wrong. First, in those halcyon days of no competition the last thing American management needed or wanted was continued investment in productivity or technology, as it turned its profits into stockholders' income and the highest wages and benefits ever enjoyed by its work force. Second, the worldwide system of free trade encouraged the emergence and ultimate success of the low-cost producers who paid their workers less while mastering state-of-the-art technology. By the mid-1960s, the race for world markets was on between the emerging low-cost, high-technology producers like Japan, on the one hand, and the United States, on the other—with a sophisticated economy and strong financial base, but whose workers demanded the world's highest wages and whose productivity growth was low and industrial technology becoming obsolete. Thus, the only way to compete was by efficiencies of production, an area in which both Japan and Western Europe surpassed the United States. In the last 20 years, however, the productivity gains which resulted from the postwar reconstruction and modernization of Western European industry have all but evaporated in the face of increasing demands for higher wages, benefits, and social services in Western European societies. The fact is that, aside from minor and temporary improvements, both the United States and Western Europe have fallen back in terms of productivity as they continue to spend their gross national product in increasingly nonwealth-producing areas, while Japan has grown to be an industrial and commercial giant, passing the Soviet Union in industrial production in the early 1980s. Today it stands as second only to the United States, and if the present rate of Japanese expansion of production and the corresponding gain of markets continue, while America more or less maintains its course, then it will be the world's first industrial power by the end of the twentieth century.

The race for industrial, commercial, and financial dominance of world markets is, then, between the United States and Japan. In nonmilitary terms and in the context of free-world trade, there are no other competitors. The outcome is not at all clear—and I am seriously concerned about America's chances.

In the 1970s, the emphasis in American industry was on *productivity*. And indeed, we made some impressive gains through massive investment in new technology and wage settlements more conducive to productivity. American managers soon realized, however, that the Japanese were able to steadily match our improvements in productivity. Furthermore, while American management was betting heavily on cost efficiency, Japan has continued to outperform us in the area of quality—for the Japanese had recognized a long time ago that *productivity and quality go hand in hand in ensuring a superior competitive position.*

As American business leaders and managers ponder these developments, they must come to the realization that today many American products are no longer competitive at home or abroad, and that the Japanese are better prepared for the remainder of the race than we are. For the race is already over in a number of events: consumer electronics, photo equipment, steel, and shipbuilding. And by virtue of their system of government–industry partnership—an ideal combination of government planning and private enterprise which is unquestionably superior to ours in directing a modern industrial state for national purposes—they are favorably positioned to win the rest: automobiles, aircraft, and computers. The case of the U.S. semiconductor industry well illustrates this point.

> On July 30, 1986, Japanese and U.S. negotiators signed an agreement that promises to protect American semiconductor manufacturers from "predatory Japanese pricing" and to open the heretofore "closed Japanese market" to increased sales of American-made semiconductor products, primarily logic and memory chips.
>
> But preventing the ultimate demise of this key U.S. industry will take a lot more than a piece of paper: The only long-term solution is to eliminate the *structural advantages* enjoyed by Japanese semiconductor producers. As of the mid-1980s, the leading edge technologies for the so-called commodity chips (produced for the open market and purchased by systems companies and other industrial users) have shifted to the Far East. Also, Japanese semiconductor producers have overtaken U.S. chip makers in the area of capital spending and by the end of 1986, Japan has owned the world's largest market for semiconductor chips. An already leading technological base and the continuing, accelerating capital spending will lead to the inevitable domination of the world's semiconductor markets by Japan within the next 10 to 15 years. In this sense, then, the new trade agreement will only postpone the inevitable route of the U.S. commodity semiconductor industry. And the stakes are much higher than the industrial decline of Silicon Valley, or the $200 billion business potential represented by semiconductor products at the end of this century. Integrated circuit technology is the base on which all other high technology industries rest—from automobiles and aerospace to telecommunications and computers. While the latter two are still adequately supplied by so-called "captive" production (by AT&T, IBM, and a few others) the main growth markets for "noncaptive" commodity chips (such as consumer electronics) are owned by the Japanese. With no significant production of television sets, compact disc players, and video cassette

recorders left in the United States, overall domestic demand for commodity chips has been steadily declining.

The most devastating aspect of the scenario, however, is that stiff, quality-oriented competition and stagnating markets occur at the same time when the cost of research and capital investments necessary to stay competitive has reached new highs. And while it is getting more difficult for American semiconductor companies to raise capital (once everyone's glamour issues, their stocks are now considered poor investment risks on Wall Street), for Japan's semiconductor producers, the cost of capital is less than in the U.S. and funding sources are always available. Consequently, the Japanese are winning the semiconductor race by simply out-investing their American rivals and thereby further increasing their lead in technology and productivity.

Creating an advanced technological base, however, is a necessary but not sufficient condition for competitiveness. In addition to lavish automation, the Japanese have introduced rigorous discipline into the management of their manufacturing and plant maintenance *processes*. As a result, they produce far more good chips than comparable American plants; they are also winning the race for *quality*. Typical yields of 256K random access memory (RAM) semiconductor chips in Japan are triple those in the U.S. today. And so, while just eight years ago the center of technology was Silicon Valley and U.S. semiconductor producers accounted for the bulk of RAM sales worldwide, that center may now well have shifted to Japan. In summary, better quality through higher yields leads to lower international prices and better competitive position.

Time is running out to stop the erosion and eventual demise of the U.S. semiconductor industry. Trade barriers are clearly not the answer. The answer is productivity and quality improvement. To enhance productivity, capital has to be raised at acceptable costs. Structural, political, and tax measures, and major changes in depreciation rates for capital equipment are needed in this essential area. Joint ventures, perhaps even with the federal government, may be the only answer to develop a generation of integrated circuits so advanced that the basic technology is still a researcher's dream today. (One possible area is the commercialization of the technologies currently developed for the Strategic Defense Initiative which are expected to yield private sector sales ranging between $5 and $20 trillion in the next few decades. One example of the types of results this program can provide is the development of gallium arsenide crystals, a new material that transmits electrons several times faster than the conventional silicon chips used in the electronics sector today. Such crystals can also be used in optical switches which could be the basic building elements of a new generation of computers and other telecommunications equipment.)

Much has been said about Japanese government subsidies for industrial development and special tariffs and nontariff barriers to trade which make Japanese markets less than open to outside competition. To be sure, certain Japanese trade policies and practices are unfair, but I believe there are more fundamental reasons behind their advantage—particularly in the area of quality.

This leads us to the second factor which should help change management attitudes about quality—that is, the *understanding of quality* proper, as well as the mentality and management approach needed to achieve it. Management needs to realize that quality is definable and measurable, that objectives and requirements can be formulated toward its achievement, and that specific programs can be implemented to ensure that requirements are met—in short, that quality is manageable.

This growing awareness about quality leads to the third factor: the realization that in the final analysis, *quality depends on people.* Every process producing goods and services employs human resources—people who in turn must (1) understand what is required of them, (2) given the wherewithal (education, tools, instructions) to achieve their objectives, and (3) most importantly, be motivated to do all this in a professional and productive manner. It is my conviction that the only way to achieve consistent quality is through motivated people. Such motivation cannot come from campaigns—although temporary motivation or even enthusiasm can be achieved by various methods and means, not the least known of which is money. But quality-oriented motivation must be more fundamental and permanent: It must be part of a mental set—an industrial culture or a work ethic—which, in the absence of outside motivators, can still be self-motivating and self-generating. Such motivation stems from *professionalism*, an outlook which is diametrically opposed to the mentality which still pervades American industry and society today. This is the mentality which has fostered the welfare state, which has led to an industrial and business community where both work ethic and practice have decayed, created consumerism oriented toward instant gratification, and changed the United States from a nation of political and social ideals to an assembly of consumers and special interest groups, all at odds with each other and their government.

It certainly goes beyond the scope of this book to suggest ways and means for a fundamental, structural change in American life and thinking to reverse these trends. But it *is* our intent to suggest that within business and industry—as well as all walks of life where services are offered—it is management's responsibility, indeed mission, to do everything in its power to bring about a change in people's thinking and to instill *motivation*, the essential ingredient for quality.

A fourth and equally compelling factor shaping management attitudes is the realization that *quality is a significant contributor to profits.* The erroneous perception that quality is an unaffordable luxury is being replaced by the realization that every dollar not spent on redoing things done incorrectly becomes half a dollar on the bottom line. In these days of high taxation and high interest rates—and the continuing cost squeeze of regulations, environmental controls, litigation, and continuing wage demands—that is a welcome help to profitability. Those profit dollars can in turn be reinvested in productivity improvements—which is really the prime purpose of quality.

> Productivity (output per unit of work time) is the general measure of a society's ability to generate a certain standard of living for its citizens. It is a basic law of

economics that no society can for long enjoy a standard of living higher than it itself is producing—for no one can share nonexisting output. The rising standard of living means to consume more, and to do so the citizens of a society have to produce more. Productivity measures society's ability to produce more of the goods and services that each of its citizens *wants* (not needs, which is an entirely different concept). Productivity is also a measure of a country's ability to compete with other countries on world markets. In the case of America, to fall behind in productivity means to fall behind in introducing the new products and production technologies that have given American products an advantage in world markets so far. If America cannot compete on the basis of productivity, then it will only be able to compete on the basis of wages that are lower than those of the world's productivity leaders. (By the way, this basic truth points out the fallacy in the argument for redistribution of wealth to raise the living standard of "the poor." While this may temporarily raise the living standard of some at the expense of others, a permanently rising standard of living can only be achieved by the increased productivity of the *entire* society.)

If productivity growth cannot be increased again, Americans can only hope for a very slow, if any, rise in their standard of living regardless how successful they are in the redistribution of wealth through public policy, lowering unemployment through public projects and at the expense of private enterprise, eliminating budget deficits, or in dealing with any other major social or economic problems. *Rapid productivity growth, coupled with quality improvement, is the key to America's economic and political future.*

The decline of national productivity is also caused by the expansion of low-productivity industries, such as services—mistakenly praised by many as the onset of the "post-industrial society." Productivity, however, should not be confused with *efficiency*. For example, technology dictates that some industries use much more capital per worker than others. This leads those industries to produce more per hour of work (high productivity) but not necessarily at higher total efficiency (output per unit of all inputs: capital, labor, materials, land, energy, etc.). Services have been slowing down national productivity growth ever since World War II—at an increasing rate. (While service productivity was 96 percent of the national average in 1948, by 1983 it had fallen to 61 percent. Every worker who now moves into services represents a 40 percent decline in productivity.) Continued growth of service industries, without an attendant reacceleration of their productivity and that of the national average, is a sure prescription for America's decline as a competitive, high-wage, technological and industrial power.

Productivity is essentially a matter of social organization or, in business terms, the management of the processes producing goods and services. Productivity will be achieved if the process meets its quality objectives. The many widely publicized stories about dramatically reduced defect rates in consumer electronics and massive dollar savings from quality improvement programs in telecommunications all support this contention. My own management experience in the information systems industry also convinces me beyond a doubt that it is always less costly to do the job right the first time and that improvements in quality always go hand in hand with increases in productivity—and, ultimately, in profitability.

The value of quality improvement and the need for its purposeful management are, then, well understood and amply demonstrated. Once this level of awareness becomes widespread, the need arises and the search begins for a practical and—more importantly—successful way to implement it. Quality management will be the primary concern for the next decade or two because the alternative would be far too costly and may mean business and commercial failure.

Before the methodologies and implementation of quality management can be discussed, however, it is necessary to dispel a few misconceptions that are, to this day, held by many managers and executives. These misconceptions cause most of the problems with regard to commitment, communication, and motivation between those who set quality objectives and those who are expected to implement them.

The first misconception is that quality is an extra or a luxury—a "gilding of the lily." People under this misconception use the word *quality* to signify the relative value of things in such expressions as "low quality," "good quality," and the like. We will get back to this subject later; suffice it to say that quality is an essential characteristic which tells us whether something—a product, a service, or an activity—meets requirements or falls short.

The second misconception—related to the first—is that quality is something nebulous or intangible, and therefore not measurable. In fact, using the appropriate definitions and methods to manage it, quality can be precisely measured in a number of ways, including one of the key measurements: its cost.

Another misconception is that quality represents added cost, that it is uneconomical. This management mentality, rooted in the "economics of quality," disallows the initial investment needed to launch quality improvement and treats quality as a low-priority objective against costs, schedules, or other management parameters.

The fourth set of misconceptions has to do with the causes of "poor quality." One of the most prevalent assumptions is that most of the problems with quality originate with the workers, who have become lazy and greedy, and the unions, which continue to foster this kind of environment. To be sure, some unions have contributed to the problem by pushing through unlimited and unaffordable cost-of-living allowances, early and full retirement plans, and the like. But the fact is that workers in shops and warehouses will work just as well as they ever did—and more productively too—given appropriate management direction and leadership. And American management has to accept just as much blame for the state of affairs in the area of wages and benefits as the unions. As long as American business was making money, it was always easy to give in to union demands and recover them later—from the consumers. American executives, unfortunately, have not been known for their interest in long-range planning. They have been too concerned about improving profits for the current year—and earning a good bonus in doing so. I blame management's "here-and-now" mentality—the instinct for quick settlement, the fixation with the bottom line even when the problems seem to originate with the workers—for having tolerated an environment in which the most expensive problems occur because of poor planning or lack of strategy; where the future is mortgaged, and quality is dismissed with a wave of the hand as something impractical or too time-consuming. Management's preoccupation with short-term objectives and its failure to correctly assess and plan for the future by predicting problems and change, along with protectionist tendencies have nurtured the waste of manpower and other resources—all of which increase the producer's cost and ultimately, the price the consumer must pay. But the American consumer is no longer willing to subsidize this waste—turning to better made, and often less expensive, imported products. The resulting loss of market by American industry, both at home and abroad, in turn leads to higher unemployment, lower wages, and a general decline of the purchasing power of the American consumer in the American marketplace. The time has come for drastic changes, both in mentality and practice. "Everyone is doing his best," or "we've tried hard," can no longer be the answer. The responsibility for introducing and managing change rests with management. The first step is to learn *why* change is necessary; the second, *what* to change; and the third, *how?* Management performance can no longer be measured only by the quarterly dividend or the annual profit and loss statement. Instead, it must be measured by its ability to stay in business on a sustained, competitive basis, both at home and abroad, to expand market share, to protect investment and earn dividends, and to ensure jobs of increasing value and productivity through technological innovation and product quality improvement.

The last misconception has to do with the responsibility for quality. A prevailing but erroneous assumption is that quality originates in the quality department and that quality professionals are responsible for quality in their organizations. Interestingly, this view is widely entrenched among the quality professionals themselves—who should know better. A corollary of this view is that quality can be improved through tighter controls or an increased level of inspection. This approach holds people responsible for resolving problems over which, in fact, they have no control. "Quality problems" are really the problems of those functions or processes in the organization where they occur—engineering problems, planning problems, manufacturing problems, administrative problems, and the like—the solution of which is clearly the responsibility of management in those areas. Building up quality departments beyond reasonable limits and making them responsible for what should be the task of all levels of management represent the principal weakness in modern quality management. It is also the first trap into which many business leaders fall as they try to implement quick-fix, short-lived quality improvement programs.

Management must take the initiative—together with the country's political leadership, the administration and Congress—to create an environment in which labor unions work closely with management and in which each side understands that its fate is bound up in the other's success. The prime ingredient in such an environment is trust, a far cry from the antagonism and mutual suspicion that has been endemic in the relationships between management and labor, government and the governed. Only in this fashion can we hope to achieve anything that will compete with the managerial partnership of Japanese government and enterprise.

Now let's get to the business of what quality management is all about and how this book can be of help in implementing it.

The Students of Quality: Perspective and Solutions

The view that quality is primarily a management responsibility and that lasting, consistent improvements can only be achieved through strong management commitment and leadership is shared by most of the well-known students of quality. This is because quality has been recognized as the most important factor leading to competitive success and business growth in both national and international markets. Success in the implementation of such a quality-based business strategy, however, varies widely by industry and business. Because of this wide variation, the search for the genuine, sound, and practical approach to quality management has become a matter of prime concern to top management all over the world. The experience of the most successful quality leaders discloses a fundamental fact for achieving continuing and consistent success: Quality is, essentially, a *way* of managing business and industrial processes. Like finance, or personnel, quality is now becoming an essential part of modern industrial and business management.

Philip Crosby's perspective[2] is that management understanding and support are the two fundamental prerequisites of a successful quality improvement effort. Based on a positive management attitude and top-down commitment, Crosby's scheme consists of the repeated implementation of a 14-step program. This program, in turn, is based on four "absolutes": (1) The definition of quality is conformance to requirements; (2) defect prevention—not inspection—is the management system of quality; (3) the only acceptable performance standard is zero defects; and (4) the measurement of quality is the cost of quality—that is, the price of nonconformance.

W. Edwards Deming's view[3] is that lack of quality results from ineffective management. He sees American management's problems as stemming from unrealistic expectations of both workers and processes, a punitive and unconstructive approach to motivation, and overdelegation in the management and control of tasks. Since management controls the processes which produce goods and services, their improvement is largely management's responsibility. Accordingly, a long-term commitment to a new philosophy based on "statistical thinking" is required of any management which seeks to improve quality and productivity. Deming's solution of the quality problem is the adoption of a 14-point program acted on day after day, year after year, on a continuing basis.

---

[2]See Philip B. Crosby, *Quality Is Free* (New York: The New American Library, Inc., 1980).
[3]See W. Edwards Deming, *Quality, Productivity, and Competitive Position* (Boston, MA: MIT Center for Advanced Engineering Study, 1982).

J. M. Juran's research[4] shows that of all the quality problems encountered by an organization only about 20 percent are employee controllable; this is the case if the worker knows what is expected, how to determine conformance, and how to correct nonconformance. All other quality problems lie beyond the control of individual employees and are, therefore, controllable only by management. To achieve quality improvement, Juran considers upper management leadership indispensable. He regards company-wide training of management and the use of three basic quality-oriented processes—planning, control, and improvement (the "quality trilogy")—as the other two important ingredients of an annually implemented quality improvement plan. Juran's solution is to focus on chronic problems which represent long-standing adverse situations and address them through a seven-step improvement program sequence which is designed to achieve a "breakthrough" to an improved level of performance.

While there seems to be little disagreement on the role or the importance of management action and leadership, and there is clearly willingness on the part of businesspeople, managers, and executives to follow the various solutions offered, few guides are available on the practical implementation of these basic principles in day-to-day problem solving.

What is needed, then, is a guide of general applicability for the implementation of a quality management effort. Such a guide needs to be based on the fundamental and well-recognized principles of *process management* and rooted in real-life management experience. This book has been written with these needs in mind.

In addition to serving as a comprehensive guide to implementation, *Quality Process Management* also includes, in a theoretically consistent framework, a number of contributions to the theory and practice of quality management:

- Quality is a binary *state* or *attribute*, not a matter of degree. Lack of quality or nonconformance, however, can be measured in continuous terms—that is, in terms of degree or extent. Nonconformance is the continuum preceding the point of conformance or defect-free state.
- Most industrial and business processes can system-theoretically be viewed as *open systems*, capable of improvement and adaptation.
- *Total process management* comprises *quality management* (prevention and control) and *process optimization* (in terms of efficiency and adaptability).
- The requirements process is a subprocess of any process under consideration. It is one of the key prerequisites for successful quality management.
- The *cost of quality* is not just a measurement but also a management tool for the purpose of (1) conscious trade-offs among functional content, cost, and schedules during the negotiation of requirements and specifications; and (2) investment and the measurement of return on investment in prevention. It also makes possible the quantitative linkage between quality and productivity, and quality management and process optimization (see below).

---

[4]See J. M. Juran, *Managerial Breakthrough* (New York: McGraw-Hill Book Co., 1964).

- In any given organization or enterprise, *quality improvement should be implemented across the board*, not in the form of "pilot" or "test" programs in designated areas, to be followed by the total effort only later on.

Methodology of the Book: Techniques and Implementation

In presenting a text on a broad and complex subject such as quality management, the subject matter can be structured in several ways. The organization and sequence of topics selected for this book are based on the conviction that, even though practicing managers are often faced with the urgent task of quality control to solve a current problem, they will never succeed in the management of the total process unless they master the initial but equally important tasks of establishing requirements and planning for quality. Far too many managers and organizations have been bogged down for years in an effort to solve an "urgent quality problem"—never giving themselves the chance of achieving fundamental and lasting quality improvement through total process management. Therefore, however tempting it may be to "get right to the bottom of things" while letting planning and organization slip to "less demanding" times, this book encourages the top-down, total management approach which includes the management of *both* intent and outcome.

Accordingly, the presentation of the material in this book is guided by the priorities of a long-term quality management effort designed for continuous quality improvement.

Chapter 1 introduces *basic concepts* and definitions, maxims, and measurements required for a thorough understanding of quality and its consistent and successful management.

Chapter 2 focuses on the management of *intent*: It presents the key preventive activities that comprise the design and planning aspects of a process. These initial activities are essential in preventing errors and defects from entering the output of a process, be it a product, service, or other offering.

Chapter 3 is about managing the *outcome*: It introduces the tools and techniques of quality control—detection and correction.

Chapter 4 introduces the *process*—be it administrative, manufacturing, or service-related; simple or complex—as the basic vehicle of quality management. Most traditional quality improvement efforts have been characterized by a product focus, supported by conventional techniques of quality control—hallmarks of managing the outcome after the fact. Beginning with the mid-1980s, the shortcomings of the traditional approach as well as relentless competitive and economic pressures led to a process orientation of quality management, with sharp emphasis on prevention and on increasing the linkage between quality and productivity. Process management, as presented here, combines prevention and control as the key ingredients of quality management, with process optimization to ensure process efficiency and productivity.

Chapter 5 describes the overall *management system*, along with the key measurement of quality improvement—the cost of quality, which is used as a management tool throughout the process.

The management of quality and the various related quality improvement programs are never-ending efforts in the life of an organization. In my view, the time it takes for true, planned, and managed improvement to set in is several years. Consequently, it will take a nontrivial amount of time to develop a fully operational and successful quality management scheme—a plan which will proceed to maturity through a number of well-defined, recognizable *stages*. Through the three stages of maturing quality management, the approach to managing the process and to the use of the various management tools, techniques, and measurements—notably the cost of quality—will also vary.

Chapter 6 illustrates the implementation of *process management*, including the management of intent and outcome, through these three stages. In this manner, the practicing manager will be able to lay out a quality management effort from the inception of the plan through its complete implementation. This approach also helps take advantage of early experiences in terms of structured, more purposeful feedback, which is an essential ingredient of the continued improvement towards a defect-free, stable environment.

Chapter 7 presents a real-life example of managing quality through the successive stages of evolution, organized in the form of a *case study*.

Quality Improvement at Sterling Forest

The quality story at IBM Sterling Forest started in 1980, when, as one among the first locations in IBM, a quality improvement program was initiated, to continue over the years ever since. Its initial implementation was based on Crosby's 14-step approach, gradually modified and enhanced with a tailored education program, quality circles, quality assurance, and defect elimination activities to fit the site's information systems environment. Many of the lessons learned during the initial implementation period were used on an ongoing basis to further tune and enhance the management effort. The commitment stage at Sterling Forest lasted little over two years; by 1983, we were well into the consolidation stage, with good prospects for approaching maturity. By this time, Sterling Forest had become known as one of the locations using the cost of quality as a prime management tool and also a site where significant elements of the process management approach were introduced.

A lot was learned through the years as the quality improvement program was put in place at Sterling Forest. Most importantly, a consistent management view and experience emerged on the use of management tools and techniques, the measurement and value of quality, and its interrelationship to other business objectives, like professionalism and productivity. The cost of quality is the one handle which managers need to make investment decisions that will prevent future defects and simultaneously improve productivity and, ultimately, the profitability of the entire business.

For I believe, when all is said and done, that the objective of quality management is to improve productivity. This in turn will enhance the profitability and competitive posture of the business. We know intuitively—and there is growing quantitative evidence as well—that there is a direct linkage between quality and productivity; therefore, quality is really serving the overall business objective of being profitable and competitive at the same time.

Quality Process Management is directed to those in business, industry, and government who are responsible for the successful operation of major processes or some parts within them. It is important to recognize that quality management, once the interest of only a few specialized people, is today the primary and growing concern of an increasingly large number of executives, managers, technologists, and others working in many key processes throughout industrial and business organizations worldwide.

This book may be used in several ways:

(1) As a reference for managers and professionals interested in a wide range of methods and techniques in quality management
(2) As an introduction to the latest practices of process management
(3) As a fundamental text in management education and development, on the subject of quality control and improvement

Part I QUALITY FUNDAMENTALS

1

BASIC CONCEPTS

A rigorous definition of the concept of quality—which is also best suited for such management purposes as objective-setting, measurements, and adaptability to change—is one essential ingredient of a successful approach to quality management. However, the acceptance and use of the set of definitions presented here will go beyond that: It will result in a gradual but consistent change of attitudes, and even mentality—another essential ingredient of successful quality management. When we talk about a change in thinking, gone will be such notions as "quality of life" or comparisons between "low" and "high" quality. For *quality is a state of conformance*, which is either there or it is not. Gone, too, will be the arguments whether quality is a perception and whether or not it should be viewed through the producer's or the user's eyes. And last but not least, gone will be the view that quality is a matter of degree in conformance—because it leads square back to the erroneous distinction between "low" and "high" states of quality.

Conceptually and philosophically, *until a state of zero defects, or measurably full conformance to requirements is met, quality will remain an objective which has to be pursued relentlessly through continuing improvement.*

1.1 Operational Definitions

Through history, members of all human societies have made use of materials and energy to create *work products* for the use and benefit of other members of the same society, or members of other societies, always with the intent to satisfy the

15

expectations and needs—real or perceived—of the recipients. Especially since the industrial revolution, the notion of quality has primarily been associated with manufactured products and related services (delivery, warranty, maintenance, and the like). With the diversification of needs in modern society and the emergence of service industries (communications, transportation, entertainment), the concept of quality has naturally been extended to all aspects of life wherever something is provided to meet a known need or expectation.

The concept of *work product* comprises, in the most general and consistent manner, all the items created, produced, and provided to meet human needs and expectations, such as:

- *Goods*: Items designed primarily for personal use, such as food, clothing, furniture, books, and the like.
- *Products*: Items of both personal and general use, and related more to comfort, convenience, and productivity, such as appliances, vehicles, cameras, office and data processing equipment, and so on.
- *Services*: Activities or capabilities related to goods and products (delivery, maintenance, and the like) or offered by themselves, such as transportation, education, electricity, and so on.
- *Offerings*: Specific combinations of products and services provided in a "packaged" form to satisfy certain specialized needs. (The products in this context are sometimes also known as *deliverables*.) Examples of offerings include education, including both instruction and course materials; information processing services comprising hardware and software as well as programming and installation support activities.

An essential characteristic of all these work products must be that they satisfy the needs of those members of society for whose use or benefit they are provided, namely, the recipients. *Recipient* is the most general and consistent definition of all those individuals or organizations for whom work products are provided.

This in turn gives rise to the concept of the *provider* which represents both individuals and organizations from whom work products originate—including agricultural producers, manufacturers, public utilities, educational institutions, vendors, and the like.

When a work product is obtained from the provider with some form of compensation in return, the recipient is known as a *customer.* If the acquisition is for the direct use of the work product, the recipient is known as the *user.* The *end user* is one who receives the intended benefit of the work product. (End users of consumable products such as food, fuel, clothing, and the like are known as *consumers.*) In acquiring a product, or service, the user is interested both in the intended benefit as well as actual use. Consumers buy milk because they want nourishment as well as the benefits of taste, convenience, and the like. Customers

buy automobiles for transportation as well as the satisfaction of individual ownership, self-image, comfort, and the specific benefits and advantages of a certain
type of vehicle.

Among providers, service industries have historically offered their work
products directly to end users, without the intervention of others, although with
the emergence of more complex and specialized offerings in a number of industries, the concepts of such intermediaries as "value-added retailers" and "service
consultants" have emerged. On the other hand, manufacturers have done most of
their selling through a number of middlemen—wholesale and retail merchants,
distributors, and the like. A thorough understanding of the flow of work products
from the provider to the end user is critical in managing quality, as each stage in
this flow becomes part of the overall process.

Without clear and consistent definitions, it is impossible to establish clear
objectives, communicate requirements, measure progress, and introduce the necessary improvements to eliminate variances between requirements and actual
status. The primary reason for lack of quality is the failure to understand and
agree on a *manageable definition* of quality. To help practicing managers produce
quality work products, such a definition must have five attributes of manageability:

(1) It must be *precise,* which means formally stated for consistency and repeat-
    ability.
(2) It must be *generally applicable.* It must apply to all work products and not
    depend on time, the availability of certain technology, management meth-
    ods, and so on. General applicability also means that the definition must be
    supportable by measurements and management methods in a wide variety of
    processes, industries, or technologies.
(3) It must be *adaptable to change*—without change in the basic concept of the
    definition itself. For instance, improvements in measurement technologies
    over time may result in a redefinition of what the measurable limits of
    conformance are, without changing the meaning of conformance itself.
(4) It must be *practical* or, in other words, communicable, understandable, and
    easy to implement. A definition is not manageable if practicing managers or
    workers cannot understand it and consequently will not be able to deliver
    what is expected of them. Without common understanding, a requirement or
    specification is meaningless—and so is any attempt to measure or establish
    performance against them.
(5) It should fit into the overall set of cultural and mental attitudes within which
    it is expected to be implemented. Many times, introducing a new view or
    definition so that it becomes workable and manageable is made difficult if
    not impossible by prevailing cultural or popular attitudes—which can only
    be overcome by directed, purposeful, and consistent education and motiva-
    tion of all involved.

1.1.1 Expectations, Requirements, and Specifications

Work products are provided to meet *needs and expectations*. The two are related but not the same; yet both are important in determining whether or not satisfaction has been achieved through conformance to both. *Need* is a lack of something requisite, desired, or useful; it is a *condition* requiring provision or relief.[1] It is also a definable state which can be stated with a reasonable degree of precision—such as hunger or cold, need for transportation or a specific type of training. Although there may be some argument about level and degree, basic human needs in a given cultural or social context are pretty well established and understood. All people need nourishment—although the amount and kind might be subject to further discussion. Children need education; workers need tools and training; manufacturers need energy and raw materials—again, with the amount and kind requiring further definition. On the other hand, *expectation* means anticipation of the future state of things, especially of benefits to be derived from satisfying a known need. Hence, expectation is a highly subjective notion, as it is related to one's perspective of how things will turn out. Expectations are much more volatile, vague, and difficult to express since they change as does the view of the future. Lack of understanding of this difference between need and expectation has caused most of the misconceptions and confusion about what constitutes meeting a need or satisfying an expectation.

Given a recognized need, the related expectation will always have two components: first, the *manner* in which the need will be met, and second, the anticipated *benefits* derived. Meeting a need is the necessary but not sufficient condition to satisfying an expectation, for not all the anticipated benefits may be derived from the manner in which the need was met.

This distinction is critical in understanding the following definition: *A requirement is a formal statement of a need and the expected manner in which it should be met.* A requirement may represent an expectation only to the extent that anticipated benefits are incorporated, along with the ways in which they are derived. Thus, a "good" requirement (sometimes also known as a requirement statement) must have three important attributes:

(1) It must be *complete*; that is, include all the needs and the manner in which they are to be met (as, for instance, timetable, price range, etc.).

(2) It must be *clear*; that is, easily understandable and unambiguous to those who will have to respond to it; if alternative implementations are available, the preferred one should be clearly identified, along with the reasons for it.

(3) It must be *timely*; that is, represent needs as they currently exist; if time is critical to meeting the stated needs, the requirement should be stated in

---

[1]*Webster's New Collegiate Dictionary*, 2nd ed. (Springfield, MA: G. & C. Merriam Co., Publishers, 1958).

terms that allow adequate time for a satisfactory response and implementation.

Depending on cultural and social environment, business or legal context, and industrial practices, the sources of requirements may be users or consumers, or other potential recipients with a need. In many situations, the needs and expectations of a set of recipients are consolidated into requirements through market research or the organized activities of consumer organizations, created for the protection and representation of certain groups of consumers. In large business or industrial organizations, the mechanism of a "chief user" or "user of record" has been created to regularly survey and consolidate the known and justifiable requirements of specific sets of users (accountants, engineers, legal staff, etc.). This is because the process of establishing requirements necessitates interaction with like users across several organizational entities and functional areas. And while good requirements will produce tangible benefits, including significant cost savings later, establishing them—especially in a large, complex business organization—requires an initial investment of nontrivial resources, including education, communications, planning, and management reviews. *Unwillingness, or the inability to recognize the need for this initial effort to establish good requirements, has been one of the key reasons for the lack of quality in American business, industry, and government.*

A requirement always represents the potential recipient's (user, consumer, or customer) *view of a work product.* The more accurately and completely a requirements statement incorporates the benefits anticipated by the recipient, the higher the probability that the resulting work product will satisfy expectations.

In practice, of course, work products are expected to meet the needs of a multitude of users and, therefore, to satisfy multiple requirements. The sum total of all stated requirements of all known users represents the *demand* for a given work product.

Although there may be a multitude of users and recipients of a work product, there are usually fewer providers or producers. It is the provider who receives—directly or indirectly—the requirements or demand. In turn, the provider converts the requirements into a set of *specifications* which will determine the work product and the process that produces it. *Specifications represent the provider's view of the work product.* They are usually stated in terms of implementation, that is, the manner in which the requirements will best be met by the producer—comprising technology, skills, resources, and cost. The relationship among needs, expectations, requirements, and specifications is illustrated in Table 1-1.

A critical factor in the total quality management process is how accurately the provider translates requirements into specifications. For once specifications are set, the work product and the process producing it can be directly measured only against the specifications; additional procedures and controls will be required to ensure conformance of specifications to the original requirements. *The existence*

Table 1-1. RELATIONSHIP AMONG NEEDS, EXPECTATIONS,
REQUIREMENTS, AND SPECIFICATIONS

	Need	*Expectation*	*Requirement*	*Specification*
Definition	*Lack of* something required, desired, or useful; *condition* requiring provision or relief	*Anticipation* of future state of things, of future *benefits*, of *manners* in which needs are met	Formal statement of *needs* and expected *manner* in which they should be met	Formal description of work product and the intended manner of providing it
Basic Classification	Definable, objective	Subjective	Recipient's view of work product	Provider's view of work product
Form of Communication	Informal surveys and reports	Informal, verbal	Document	Document

of differences between specifications and requirements has been another funda-mental cause of quality failures in the past. In the final analysis, however, failure of the work product to meet user requirements is all that counts.

In our complex economy, work products are often components of another more complex work product and these, in turn, are used to build still others. In the sequence of events and the staged buildup of work products from the simple to the more complex, it is always critical to keep the provider–recipient, supplier–customer relationship in focus. It is generally clear who the end users or consumers are. But in large organizations such as NASA, General Motors, or IBM, the *business process* of producing the end product or service is made up of a number of individual *subprocesses or activities*. These pass their work products to one another. As an example, in the automobile industry, the assembly plant is the user of the engine factory's products. In the computer industry, the assembly process is the user of the work products produced by the manufacturing process, that is, chips, modules, cards, and the like. In general, the user of a work product is the entity to whom that product is provided or supplied: therefore, the user can be the next individual in the production line, an intermediary in the administrative process, or the customer in the traditional sense. But no matter whether the recipient is within or outside the process producing the work product, the same principle applies with respect to meeting requirements. These must be established so that the resulting work product meets the needs of the *next recipient;* outputs of one process must be acceptable inputs to the next. If one examines the logic of this statement carefully, one will find that it leads to *the process view of quality management* which encompasses managing both requirements and conformance, both intent and outcome. This view is exceedingly important for the successful design and management of the process itself—the fundamental task for the practicing manager in producing work products that meet user requirements—with the ultimate assurance that this process will also satisfy user expectations.

1.1.2 Quality

As stated earlier, work products are provided to meet the needs and satisfy the expectations of their recipients. This concept is universal and applies to all products, goods, services, and offerings. The stated, formal representation of expectations (needs and benefits) is embodied in requirements which, therefore, provide the basis for any further measurement, evaluation, and management action. If we accept the assertion that quality cannot be achieved unless it can be measured, and it cannot be measured unless it is first defined, it is logical first to establish the definition that *quality means conformance to requirements.* Accordingly, the *definition of a quality work product is one which meets the requirements established for it.*

This definition applies regardless of who establishes requirements—end users or customers; their chosen representatives or market research staffs; those who build the work product or those who design the process producing it—or whether the requirements are general or detailed. This definition also means that *quality is more than meeting specifications*; for specifications may or may not accurately represent stated requirements. Nor does quality equate to satisfying expectations; again, because expectations may or may not be correctly reflected in the requirements.

Now all we need is to demonstrate that the definition of quality is a manageable definition, that is, it incorporates the five attributes of manageability.

"Conformance to requirements" is a precise and consistent definition; based on this, quality can be verified again and again by comparing a work product to its stated requirements; either they are met or they are not. The definition is also generally applicable, because specific requirements can be established, not only for each class of products and services, but also for each step within a complex process. It is adaptable to change as it does not depend on technology, resources, standards, or procedures. Furthermore, "conformance to requirements" is clearly understandable and easy to implement—as long as good requirements are available and the process of producing the work product and measuring conformance are defined. Lastly, the definition is not in conflict with the emerging views of quality and related attitudes: Requirements can be established to promote the goals of individuals as well as organizations, and people can be educated and motivated to achieve the level of professionalism which will result in defect-free, quality work.

Satisfying these attributes is not trivial, and this is what this book is all about. But it does not present philosophical or conceptual problems, and one can conclude that "conformance to requirements" is not only a manageable definition of quality, but the only one that will produce consistent results.

Once the definition of quality has been established, it is possible to examine some of the popular views about it, to learn how they help or hinder the implementation of this formal definition, and to deal with them as appropriate.

"Conformance to requirements" means that *quality is a binary state:* it is either present or absent; conformance is either achieved or it is not. This definition of quality, then, disposes of the view that quality is a matter of degree—that there is such a thing as a "low," "high," "minimum," or an "acceptable" level of quality. In fact, *there is only one level of quality, and that is a defect-free state.*

Several decades ago, the term "fitness for use" gained wide acceptance to designate quality. However, as mentioned later, this definition has limitations when it comes to attributes not directly related to use, such as price, reliability, manufacturability, and the like. In particular, reliability engineers contended that product performance over a period of time was something different from "fitness for use" and, therefore, reliability should be considered an attribute equal to quality. Acceptance of these contentions led in the 1960s to the term *quality and reliability* as an overall designation. Then, as more and more performance and process characteristics came into focus, the idea of creating combined phrases by stringing together numerous attributes came into vogue, as for example, *reliability–availability–serviceability* (RAS). Soon, however, these were discarded as too cumbersome, and ever since the search has been on for a single, generally applicable phrase to designate quality in all situations. The search is now over; for if quality is defined as conformance to requirements, the specific and measurable attributes of manufacturability, reliability, availability, serviceability, and the like can be incorporated in the overall requirements statement and become part of the quality measurement.

The definition of quality as conformance to requirements *includes* the concept of "fitness for use"—which in itself is a functional, albeit broadly applicable characteristic, useful and applicable primarily to consumers and end users of industrial products and services.[2] When used as a definition of quality, "fitness for use" lacks the key attribute of general applicability since it is cumbersome to incorporate such aspects as price, delivery schedule, reliability, etc. Fitness for use is a valuable concept, especially when it comes to designing a product. But in the broader context of extending the definition of quality to the general management of business processes—where work products can also comprise information, a variety of services, and "value-added" activities, and where requirements are not always expressed in terms of use or usability—"fitness for use" becomes limited. In addition, since

---

[2]J. M. Juran, F. M. Gryna, Jr., and R. S. Bingham, Jr., *Quality Control Handbook* (New York, NY: McGraw-Hill Book Company, 1979), p. 2-2.

"fitness for use" is always determined by the user or recipient, it is more related to expectations than stated needs.

Other definitions of quality abound. Scholars in such disciplines as philosophy, economics, marketing, and operations management have considered the subject, with each group having a different view. The result has been a host of competing and confusing perspectives, resulting in different terminologies and definitions. Garvin[3] identifies five approaches to the definition of quality. One of these, the transcendent definition, is totally useless for management purposes because it considers quality an intangible, similar to truth, beauty, or goodness. All the other categories are based on degree or level—with only one definition indicating basic nature or kind of state: *conformance to requirements.*[4]

> Traditionally, three factors have been considered to influence the customer's purchase of a product and subsequent satisfaction with it: quality, price, and delivery. If we accept that a customer's requirement can include an expected delivery date and also establish a price range determined by the customer's available resources and other economic circumstances, then the definition "conformance to customer requirements" is still the most manageable, practical, as well as concise one. (The fact that in the vast majority of products bought by individual consumers, the customer's requirements are not recorded in a specific requirement statement, is easily compensated for by the various marketing processes that define a group of customers for which then a general *market demand statement* is produced.) If affordable price is part of the customer's requirement, then the argument becomes academic and of no relevance, whether a Volkswagen or a Cadillac is a "higher quality" car. This point, by the way, also illustrates the importance of a complete, clear requirement statement that will lead away from the traditional distinction between quality, price, and delivery—they should be really part of the same customer requirement.[5]

Still another popular view of quality is that it means the ideal or the perfect. Related to the belief that quality means perfection is the idea that it is a superior trait, implying a "touch of class." In this sense, quality is associated with the upper classes of society, and a restricted class of activities and products, such as art, jewelry, and other items of luxury. (In this vein, we usually do not speak of quality housecleaning or dishwashing, quality trucking or quality pest control.)

If quality means conformance to requirements, then there cannot be a

---

[3]David A. Garvin, "What Does 'Product Quality' Really Mean?", *MIT Sloan Management Review*, 26 (1984), 25–29.

[4]The definition of quality, adopted by the American Society for Quality Control (ASQC), also implies degree: "Quality is defined as the totality of features and characteristics of a product or service that bear on its ability to satisfy a given need." (*See* [3] in the Bibliography.)

[5]A technique called Operating Profit through Time and Investment Management (OPTIM), developed by Westinghouse Electric Corporation, can link cost, schedule, and quality through an inventory flow model, known as the *cost-time profile* for a given process. (See E. Sullivan, "OPTIM: Linking Cost, Time and Quality," *Quality Progress* [April 1986]: 52–55.)

distinction between "quality" requirements, "product" requirements, or "business" requirements. The concept of quality simply means that requirements of all kinds—be they product, business, or performance-related—are met at every stage of the process producing the work product.

Clearly, a requirement statement should not include items that are in conflict with one another and therefore cannot be implemented; or items that are not easily measurable. Therefore, it is true that *establishing good requirements is an extremely challenging task, and one fundamental of successful quality management.*

1.1.3 Conformance

Conformance means agreement; it means that the substantive, observable, and measurable attributes of two or more entities are identical. Accordingly, conformance is a *state*, or binary variable: it exists or it does not.

The measuring and judging of conformance, obviously, is critical to establishing quality. Depending on the requirements to be met and the nature of the work product, the measurement of conformance may range from the trivial to the most complex of tasks.

When conformance is measured in terms of *attribute data* (data that can be counted)—that is, when meeting a requirement means attainment of a stated number of countable attributes—then conformance means the total absence of all defects: the state of "zero defects," or a defect-free work product.

When conformance is measured in terms of *variables data* (quantified attributes measurable along a continuous scale)—that is, when meeting requirements means the attainment of quantifiable attributes within the stated error of measurement (tolerance)—then conformance means the absence of deviation in all data measurements, within tolerance, from the quantified requirements.

Examples of attribute data include characteristics such as the presence of a required label, the absence of a warning light, the occurrence of spelling errors in a document, the installation of a required washer, and so on. Other examples of characteristics that are inherently measurable and in which the results can be recorded in a binary fashion (yes/no), are the presence (absence) of engineering changes on a drawing or the acceptability of a dimension when measured on a go/no-go gauge.

Examples of variables data include the diameter of a shaft measured in millimeters, the lifting capability of a fork lift in kilograms, or the concentration of a solvent in percent.

Work products sometimes mean discrete *units*, as, for example, a bolt, a lightbulb, or a document. A collection of discrete units is called a *lot*, where variations may exist between individual units in terms of conformance to requirements. Products can also exist in *bulk*, such as containers of chemicals, rolls of paper, coils of wire. Still other work products can represent a *service*, such as a course or a television program, or a complex *system*, such as a transportation network or a weapons system. For all these cases, the measurement of conformance is just as complicated as the requirement statement with which the work product must be in agreement. Measuring and judging conformance may require the installation of elaborate quality planning and control functions, as well as inspection and test programs with a coordinated series of tests at successive levels of the process. Subsequent chapters will deal with some of the specific aspects of planning and managing conformance.

This notion of conformance and the definition of quality as conformance to requirements obviates such concepts as "quality of conformance,"[6] which in reality refers to conformance to specifications. This concept is only helpful in the overall context of quality management if there is reasonable assurance that specifications accurately represent requirements.

In a similar vein, the term *quality of design* has a meaning only as it becomes a specific phase of the overall quality management process. Also known as the "grade of quality," it establishes a relationship between specifications and the expectations of the end user—a relationship difficult to measure at best. Since the basic, tangible input to quality management is the requirement statement, the concept is helpful only if requirements fairly and accurately represent user expectations.

The interrelationship among expectations, requirements and specifications, conformance, and quality is shown in Figure 1-1.

1.1.4 Process

Achievement of conformance to requirements involves the performance of a number of separate activities in a prescribed, logical sequence. *A process can be defined as the logical organization of people, materials, energy, equipment, and procedures into work activities designed to produce a specified end result (work product).*

A *manageable process* must have measurable inputs and outputs, and it must be *adaptable* to change. In addition, the resulting work product must have a *value* (measurable in some convenient form) greater than that of the original inputs to the process. Although the properties of effectiveness, efficiency, and productivity may not be needed for process manageability, they certainly figure in acceptable process performance (see Figure 1-2).

Process management emphasizes conformance to customer requirements by means of defect-free output (quality management) in the most efficient and productive manner (process optimization) and the planning and implementation of changes to the process in a timely and orderly way to meet changing requirements and other needs anticipated in the future (adaptability).

A process may or may not yield quality results, that is, its resulting work product may or may not conform to requirements. If it does not, a predetermined

---

[6]Juran et al., *Quality Control Handbook*, p. 2–4.

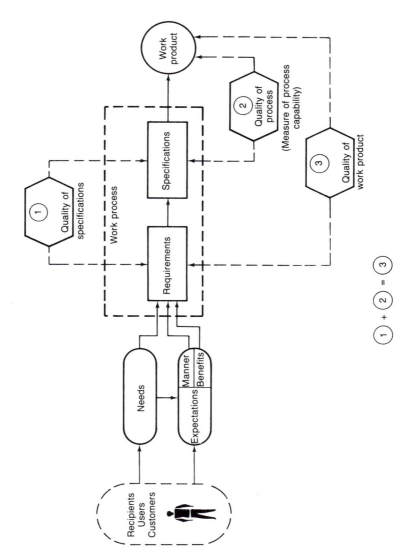

Fig. 1-1. Interrelationship among expectations, requirements and specifications, conformance, and quality.

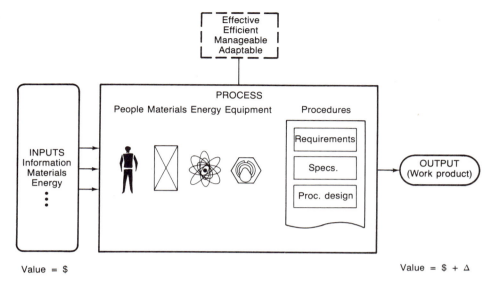

Fig. 1-2. Basic process schematic.

series of changes and management actions are required, known as *quality improvement*. (Since quality by definition is a singular state, the term *quality improvement* is really a misnomer, because it implies improvements to assumed levels of quality. A more appropriate expression would be *improvement toward quality*.)

A process can involve any aspect of a business; in turn, every business or industrial function (design, manufacturing, administration, and so on) can be characterized as a set of one or more interrelated processes. The definition of a process can actually encompass a small activity or a very large, complex business or industrial operation. For purposes of measurement and control, it is convenient to define elementary processes—or *tasks*—which are manageable by a single individual and in which work activities are carried out by one or more people but always under the control of a single supervisor or manager. *A task is the smallest measurable activity within the process.*

Another key concept in process management is *process control*—the set of activities through which a process is maintained in or returned to a desired state. *Statistical process control* is the use of statistical techniques to analyze a process through its various outputs so as to take appropriate actions toward maintaining or improving process capability.

A third key concept for managing processes is known as *process capability.* Theoretically speaking, a process is termed capable if it produces work products which meet specifications. The process view of quality management requires efforts to improve process capability, consistent with the philosophy of never ending, continued improvement toward defect-free output. In a broad sense, output of a process includes not only the work product, but also any intermediate outputs that indicate the operating state of the process, such as temperatures, pressures, flows, throughput, yield, and so forth. The gathering, measurement, and correct interpretation of this information is part of process management, and it leads to decisions whether or not action is necessary to improve the end product just produced, or the process itself.

Still another important process-related concept is that of *dominance*. This recognizes that various components of a process—usually represented by process variables—are not always equally important in their effect on the outcome, that is, the quality of the work product. Usually a single variable or a set of variables dominates the others. Identifying the dominant subprocesses or components in the overall process is important to process management because it focuses on high-leverage variables that will yield the greatest return on an investment in quality improvement. Variables representing dominant components or subprocesses are also referred to as *critical success factors*.

1.1.5 Performance

The total performance of a process comprises both the quality of its work product and the efficiency and productivity of the process. Process performance depends both on how the process has been designed, as well as how it is constructed and operated.

> The term *performance* is used in this book both as an attribute of the work product itself and as a general process characteristic. The broad performance characteristics that are of interest to the management of a process are *quality* (effectiveness), *cost* (efficiency), and *schedule*. Of course, each of these performance areas can be further broken down for ease of measurement and corrective action. Also, various performance characteristics can be interrelated, while the process itself can be optimized around one or more of them, necessitating management trade-offs. For instance, a schedule is affected by such things as the availability of skilled people, timely delivery of materials, and the availability of timely requirements. Process costs will be affected by the costs of labor, energy, and any corrective action needed. Quality will be affected by the education and motivation provided to people and by the availability of clear and complete requirements, as well as a whole host of attributes related to the process itself. As will be seen later, cost is the one convenient and highly effective common measurement which links the quality of the work product to process efficiency and productivity.

Information about performance can be gained by studying the various process indicators. If this information is gathered and interpreted on a timely and correct basis, it will show whether or not corrective action is necessary to restore the process to its intended state—that is, to ensure conformance of the output to requirements.

1.2 Maxims of Quality Improvement

The maxims of quality improvement provide the educational and motivational base upon which all implementation efforts for continued quality improvement can be built.

A maxim is a statement of a general truth with the purpose of providing a base for general direction or conduct in an area of endeavor. The maxims of quality improvement are:

(1) Quality improvement is a *business objective* because it (a) enhances competitive position, and (b) contributes directly to profitability through increased productivity and reduced costs in an environment of rising labor and service costs, increased cost of education, and ever more stringent government regulation and environmental controls.

   (Corollary: It is always less costly to do a job right the first time. The total cost of defect-free work is always less than the cost of work in which defects are present and which, therefore, requires corrective action—scrap, rework, or repair.)

(2) Quality improvement is a *management responsibility* which results from direct management commitment and action.

(3) Quality improvement requires *everyone's involvement* (it cannot be delegated and it is not a part-time staff assignment).

(4) *No level of defect or deviation is acceptable*; hence, quality improvement must be a continuing effort toward the state of full conformance to requirements.

(5) Continuing quality improvement requires purposeful management of the work process, also known as *process management*.

These maxims determine the thrust of management efforts needed for the successful overall improvement toward quality (see Figure 1-2).

1.3 Basics of Quality Management

In today's complex and competitive business environment *the achievement of quality means the successful management of the work process*. To this end, management has to satisfy several fundamental requirements of process management. Also, it takes time for every organization—no matter how well it has planned and how much it has invested in its quality improvement effort—to evolve to a point where a well managed process is in place, producing quality output. In this section we discuss the fundamentals of process management and the major stages of evolution toward it.

1.3.1 Management Concept

The purpose of quality management is to eliminate nonconformances. Although this can be approached in many ways, *process management* is the only way to assure continuing improvements toward zero defects, *as well as* process optimization. Using process theory, business processes (ranging from the simplest office procedure to the most complex technological and industrial operations) can be defined and built such that they will behave and respond in a predictable manner.[7]

In management terms, elimination of nonconformances means the removal of both worker-controllable and management-controllable defects and their causes. In terms of statistical process control, this is equivalent to removing both special causes and common causes of variation in the process output. In turn, the removal of special causes means bringing the process under (statistical) control. The removal of common causes means improving the capability of the process to meet specifications and, ultimately, user requirements (continuing quality improvement). A schematic representation of these concepts is shown in Table 1-2.

Table 1-2. QUALITY MANAGEMENT OVERVIEW

Management Attribute	Process Control	Process Improvement
Action	Detect special causes	Detect common causes
Correction	Eliminate special causes	Eliminate common causes
Applied to	Output	Process
Characteristic	Worker controllable	Management controllable; worker controllable to some extent
Result	Stability (statistical control)	Process improvement (improved capability)

Note: All management-controllable actions are upon the process, but not all actions upon the process are management controllable (some can be controlled by workers).

In quality management terms, designing and building a process and deploying resources for its future operation, including measures to prevent the occurrence of nonconformances, is known as the *management of intent*. The *management of outcome* comprises the *detection* and *correction* of nonconformances. Since all this requires time and resources, it is important that (1) priorities be established for the continuing improvement toward quality and (2) the expenditure of resources to accomplish this be consistent with the objective of

---

[7]If the process is designed and operates on the basis of the *basic feedback loop*, it will be responsive to subsequent, organized management action.

process optimization, that is, improved efficiency and productivity. The most important management tool in this regard is the *cost of quality*, which has multiple and specific uses both in quality management and process optimization.

1.3.2 Process Management

In the management of quality, it is usually the single activity that is missed or out of control which creates the quality problem. The process management approach provides a company with integrated, overall, and continuous control of all key activities required for conformance. This is true whether the problem is one of reliability, function, serviceability, performance, or any other major component of a user's requirements. Since the performance of any key activity in a department or an enterprise can substantially affect overall quality performance, the key to the modern process management approach can be stated as follows: The process must be designed and operated such that the interrelationships of all key components (people, equipment, information flow, materials, procedures) and the resulting key activities must be established not only for their own effectiveness but for their interrelated and cumulative impact on total quality performance. The significance of the process management approach is that it adds to the traditional principle of improvement through division of effort the complementary principle of *improvement through integration into a precisely defined process*. In fact, the hallmark of process management is the integration of people, equipment, information, and procedural structures to ensure conformance in an economically optimal manner. The fundamental ingredients of process management comprise:

(1) Process *ownership*: The management concept which assigns key responsibilities for designing and establishing the process and for implementing the mechanisms for measurement and corrective action (see also Section 4.2.2).
(2) Process definition, design and documentation: A structured and disciplined approach to the understanding and formal documentation of all the major components of the process and their interrelationships (see Section 4.1). The *process plan* (along with user requirements and work product specifications) is one of the five key documents in the overall quality management effort.
(3) Process *control*: The managerial function of ensuring that the process output meets specifications. It includes the functions of detection and correction. The basic process control mechanism is the *defect elimination cycle* (DEC)—essentially a feedback loop which allows management to control the process and facilitates process capability improvement. Correction comprises (1) *action on the output* (past-oriented, as it involves restoring or replacing nonconforming work products); (2) *action on the process* (future-oriented, as it is taken to prevent production of defective output); and (3) *feedback* aimed at changing specifications or process design, to ensure continued conformance to specifications.

(4) Process *measurements*: Based on the variables which dominate the process, a hierarchy of measurements is established such that they map into the user requirements as well as the measurable attributes of the work product. Along with measurements, criteria for their accuracy, precision, and frequency are also determined. Measurements are a key and essential aspect of detection. Output of every subprocess must be specified, deviation of output must be measured and identified, and actions must be taken to ensure conformance at every step in the process.

(5) Continuous process *improvement*: This is the managerial process to ensure that improvements become permanently embedded in the process, and that process output consistently meets user requirements. The object is to turn defect removal into prevention through *defect cause removal*, which in turn may require formal process changes that will become permanently embedded, as for example, process capability improvements. Continuing improvement of the process is predicated on the attribute of *adaptability*.

(6) Process *optimization* in terms of efficiency and productivity.

To be successful, a quality improvement effort needs management commitment and support so that it is equally effective in every part of the organization. The process management approach makes this eminently possible, because processes permeate the organization and cut across functional lines. Because of this, all functional areas within the business must strive for the consistent implementation of process management concepts so that the organization as a whole can deliver quality outputs both at the subprocess and at the process level. To ensure that all functional areas implement the same management techniques, there must be guidance from those to whom all functional areas report—top management. If top management understands that quality is achievable and the best approach to its management is the process approach, then the organization will succeed in achieving continual quality improvement, along with assured improvement in productivity and profitability (see Figure 1-3).

1.3.3 Stages of Quality Improvement

The implementation of quality management means to set up a process and a related management system that will prevent defects from happening anywhere in the organization. To accomplish this, investments have to be made and actions taken early in the game so that rewards are gained later. Management has to put plans in place and commit funds in advance to conduct quality testing, say, two years later, and to ensure that corrective actions can be taken and the overall process improved perhaps another year after that. A training program that costs a lot of time and money must be set up right at the beginning, even though it will produce benefits only some time later. Organizational changes—changes to the accounting infrastructure and the establishment of measurement and detection mechanisms, as well as corrective procedures—have to be made before problems

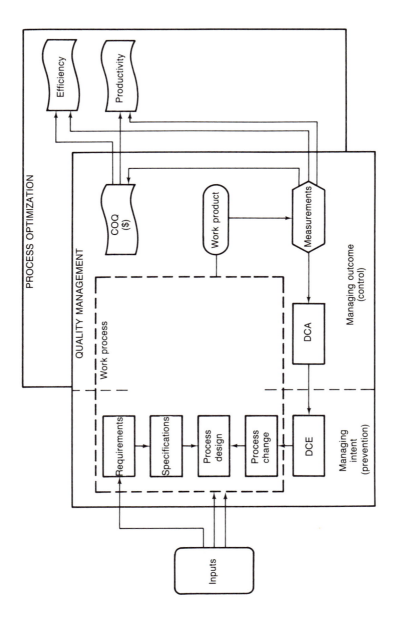

Fig. 1-3. Process management.

become big enough to have disastrous effects. Detective and preventive measures are not hard to take by themselves, but it is hard to justify them when most of the rewards lie far—perhaps years away—in the future.

The fact is that it takes time—several years in most cases—for a quality management effort to mature and produce consistently defect-free results. It takes a considerable amount of time to plan, implement, and tune the process before its work product fully conforms to requirements.

Most organizations will go through a number of distinct *stages* of evolution during their continuing quality improvement effort[8] as shown in Figure 1-4.

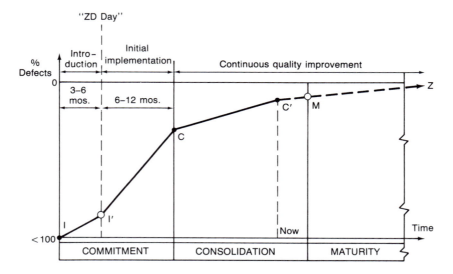

Fig. 1-4. The three stages of quality improvement.

(1) *Commitment* (Table 1-3): Management has recognized that quality improvement is needed and the decision is made to go ahead and conduct a formal, planned, and measured program. Detection efforts are put in place, and methodologies are established for problem analysis, defect removal, and the

---

[8]This staged development has been recognized by several authors and practitioners of quality management. Among others, Philip Crosby divides the process into five stages: uncertainty, awakening, enlightenment, wisdom, and certainty, each stage representing a recognizable pattern of behavior within the organization and its management (P. B. Crosby, *Quality Is Free* [New York: The New American Library, 1980], pp. 26–29.) My experience shows that it is most convenient—and operationally, more meaningful—to identify the development of a quality management effort through three distinct stages: commitment, consolidation, and maturity. These map quite easily into Crosby's five stages; leaving uncertainty off as a stage representing inaction and confusion, awareness and enlightenment map very conveniently into commitment, and wisdom and certainty will correspond to consolidation and maturity, respectively. My definition of consolidation covers some of the management actions and behavioral patterns identified with the beginnings of Crosby's stage of certainty.

Table 1-3. THE COMMITMENT STAGE OF QUALITY
              IMPROVEMENT

	Quality Improvement: Stage 1 (Commitment)
Motto	*Commit to quality*
Goal	Conformance to requirements
Objectives	1. Management commitment to quality improvement 2. Management infrastructure 3. Process selection and ownership 4. Completed defect elimination cycle (DEC)
Accomplishments	Quality policy statement Quality attitude Initial quality education Management of outcome dominates Detection Problem analysis Defect removal (special cause elimination) Cost of quality database
Measurements	Cost of quality (reporting)/Efficiency Reduction of failure costs (initial) Defect reduction/Effectiveness
Process Management	Overall process defined Process control (stability) Process performance rating "4" to "3"
Organization	Quality improvement team/Process ownership/Cross-functional management mechanism

calculation of the cost of quality. The approach for education and motivation is put together, based on the *maxims of quality improvement* (Section 1.2). With the establishment of a formal *quality policy* and an appropriate management infrastructure comprising the basics of process management, management makes the necessary commitment to quality. The commitment stage has two phases within it: (1) *introduction* and (2) *initial implementation*. The quality improvement effort in this stage is primarily *control* oriented. Its motto: "Commit to quality."

(2) *Consolidation* (Table 1-4): All components of quality management are in place; when defects appear, they are handled and they disappear, along with their causes; the process gets adjusted. Consolidation is the stage at which heavy investment is made in prevention: the organization has the chance to make process improvements permanent. Because of this, it may be the most critical of all the stages. The quality improvement effort is continual and it includes the management of both *intent* and *outcome*. Motto of the consolidation stage: "Manage quality."

Table 1-4. THE CONSOLIDATION STAGE OF QUALITY
           IMPROVEMENT

	Quality Improvement: Stage 2 (Consolidation)
Motto	*Manage quality*
Goal	Continuing quality improvement
Objectives	1. Conformance to requirements
	2. Management by cost of quality trade-off
	3. Continued improvement of process efficiency and productivity
Accomplishments	Continuing quality education
	Balanced management of intent and outcome
	Defect elimination (common cause removal)
	Quality objectives in managers' performance plans
Measurements	Cost of quality (reporting and analysis)/Efficiency
	Reduction of failure and appraisal costs (planned)
	Defect elimination/Effectiveness
Process Management	Permanent changes to process
	Improved process capability
	Process adaptability established
	Process performance rating "3" to "2"
Organization	Process ownership/Participative management

(3) *Maturity* (Table 1-5): Quality management—through the pervasive management of the process—is part of the "management fabric." Quality output is produced routinely and process management is heavily focused on prevention—the process is a *preventive* system. The result is that very few significant defects ever actually occur. The cost of quality, in absolute dollar terms, is down to where it consists almost entirely of the cost of prevention. The contribution of quality to productivity and profitability, therefore, is also part of the business measurement process. Motto of the maturity stage: "Quality—A way of life."

In terms of schedule, quality improvement is a continuous process. In other words, there is no finite time scale within which to finish it. Its initial stages, however, are finite and can be put in a schedule-related context.

During the commitment stage, most enterprises must make extensive changes in their existing organizations and procedures. Currently most do not have the foundations to satisfy the demands that a comprehensive quality effort would imply, and preliminary steps must be taken to get their house in order. This in turn requires resources. These will not be forthcoming until management is convinced that their use is justified. Thus, the strategy in Stage 1 is to gain management commitment and support for the overall effort; the key contribution of the commitment stage is the profound change in management attitudes.

Table 1-5. THE MATURITY STAGE OF QUALITY IMPROVEMENT

	Quality Improvement: Stage 3 (Maturity)
Motto	*Quality—A way of life*
Goal	Total process management
Objectives	1. Management by return on investment in prevention 2. Optimized process efficiency and productivity 3. Competitive and adaptable process
Accomplishments	Quantified linkage between profitability and quality Quantified linkage between productivity and quality Management of intent dominates Quality objectives in individual performance plans
Measurements	Cost of quality (return on investment) Conformance measurements integrated into business measurement system Productivity and efficiency improvements Contribution of quality to profitability and competitiveness
Process Management	Process optimization Permanent improvements to process Improved process efficiency and productivity Adaptability Process performance rating "2" to "1"
Organization	Process ownership integrated into business management

The consolidation stage shows tangible benefits by attaining conformance and significantly lowering the cost of quality; its real contribution, however, is the change in everyone's attitude toward quality. Before consolidation starts, most people accept intellectually that there will be benefits. But when costs really do come down dramatically in Stage 2, intellectual acceptance turns into identification and commitment by all.

At this point, maturity sets in. When people really believe in quality and have built a solid base, Stage 3 is entered, and they begin to ask basic questions: How do we manage the new, improved process? What investments do we have to make, not only in terms of quality, but also productivity and efficiency? The maturity stage rests on an understanding that quality management is an integral part of the overall management of resources, and that process management is the vital, pervasive vehicle to accomplish it.

From a broad perspective, the three stages of quality improvement are sequential: Understanding and commitment is followed by permanent changes to and consolidation of the work process, followed by improved functioning in a new, more efficient, and mature environment. It is inevitable, however, that the pace of improvement and the progression through these stages in a large business or industrial organization will differ from group to group, function to function.

One of the critical responsibilities of top management is to prevent excessive drift and differences from developing because they will cause serious stresses in the evolution of a pervasive process management approach to quality. *Common implementation* is a key concept in the overall quality management approach: It means that every group and function within an organization should start at about the same point and at about the same time and experience progression through the stages of improvement in a more or less synchronized fashion.

> Some students of quality have suggested that staggered progression through the stages of evolution can be beneficial by providing a leading-edge group to serve as a role model for those that lag behind. A few implementations of quality management even went to the extreme of first establishing "pilot quality efforts"—which is exactly the wrong, time-consuming, and costly approach.

1.4 Cost of Quality

Historically, quality management has always suffered from the lack of an obvious method of measurement, which executive management can always easily understand. In the past, quality management was not considered to be a business management function, but rather a statistical or technical one. The reason is that until now quality has never been looked at in financial terms the way everything else in business is. By bringing together easily assembled costs like rejects, rework, warranty, inspection and test, error correction, and the like, an accumulation of expense can be shown to line management which will make them listen. Thus the first important role of the cost of quality is to gain management's attention.

Certainly, conformance costs money. It costs money to produce defect-free work products, and it also costs money to remove defects and improve products to the point where they meet requirements. But it costs even more money to operate faulty products, use erroneous reports, or to have to depend on service call after service call because of continuing, poor product performance. Work products that fail to meet requirements can cause delays, loss of productivity or assets, accidents, and the like. In assessing quality, all costs must be measured— the total impact on the "bottom line" is the important issue.

The concern of management is to minimize the total amount spent in the quality area—the cost of achieving quality and the penalty for failing to do so.

1.4.1 Definitions

The cost of quality may be divided into two areas: the cost of nonconformance (failure and appraisal) and the cost of conformance (prevention and some appraisal). The cost of nonconformance comprises all the expenses caused by doing things wrong; the cost of conformance is what is necessary to spend to make things come out right the first time.

Specific cost elements in the quality area are usually classified into three categories:

- *Cost of prevention:* Money required to prevent defects and to "do the job right the first time"; to minimize failure and appraisal costs. This category includes the cost of activities undertaken to prevent defects in design and development, and other aspects of process design and quality planning. Also included are the costs of education and training; procedural and preventive actions and measurements conducted in the business process; process design review; requirements, specifications, and specifications review; process improvements; and so on. Prevention money is usually spent *before* the work product is actually produced; therefore, it can also be considered as *the cost of managing intent.*

- *Cost of appraisal:* This category includes all the costs incurred while conducting inspections, tests, and other planned evaluations used to determine whether a work product conforms to requirements. Also included are costs of product inspection and test, maintenance of test equipment, and so on. Appraisal money is spent *after* the work product is produced but before it is released to the recipient or the user; therefore, it is *part of the cost of managing outcome.*

- *Cost of failure:* Money spent on correcting defects or using defective work products; cost associated with things that have been found not to conform to requirements, as well as the evaluation, disposition, and public relations aspects of such failures. This category includes the cost of repairing products to make them meet requirements as well as the cost of operating faulty products and the damage incurred by using them or because of their unavailability. *Internal failure costs* are caused by defects which exist in a work product prior to shipment to the user. They comprise: repair/rework and scrap; reinspection/retest; down time, lost production, and yield lost. *External failure costs* are caused by defects detected by the customer after shipment. They comprise: cost of returned defective products; complaint administration and warranty costs; and cost allowances (concessions made because of nonconformance). In some cases, the customer's cost, caused by a failing product or service, is also included.

The sum of the costs of prevention, appraisal, and failure is commonly known as the cost of quality (COQ). Since the aim of management is to minimize the total cost of quality, it makes no difference whether this is achieved by the reduction of all three components or by increasing the cost of prevention to decrease the other elements in order to lower the total. Hence, the cost to achieve quality (cost of prevention) may rise as long as this is more than offset by the savings resulting from a reduction in the penalty paid for nonquality (cost of appraisal and failure). *Any reduction in the total cost of quality translates directly into bottom-line profits for the business.*

The largest component in the cost of quality is usually the cost of failure. Therefore, to effectively cut the cost of quality, failure costs must be reduced to a minimum—if not totally eliminated. The way to do this is to invest more in prevention. This is the financial mechanism which makes the cost of quality an *investment tool* and which also ensures that it is always less expensive to do the job right the first time than to do it over. Money spent on prevention is more than compensated by the decreasing costs of appraisal and failure (see Table 1-6).

The cost of quality is also a *management tool for trade-off* against other process parameters (cost, schedule), and it is the universal measurement across the process, a common financial denominator which ensures ultimate consistency of measurement, and linkage to productivity and profits.

What has, then, emerged here is a concept of defining and tracking quality costs and then using them for three different, but interrelated purposes:

- To provide a new reporting mechanism as an added form of cost control
- To establish an analytical tool to identify opportunities for management trade-offs and the reduction of quality costs
- To provide management with an investment tool for planning prudent increases in the cost of prevention, ultimately to achieve the overall cost of quality reductions identified earlier

Note that the term *cost of quality* is associated solely with defects—the cost of making, finding, repairing, or avoiding them. In a process, there are many other costs which are not a part of the cost of quality and which contribute in a direct way to producing work products. Also, the total cost of quality is strongly influenced by the interplay among the various cost categories. We will return to this subject in more detail in Chapter 5.

1.4.2 Leverage on Productivity

The aim of this section is to define the relationship between quality and productivity and to illustrate with simple examples that productivity increases with improvement toward quality. Lack of quality means high costs, low profitability, and an erosion of competitive position.

> There is a popular belief in American business that quality and productivity are incompatible: we cannot have both. A corollary to this belief is the folklore that quality and tight schedules are also incompatible. If we want to meet a target date, quality will suffer; if we push quality, time will be lost and schedules will not be met. Deming[9] relates the case of a meeting with 22 production workers and union

[9]W. Edwards Deming, *Quality, Productivity, and Competitive Position* (MIT Center for Advanced Engineering Study, 1982), p. 80.

Table 1-6. TYPICAL EXAMPLES FOR COST OF QUALITY
COMPONENTS

	Cost of Quality	
Components	Examples	Quality Management
Prevention	Quality education Process design Defect cause removal Process change Quality audit Maintenance (preventive)	Cost of managing intent (cost of conformance)
Appraisal	Test Measurements Evaluations and assessments Problem analysis Detection Inspection Maintenance (test equipment)	
Failure (Internal)	Reinspection and retest Scrap Rework Repairs Service Defect removal Lost production	Cost of managing outcome (cost of nonconformance)
Failure (External)	Returned products Legal exposure and costs Liability and damage claims Poor availability Malfunction Replacement Poor safety Complaint administration and warranty	

representatives whose answer to the question, "Why is it that productivity increases
as quality improves?" was: "Less rework." These people knew that quality is
achieved by improvement of the process; in turn, improvement of the process
increases uniformity of output and reduces rework and defects. The savings in
human resources, machine time, and materials actually increase output with less
effort, which by definition is productivity.

Traditional thinking has held that manufacturing operations could only be effective if
they were optimized with respect to one, or certainly not more than a small set of
objectives. Cost efficiency, quality, rapid delivery, adaptability to volume changes,

and new product introductions were thought to be mutually incompatible objectives, requiring trade-offs, as any one objective could only be achieved at the expense of others. Recent experience in high technology manufacturing, notably in Japan and here in the U.S., has shown that products can be produced that meet both the objective of quality and that of low cost. This means that the traditional concept of manufacturing trade-offs and productivity has to be reexamined as many traditional assumptions no longer apply.

Conversely, the benefits of improved quality are lower costs, higher profits, and a better competitive position—which also leads to more jobs for the workforce.

Reduction of waste transfers resources (people, equipment, energy, and materials) from the manufacture and repair of defective products into the manufacture of more defect-free products. In effect, *the capacity of the production line is increased.* The benefits of better quality through improvement of the process are therefore not just better quality and the long range improvement of competitive position that goes along with it, but greater productivity and better short-term profits as well.

Discussions of the relationship between *quality and cost* fall into two distinct categories. One view, which draws on the operations management experience, sees quality and cost as inversely related because the cost of improving quality is thought to be less than the resulting savings in rework, scrap, and warranty expenses. According to this view, which is widely held among Japanese and U.S. high-technology manufacturers and which explains much of their dedication to the goal of *continuous quality improvement*, quality is synonymous with the absence of defects and the costs in question are the cost of quality.

Another view, which is an extension of the first, is that improved conformance will eventually lead to a reduction in long-term manufacturing costs. The justification for this claim is the link between quality improvement and productivity gains. For example, simplified, prefabricated and easy-to-assemble designs should require fewer workers at the same time that they reduce defects. Investment in automation should result in more consistent production as well as improvements in worker productivity. Quality improvements are also expected to lead to further savings in the form of experience-based scale economies, through their impact on market share and cumulative levels of production.

These ideas are basic to any discussion on productivity: a work process converts inputs into outputs. Productivity is an attribute of that process and it is measured by comparing the work outputs to the work inputs. An *effective* process is one that produces a quality product, and the measure of process performance cannot be satisfactory if it concentrates on the quantity of output while ignoring its quality. We must recognize that the purpose of a work process is not just to produce an end result but to produce it in conformance to certain requirements. Hence, *quality output is the basic objective of the work process* and also the basic measure of productivity.

Examination of these and similar questions shows further, that the purpose of the process is more than producing products that meet requirements; the purpose is *to create value*. The productivity of work is measured by the incremental value of the products produced. A work product need not be "useful" or utilitarian—artists can be productive even though their products are not "used." But for work to be productive, it must satisfy a need and have value *to the recipients* who will use it or benefit by it. Thus, the measure of productivity of a work process is the *value added* to the work product by that process, divided by the value of the labor and capital consumed.

Value can be determined in two basic ways: by mandate, or by the marketplace through the laws of supply and demand. Value measures quality, but it also measures the very requirements against which quality is judged. Each of two providers can produce similar products, but one organization is more productive than the other if its products are in demand while the other's are not. In other words, an organization producing what the market requires is more productive than one producing unneeded items, however well they conform to some specification. *This is one essential difference between requirements and specifications; requirements must be based on a stated or recognized need.*

Efforts to improve productivity are hampered by three widely held misconceptions: (1) that the solution to the productivity problem is increased capital spending; (2) that productivity gains are difficult to achieve in service and white-collar industries; and (3) that the problem with productivity only revolves around the workers—they do not want to work and they certainly do not want to improve productivity.

In fact, to have any major impact on productivity, management action is required. To define productivity measures, it is necessary to assign a value to each work product, balance these into a consistent pattern, and adjust the whole to match short- and long-range productivity objectives. Productivity and quality are closely linked: a quality work product always contributes positively to the recipient's productivity. With value determined, productivity gains can arise only through adjusting the work process or the work inputs. Generally, adjustments to the process yield the greatest long-term gains. In summary, if the goal is productivity and reduced costs, the way to achieve it is through continued process improvement.

The cost of quality is in itself an overall productivity indicator, because quality improvement automatically brings a lower cost of quality, which is inversely proportional to improved productivity.

1.5 Quality, Productivity, Profitability, and Competitiveness

The purpose of this section is to assess the effect of quality and improved productivity on *profitability* and the *competitive position* of a business.

Short-term profits are not a reliable indicator of good management. Anybody can pay dividends by deferring maintenance, reducing research, or by acquiring another company.[10] A better indicator of the health of a business is the effect on production. Paper profits, the yardstick by which stockholders and boards of directors often measure the performance of management, make no contribution to the material well-being for people anywhere; they do not increase wealth, nor do they improve the competitive position of a company or of an industry. Paper profits do not create assets; improvement of quality and productivity do.

Value (and therefore price) has no meaning without a measure of the quality of the product being acquired. Without adequate measures of quality, business tends to drift to the low bidder—lack of quality and high cost being the inevitable results. American industry and government—federal, state, and municipal—are being ruined by rules that simply award business to the lowest bidder.

> The Wollman Memorial Rink in New York City's Central Park is a sad example of how the low bidder eventually turns out to be the most expensive one—in terms of the astronomical costs of inspection and reinspection, repair and rework of shoddy workmanship, cost of litigation, and the resultant delays.[11] When it finally opened after six years of bungling by the City and the waste of millions, it provided ample proof for how the requirement for multiple, low-bid contracting in fact discourages quality work by responsible bidders.[12] A host of examples show that municipal agencies and especially transit authorities are regular targets for legalized plunder, inviting corruption and wholesale cheating by their policy of doing business with the lowest bidder. They are, in turn, forced into this policy in the United States by state agencies and the federal government, which by law grant funds only to the lowest bidder. The many bad experiences in urban transportation, because of erratic performance of equipment purchased on the basis of the price tag alone, may have retarded by a generation the expansion and modernization of mass transit in the United States.

When purchasers require a commitment to quality, such as statistical evidence of process control, in the purchase of critical parts, they will experience a drastic reduction in the number of vendors they deal with. Determination to reduce the number of vendors, and to require evidence of statistical quality control, requires time, learning, and cooperation. In the long run, however, a

---

[10]Corporate restructuring, resulting from or under the threat of takeover by "corporate raiders," is the most extreme case of the unproductive utilization of assets in that *equity is retired in exchange for increased debt*. American enterprise, at a time when all its assets and management skills are needed to improve its long-term competitive position, is being driven by the takeover campaign into massive restructuring and other protective measures whose entire focus is on short-term payoffs. To be sure, enhancing competitiveness through the continuing improvement of business processes will undoubtedly lead to the redeployment of assets—but this must go hand-in-hand with productivity growth, quality improvement, and the creation, rather than destruction, of equity.

[11]*New York Times*, August 26, 1985, pp. B1–B5.

[12]*New York Times*, November 13, 1986, p. A30.

relationship between purchaser and a single supplier has significant advantages and is necessary for best economy. There are operational advantages, too—the simplification in accounting and paperwork being just one.

In summary, productivity will be increased by (1) ceasing dependence on mass inspection and substituting the demand for statistical evidence of quality; (2) ending the practice of awarding business to the low bidder and depending instead on meaningful measures of quality along with value and price; and (3) reducing the number of suppliers traditional in the competitive bidding system and requiring instead statistical evidence of quality that leads to a lasting relationship with a single source, based on mutual trust and cooperation. These measures will by definition result in a significant improvement toward quality, with a resulting positive impact on productivity and profitability as well.

The argument about the relationship between *quality* and *price* runs in both directions. Quality and price may or may not be positively correlated, depending on the amount of information available to consumers and users. The empirical results are equally mixed. Although a number of studies have found a positive correlation between quality and price, these studies were based primarily on experimental evidence rather than on market data. When such data were introduced, the results differed by product category. Hence, quality assessment is guided less by price than by other variables—in other words, high price does not necessarily mean quality.

But if quality is defined as conformance to requirements, superior aesthetics, or on-time delivery, it need not be accompanied by premium prices. In this case, quality and market share are likely to be positively correlated. Based on empirical data and market research done on this topic, analysts have found a strong positive association between *quality and market share.*[13] Those businesses that improved their quality performance in the 1970s increased their market share five or six times faster than those that did not ship quality products, and three times as rapidly as those whose relative quality remained unchanged.

Figure 1-5 shows two ways in which improved quality might lead to higher profitability. The first route is through the *market* side: Improvements in performance, function, and other aspects of conformance lead to increased sales and larger market shares—or, alternatively, to less elastic demand and higher prices. Assuming that the cost of achieving these gains is exceeded by the increases in contributions received (revenue, income), higher profits will result. Secondly, quality improvement may also affect profitability through the *cost* side. Fewer defects or field failures result in lower manufacturing and service costs; as long as gains exceed any increase in expenditures on defect prevention, profitability will improve. Empirical studies confirm the strong positive association between *quality and profitability.* Quality produces a higher return on investment (ROI) for any given market share. Quality improvements, by increasing market share, also

---

[13]Garvin, "What Does 'Product Quality' Really Mean?", pp. 34–39.

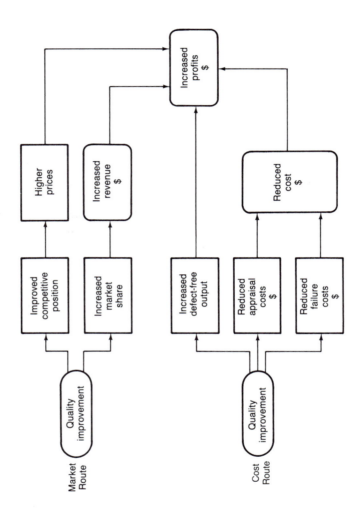

Fig. 1-5. Quality, productivity, and profitability.

lead to experience-based cost savings and further gains in profitability. The market-based link between quality and profitability is, therefore, well supported by the available evidence.

The second linkage described in Figure 1-5 is also well established. As we have stressed thoughout this chapter, quality is conformance to requirements and its cost needs to be understood as the total cost of quality. But since this total cost is actually lower than the cost of nonconformance—that is, the cost of a random, slipshod process—*the relationship between conformance to requirements and the total cost of quality is an inverse one.*

DISCUSSION QUESTIONS

1. Name the five key attributes of a manageable definition.
2. Define the terms *customer, consumer, user,* and *end user.* Explain differences.
3. Discuss the difference between need and expectation. Explain why distinction between the two is critical in understanding the formal definition of a requirement.
4. Name the three important attributes of a requirement statement.
5. Explain why an initial effort to establish requirements is essential to successful quality management.
6. Explain the difference between requirements and specifications. Is it correct to state that they represent two different views of the same work product? Whose views?
7. Define *quality.* Show that your definition incorporates the five attributes of a manageable definition.
8. Review and discuss at least two other definitions of quality. Explain why quality is a matter of state, not degree.
9. Define the terms *attribute data* and *variables data.* Explain the difference.
10. Define *conformance.* What does it mean when measured in terms of attribute data? In terms of variables data? Name a few examples for each.
11. Define a *process.* What is a manageable process? Name the key attributes of such a process.
12. Define and explain *process capability.* Explain how statistical process control is used in connection with process capability.
13. Name and explain the six fundamental requirements of process management.
14. Name and explain the three major stages of quality improvement over time.
15. Define the *cost of quality.* Name its three major component categories. Explain the three major uses of the cost of quality in quality management.
16. Show at least two ways in which quality can lead to higher profitability. How does quality contribute to increased productivity?

2

PREVENTION: MANAGING INTENT

Prevention means dealing with a situation beforehand: hindering or averting the occurrence of something through *planned* countermeasures. In the context of quality management, it means ensuring the intended outcome, that is, conformance to requirements. Prevention is intended to create obstacles to the occurrence of defects and thereby to ensure ultimate quality.

The planning and creation of a work product occur in several phases. Among these, *requirements, planning, appraisal, and process improvement,* are part of prevention—the management of intent.

The immediate objective of quality management, of course, is to ensure conformance—but this has to be an integral and compatible part of the overall set of objectives set by the enterprise. In fact, in modern business and industrial organizations, quality is one of the major business objectives.

2.1 Business Objectives and Quality

It is useful to define some of the fundamental concepts related to the purposeful, planned conduct of business and the related management of quality, all of which will be frequently discussed in this chapter and throughout the book.

- An *aim* or *goal* is that which one proposes to accomplish or attain, with an implication of sustained effort and energy directed to it over a longer range.[1]
- An *objective* has more specificity and implies attainability over a period of time. An objective, then, is a statement of the desired result to be achieved within a specified time; by definition an objective always has an associated schedule.
- A *strategy* is a broad course of action, chosen from a number of alternatives, to accomplish a stated goal in the face of uncertainty.
- A *plan* is a specific course of action, designed to attain a stated objective.[2]
- A *policy* is a statement of principles and beliefs, or a settled course, adopted to guide the overall management of affairs[3] usually in support of a stated aim or goal. It is mostly related to fundamental conduct and usually defines a framework within which other business and management actions are carried out (e.g., fiscal policy, employment policy, and the like).

Every business has at least two major goals: *profitability* and *competitiveness*. The two are essential for the survival and success of any business or industrial organization in the free enterprise system.

These fundamental goals may be complemented by other, more specific objectives. As a matter of interest, the stated business goals of the IBM Corporation for the 1980s are:

- Enhanced customer partnerships
- Growth with the industry
- Product leadership and excellence in technology, value, and quality
- Low cost in producing, selling, and servicing products and in administering the business
- Sustained profitability

It is easy to show, however, that these four—or indeed any set of similar—objectives can be related directly to the two fundamental business goals mentioned above.

Profitability can be fueled from either the cost side or the income side—or from both. Quality also contributes to both. On the *cost* side, cost reductions through consistently decreasing the cost of quality and increasing efficiency (lower unit costs) contribute directly to the "bottom line." On the *income* side,

---

[1]*Webster's New Collegiate Dictionary*, 2nd ed. (Springfield, MA: G. & C. Merriam Co., Publishers, 1958).

[2]While implementation of a strategy is a stochastic or probabilistic process, implementation of a plan is deterministic. In this context, then, the expression "strategic plan" is meaningless—although a strategy can be supported by several interrelated plans.

[3]Ibid.

quality improvements lead to increased productivity, which manifests itself in increased output and, therefore, most likely in increased revenues—which again contribute directly to overall profits. (A further, indirect way in which quality contributes to profitability is through the resulting increase in market share, which is a logical consequence of increased output. See also Section 1.5.)

Competitiveness, unlike profitability, is not directly measurable—but it is directly proportional to such other indicators as market share, customer or user satisfaction, revenue, image, and the like. Quality contributes to competitiveness through increased productivity, for example, in ensuring the position of a low-cost vendor and in allowing more flexibility in competitive pricing. Quality work products lead directly to product leadership and a superior quality image in the marketplace—both resulting in measurable increase of user satisfaction and market share.

Everything an enterprise does, all of its business processes (including planning, service, purchasing, billing, administration, and so on) must be consistent with both overall business goals and stated objectives. Processes must also be *adaptable* to change as they are carried out not only in a changing external environment but also within a changing business and technological framework.

The management of quality must be such that it consistently contributes to the attainment of those objectives—which means it must encompass the entire span of the business through the *process management* approach. This in turn will inherently lead to the philosophy of *continuing improvement toward zero defects*. Although this approach was first practiced primarily in the development and manufacturing processes, it applies to any process within a business, industrial, or government organization and is the fundamental methodology discussed in this book.

2.2 The Requirements Process

As defined before, a requirement is the foremost statement of user needs and expectations with respect to a work product. As such, it is one of the most critical phases of managing intent. A "good" requirement must be *clear, complete, and timely.*

However, producing a requirement is not a single act; rather it is a repetitive process. User needs, the environment, technology, and competitors are factors that are constantly in flux. Exactly because requirements must be timely—that is, they must represent current user needs and optimal ways of satisfaction—they are not immutable entities and they, too, have to be *adaptable* to change.

An adaptable requirement is one that can, within a predefined and systematically controlled framework, be changed without impact on its other attributes. Once a requirement possesses all the characteristics of clarity, completeness, timeliness, and adaptability, it is termed a *manageable requirement*.

Management of requirements is carried out through the *requirements process*—itself a subprocess in the context of the overall process producing the required end product (see Figure 2-1).

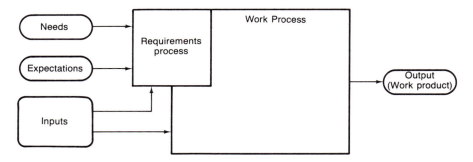

Fig. 2-1. The requirements process.

The requirements process comprises three major steps:

(1) Requirements *creation*, which begins with data gathering through such means as market research, user surveys, service feedback, standards, regulatory and environmental information, technology, and the like. The gathering of data is followed by a consolidation effort, which is a set of activities comprising (a) the elimination of conflict, (b) the grouping of data into such categories as function, performance, reliability, aesthetics, and the like, and (c) prioritization. Finally, the act of documentation results in the work product of the requirements creation step, namely the *requirement statement*.

(2) Requirements *review,* which ensures the clarity of the requirement statement document and its completeness from a functional standpoint. Requirements *assurance* is a formal activity whose objective is to ensure that (a) requirements accurately represent current user needs and expected benefits, and (b) the requirements statement is manageable. Requirements assurance verifies the quality of requirements and usually results in a *requirement acceptance statement* by the provider of the requested work product. Although it is preferable for each provider to be involved in the requirements process from the very beginning, the review stage is the latest point at which a provider should be included (see also Section 5.2).

The requirements process itself has objectives, schedules, and resources (people, funds, and so on) associated with it. Managing the requirements process is one of the most critical aspects of the overall quality management effort.[4] Two of the key

---

[4]The other critical aspects include people management, the cost of quality, and process improvement.

problems that have made the management of quality difficult, if not impossible, in the past were *incompleteness* coupled with the *rigidity* of the requirements. Incompleteness is usually the result of finalizing a requirement statement under time pressure so that it is unlikely that all of the users' needs are included or even known. (Such is the case in numerous product development efforts when a new or improved product is deemed necessary to counter competitive moves, accommodate legislative action, or respond to new regulatory or environmental guidelines.) In most cases, rigidity of requirements is really traceable to the lack of a flexible requirements creation mechanism and the ability to control changes to be introduced later: in short, the lack of adaptability.

(3) Requirements *adaptation* is the set of activities which ensures the continued, controlled updating of requirements so that they can still be used as valid input to the work process. Requirements adaptation is similar to the creation of requirements: It has its own data-gathering and consolidation activities, but includes one additional, important aspect: *change control.*

Once stated and finalized, a requirement should not be changed unless there is a control mechanism in place which ensures the disciplined adaptation of changes and additions to the original requirement statement. In many cases, a changed requirement is again subjected to requirements assurance.

What is the correct documentation level for requirements? If they are too general, they are not useful to the work process; if they are too detailed, very few people will read them. What will work for one organization will not work for another. Each organization must learn through experience what is an acceptable level. But there is one critical test: Requirements must be of sufficient detail to be translated into workable *specifications,* against which the work product can be produced.

If the requirements process is an ongoing set of activities, the level of detail can always be adjusted based on need, experience level, and results. Assuming that there exists a monitoring process to signal needed changes and to incorporate improvements, it is considered to be more efficient to start with a less detailed version. In any dynamic organization, too many things have to be changed and requirements of an overly detailed nature may become obsolete before they can be published.

Requirement statements are usually delivered in draft form for review by the provider's (producer, manufacturer, vendor, etc.) marketing and product-planning functions. Approved changes will be incorporated, and marketing, which is ultimately responsible for meeting user requirements, will approve the final statement. This document will then serve as the basis for design, which in turn will result in *work product specifications*: the producer's view of what has to be done. In turn, marketing participates in the review of the specifications as these will provide the base for the *process plan*. Since both specifications and process plan contain resource-related items (various costs, including that of human resources), they will be reviewed and approved by the appropriate functions within the business organization, most notably the controller's office. Approval of the requirement statement constitutes the beginning of the design phase for the work product.

2.3 Planning for Quality

Planning for quality involves both the *work product* and the *process*. However, care must be taken to keep them separated and manageable—otherwise control is lost and quality will ultimately suffer.

A business process comprises the decisions and activities that must be accomplished to produce a work product. Although these activities have a complex relationship and are usually carried out concurrently rather than consecutively, they are nevertheless distinct enough to be considered separately. (The activities and their interrelationship have been illustrated in Figure 1-3 and are described in the following list.)

- *Setting objectives* involves the definition of requirements and other success factors to be attained.
- *Planning* involves developing the course of action that has to be implemented, by whom, with what resources, and within what schedule. It also involves direction for obtaining and combining the human and physical resources needed for the work activities to be performed in order to meet the stated objectives.
- *Implementation* involves carrying out the work activities called for in the plan.
- *Control* includes detection and possible corrective action. Data are gathered about the progress of work activities through measurements and comparing actual progress against the plan to see whether desired objectives are being met or if the results have deviated from the plan. In the latter case, appropriate corrective action is needed.

Under normal conditions, the control functions verify that the work activities are in agreement with the stated plan. If the comparison shows a deviation between the plan and the results of the work activities, a decision must be made as to which of them is deficient and what is to be done. *Redeployment* of resources may bring the work activities in line with the plan. *Replanning* may be required if external factors or the environment have changed. It is also possible that the original objectives may no longer be relevant or attainable.

The *level concept of planning and control* was first presented by Robert

Anthony of the Harvard Business School in 1965.[5] His work considered three levels of planning and control:

- *Strategic* (long-term, usually five years or more): Concerned with adjusting the process over time according to the ever-changing conditions and requirements of the environment (society, business, the market, technology, and so on). It involves the setting of long-range business goals and the selection of strategies to meet them.
- *Tactical* (short-term, covering a one- to two-year period): Concerns the planning and control of resource management within the framework of established strategies. It involves breaking down longer range goals into shorter range objectives, determining the resources needed, and establishing specific plans to attain them. Budgeting and other financial functions play a key role at this level, because they provide information about the combined financial effects of other tactical, process-related decisions in the business.
- *Operational* (current term, usually daily, weekly or monthly coverage): Directed toward the planning and control of individual activities and tasks within the framework of a process. It is primarily responsible for seeing that assigned tasks are carried out in the best possible manner and that resources are used productively and efficiently.

An example of quality planning activities for a manufactured new product is shown in Table 2-1.

The planning phase itself is triggered by a completed requirement statement and will produce:

- *Specifications*: a translation of the requirements statement through design activities.
- Implementation or *process plan*: a comprehensive plan resulting from process design. (The interrelationship of these concepts is shown in Figure 2-2.)

Accordingly, there are two closely interrelated design activities in the planning phase: design of the *work product* (resulting in documented specifications) and design of the *process* (resulting in the process plan—also known as plan for control).

In this context, there is no meaning to such terms as "design specifications," frequently encountered in the literature.

The terms *quality of design* or *quality of specification* simply mean the conformance of specifications to the requirements—that is, agreement between two documented sets of information. Such is the definition in this book and, in this context, the quality of design has nothing to do with such concepts as "grade," "degree of

---

[5]Robert N. Anthony, *Planning and Control Systems: A Framework for Analysis* (Boston, MA: Graduate School of Business Administration, Harvard University, 1965).

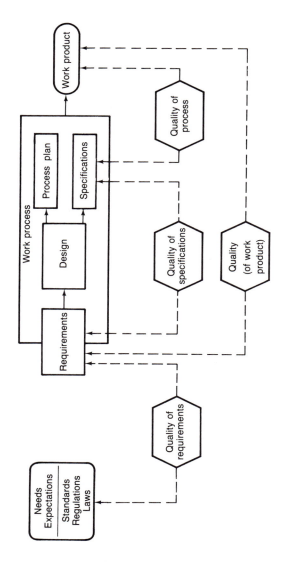

Fig. 2-2. Planning for quality: Interrelation among its components.

Table 2-1. QUALITY PLANNING ACTIVITIES FOR NEW MANUFACTURED PRODUCTS

Phase	Quality Improvement Stage 1	Stages 2–3
0. Initial Proposal	Requirement statement Product concept definition Initial business assessment Initial technical and service review Environmental impact assessment (EIA)	Quality opportunity assessment (user needs, competition) Reliability and availability objectives
1. Study	Customer and service information objectives Initial functional specifications Initial performance specifications Initial manufacturing (process) plan Industrial design Initial usability plan and test Initial comprehensive test plan EIA	Preliminary quality plan Prototype design
2. Design	Detailed functional specifications Updated manufacturing (process) plan Service plan Final usability plan Reliability planning Updated comprehensive test plan Order process plan EIA	Updated quality plan Pilot process design

Phase		
3. Development	Final functional specifications Installation plan Updated manufacturing (process) plan Design verification test (DVT) Usability test Updated comprehensive test plan Order process plan EIA	Performance design verification Updated quality plan (inspection plan) Pilot process implementation Process control and capability planning
4. Manufacturing	Updated comprehensive test plan Final customer and service information Final usability validation Manufacturing verification test (MVT) Product assurance support EIA	Initial cost of quality analysis Updated quality plan Feedback for process improvement
5. Volume Qualification and Shipment	Customer and service information maintenance Field performance reports Usability field survey EIA	Reliability, availability, and serviceability measurements Final cost of quality analysis

excellence," "level of quality," or "level of expectation" used in the literature. These are inherent to the requirements proper and are dealt with in the requirements consolidation phase. Similarly, the term "quality of conformance" is in itself misleading and incomplete, since it immediately raises the question: Conformance to what?

This text will use the following definitions of conformance in the framework of process management (see Figure 2-2):

- *Quality of requirements* means conformance of requirements to user needs and expectations.
- *Quality of design* is the conformance of specifications to requirements.
- *Quality of process* means conformance of the work product to specifications.
- *Quality* (of the work product) means conformance to user requirements.

For consumable work products (food, fuel, gas, electricity, and the like), quality of design and quality of process are sufficient prerequisites for determining overall conformance to requirements (that is, generic quality). For nonconsumable or long-life products (durable goods, manufactured products, systems, and the like) requirements must include such attributes as availability, which in turn is dependent on reliability, maintainability, and serviceability (see Section 2.3.1.). Also, two additional characteristics enter the assessment of process quality, namely, manufacturability/producibility and traceability/auditability. Before such a product is actually built, the following two steps of *qualification* are carried out:

(1) Design evaluation and qualification to verify reliability characteristics of the design (reliability prediction)
(2) Process qualification to ensure that the design is translated into a reliable product (manufacturability, manufacturing scale-up)

Whenever a major new product or service is launched, quality must be an all-pervasive objective. In addition, the growing emphasis on long life and reliability demands that the design effort encompass the entire life cycle of the product from specifications through end use and service, in other words, "from cradle to grave." This type of quality planning involves:

(1) An understanding of business goals, policies, and strategies and of user requirements, as well as the concept of quality itself—all inputs to the planning effort.
(2) Work product design, resulting in specifications and plans.
(3) Process plan:

- A listing of all the procedures, measurements, and control points throughout the work process, whether inside the company or outside, in order to achieve conformance to requirements.

- A detailed, phased breakdown of the activities to be performed throughout the work process. (Table 2-1 is a summary of such quality activities associated with the various phases in the life cycle of a new manufactured product.)
- A schedule showing when tasks within the process are to be started and finished. This can be presented either in a Gantt-chart, or more elaborate critical path diagrams (see also Section 2.5).
- Assignment of responsibilities and controls to ensure that activities are completed on time and within cost.

2.3.1 Design of the Work Product

When it comes to the design of manufactured products, public works, or complex systems which perform certain functions or services, we are looking at a problem basic to the engineering profession. Engineering is characteristically a quantitative and implementing activity, concerned not only with ideas, concepts, and inventions, but also with their translation into specifications and working reality for practical, safe, and economical applications for human use. This last aspect, namely economy, leads to the type of design most engineering activities are concerned with, namely *optimum design*, which means the selection of the *most economical* design alternative.

With user requirements clearly in mind, the engineer first conceives in general terms a solution scheme—or design alternative—that will satisfy them. At this point professional experience and judgment are applied to a significant degree, for only these give reasonable assurance that the initial choice of design parameters will reasonably well approximate the optimum design.

The next step is to analyze the initial design to see whether it will satisfy all the user requirements, especially those of a technical nature. Should the requirements not be met, some or all of the assumed initial design parameters must be modified and the procedure repeated until a solution sufficiently close to the requirements is obtained. The more routine part of the design process now includes the gradual development of a cost figure; however, at this point it is only in approximate terms, as the cost for any one design alternative may be greatly affected by a slight variation of the design parameters. Having obtained a suitable number of design alternatives with their associated cost figures, the engineer is now able to decide upon an optimum design.

For today's complex products, many companies have adopted a design process which also includes various aids to the designer:

- Design documentation aids
- Design data collection, analysis, and management
- New design disciplines, requiring formalized, quantified approaches (such as CAD/CAM, simulation, and so on.)

Once the optimum design alternative has been chosen and appropriately *reviewed* for such attributes as technical feasibility, usability, performance, financial soundness, and so on, the final process of *detail design* can begin. This is the phase in which an exact plan for implementation is laid out, which will become known as the *product specifications*. These specifications, which usually take the form of detailed drawings, blueprints, and documentation, will serve as the basis of *implementation* (that is, manufacturing or construction) and *operation* if the product is to perform a stated function such as an aircraft, a locomotive, or an appliance.

The design process, then, consists essentially of five parts: (1) A concept of the solution, usually in very broad terms, called conceptual design or *general design*; (2) an *analysis* of the design, that is, the evaluation of alternative designs and the methodical variation of design parameters to verify if they meet requirements (tests of feasibility); (3) some sort of *optimization*—the selection of an optimum design alternative with respect to performance, cost, or other significant factors; (4) the *design review*; and (5) *detail design*.

> The design of nonmanufactured work products, resulting from such non-product work processes as administrative, educational, or service activities, follows essentially the same pattern as engineering design, from general to detail design, with more or less emphasis on the interim parts (analysis, optimization, and design review).

RELIABILITY

In the early 1950s, the need arose to better define and quantify such attributes as reliability, availability, and maintainability.

The term *reliability is defined as the probability of a product entity performing its specified function under prescribed conditions without failure for a specified period of time.*[6]

Further analysis of this definition results in these prerequisites for the *quantification* of reliability:

(1) The quantification of reliability must be in terms of probability (stochastic definition).
(2) The definition must be stated in terms of the environment in which the work product must operate and for which reliability is quantified.
(3) The definition must also include a statement of satisfactory product performance, that is, conformance to requirements.
(4) The definition must also specify the required operating time period between failures.

It soon became evident that newly created specialty areas would be needed to help industry enter the era of quantification and measurement of these reliabil-

---

[6]Report by the Advisory Group on Reliability of Electronic Equipment, Office of the Assistant Secretary of Defense (Research & Development), June 1957.

ity parameters. In some cases the need for these specialists led to the creation of such specialized departments as reliability engineering, reliability control, and so on.

To achieve high reliability, it is necessary to define the specific tasks required and then to translate them into measurable quantities. Thus reliability is a design parameter just like weight, dimensions, or compressive strength, and it can be made part of a requirements statement, translated into specifications, and submitted to verfication by measurement and test.

The quantification of reliability has become increasingly important with the evolution of complex systems with many time-dependent characteristics.

As an example, consider a mechanical part which is placed on a test bench and operated until it fails, with the failure time recorded. The part is then repaired, again tested to failure, with the time of the next failure again recorded. This procedure is repeated to accumulate the *failure data* shown in Table 2-2. From these data, the *failure rate* is calculated as the number of failures per unit time. When plotted against time, the results often follow a familiar pattern known as the "bathtub curve" (Figure 2-3a). This curve shows three distinct phases, which differ both in the frequency and the causes of failure:

(1) The *startup* phase is characterized by high initial failure rates. Normally, these early failures are the results of undetected errors in design or production, or misuse and

Table 2-2. TEST-BENCH FAILURE DATA
FOR MECHANICAL PART

Time of Failure, Hours		
Startup	*Normal Operation*	*Wearout*
	20.1	
5.1	21.2	
5.2	22.1	
5.3	23.1	
5.4	23.9	40.1
5.6	25.2	40.8
5.9	26.3	41.5
6.4	27.4	42.2
6.7	28.2	42.8
7.1	29.4	43.3
7.6	30.4	43.8
8.2	31.6	44.2
8.1	32.7	44.5
9.2	33.8	44.8
9.5	34.8	
9.9	35.7	

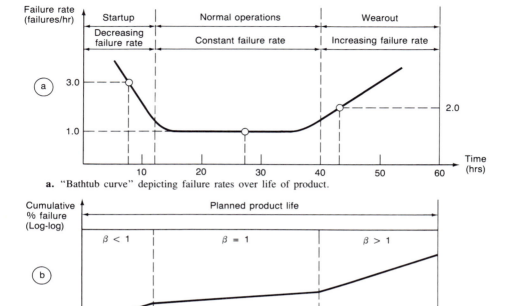

a. "Bathtub curve" depicting failure rates over life of product.

b. Corresponding Weibull plot.

Fig. 2-3. Reliability prediction: Failure rates and cumulative failure rates in time.

Source: Adapted, with permission of the publisher, from *Quality Planning and Analysis* by J. M. Juran and F. M. Gryna, Jr. (New York: McGraw-Hill Book Co., 1980).

misapplication on the part of the user because of lack of training or unfamiliarity with the product. Once corrected, early failures do not occur again.

(2) In the *normal operating* phase failures result from the limitations inherent in the design, changes in the environment, accidents caused by use or maintenance, and other operational failures; the failure rate is constant. Although failure rates can be held down by good operating and maintenance procedures, their total elimination is only possible through a basic redesign of the product.

(3) In the *wearout* phase failures are mostly material failures due to fatigue or wear; metals corrode, plastics become brittle, insulation dries out, wood rots, stone cracks, and so forth. A reduction in wearout failure rates requires well-planned and consistent preventive maintenance and the replacement of aging components.

Figure 2-3b shows the *Weibull plot* which corresponds to the bathtub curve shown in Fig. 2-3a. A value of β less than 1 indicates decreasing failure rates; a value of 1 indicates a constant failure rate, and a value greater than 1, an increasing failure rate. (See also the Weibull probability distribution in Appendix A.)

Beyond their concern for failure during the life of a product, users are also interested in the length of time that it will operate without failure. For repairable products, this parameter is called *time between failures (TBF)*; for nonrepairable products, it is the *time to failure (TTF)*.

Mean time between failures (MTBF) is defined as the average time between successive failures of a given product. (In other words, *MTBF* is the mean of the *TBF* distribution for a product which can be repaired and returned to operation after each failure, an infinite number of times.)

From the 16 failure times shown in the constant failure rate section of Table 2-2, 15 values of *TBF* can be derived by tallying them for successive failures. These can then be formed into the *frequency histogram* of Figure 2-4a. The shape of the

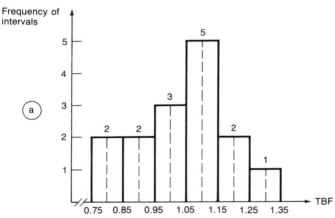

a. Histogram of time between failures (*TBF*).

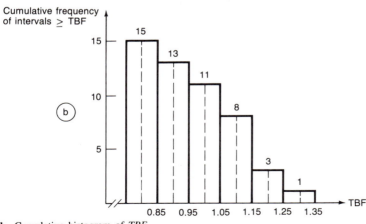

b. Cumulative histogram of *TBF*.

Fig. 2-4. Histograms.

distribution indicates an *exponential distribution* of time between failures for constant failure rates. The well-known exponential formula of reliability is derived from this fact.

The probability of achieving failure-free operation *for a specific time period t or longer* can be derived by changing the *TBF* frequency distribution to a *cumulative* one, showing the number of intervals equal to or greater than the specified time period *t* (Fig. 2-4b). Using the appropriate terminology, these frequencies become estimates of the *probability of survival*. For failure rate λ = constant, the probability of survival is called *reliability*:

$$R = e^{-t\lambda} \tag{2.1}$$

where *e* = 2.71 . . ., and *t* = time period of failure-free operation.

This formula is the exponential probability distribution rewritten with reliability as the dependent variable (see also Appendix A).

For constant failure rate the probability of failure-free operation for a period equal to or greater than its *MTBF* is 0.37, as derived from the exponential probability distribution. (In other words, *R* = 0.37, when *t* = *MTBF*.) This is contrary to the intuitive view that there is a 50 percent chance of exceeding the *MTBF*. Increasing the *MTBF* does not cause a proportional increase in reliability. Therefore, while *MTBF* is a good measure of reliability for many products, its use is not appropriate in all situations. Furthermore, *MTBF* should not be confused with such parameters as "operating life" or "service life." (Other reliability indicators are shown in Table 2-3.)

Reliability quantification for complex products comprises three basic steps:

(1) The allocation of relative reliability objectives among the various components which in the aggregate make up the more complex product or process.
(2) The application of probability theory, using historical performance data, to predict the expected failure rates for the various components identified in step 1.
(3) The analysis of predicted values to identify the strong and the weak aspects of the design, to serve as a basis for improvements, trade-offs, and similar management actions.

So far, experience with reliability prediction has shown that, in general, reliability predicted by paper analysis or demonstrated by laboratory tests is found to be higher than actual reliability experienced in operational use. Therefore, reliability prediction must be a continuous process starting with paper predictions and ending with an evaluation based on reliability measurements of actual field use of the product.

While the ultimate objective of prediction is to arrive at quantified reliability numbers, the *process* of prediction is usually just as important as its results. This is so because the prediction cannot be made without obtaining rather detailed

Table 2-3. RELIABILITY PARAMETERS

Reliability Parameter	*Description*
Mean time between failures (*MTBF*)	Mean elapsed time between successive failures of a repairable product
Mean time to failure (*MTTF*)	Mean elapsed time to failure of a nonrepairable product; mean elapsed time to first failure of a repairable product
Mean time to first failure (*MTFF*)	Mean elapsed time to first failure of a repairable product (same as *MTTF*)
Failure rate	Frequency of failures (number of failures per unit time)
Reliability	"Chance of survival"; probability of failure-free operation

data on requirements, critical material and component histories, environmental factors, and the like. Acquiring this information often gives the designer in-depth knowledge and understanding not previously available.

AVAILABILITY

Availability is defined as the probability that a product entity, when used under prescribed conditions, will perform satisfactorily every time it is called upon.

Availability is measured as the total time in the *operative* state, also called *uptime (UT)*. It is made up of the time spent (1) in active use and (2) in the ready state. On the other hand, the total time in the *inoperative* state, also called *downtime (DT)*, is made up of the time spent (3) in active repair, and (4) idling, that is, waiting for spare parts, supplies, personnel, administrative action, and the like. These time components of availability are shown in Figure 2-5.

Formulas for the quantification of availability take into account the operating time of the product and the time required for repairs. Availability is calculated as *the ratio of uptime to uptime plus downtime.*

Downtime, in turn, can be defined in two ways:

(1) Overall downtime (DT_o) includes active repair time and idle time.

When overall downtime is used, the resulting ratio is termed *operational* availability (A_o):

$$A_o = \frac{UT}{UT + DT_o} \qquad (2.2)$$

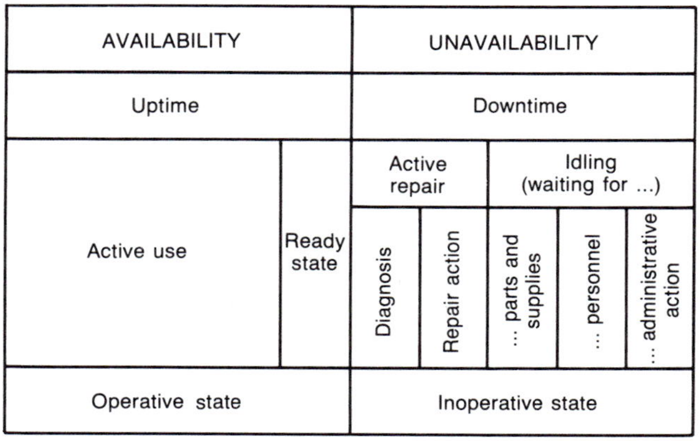

AVAILABILITY		UNAVAILABILITY				
Uptime		Downtime				
		Active repair		Idling (waiting for ...)		
Active use	Ready state	Diagnosis	Repair action	... parts and supplies	... personnel	... administrative action
Operative state		Inoperative state				

Fig. 2-5. Time components of availability.

(2) When downtime equals active repair time, the resulting ratio is termed *inherent* or *intrinsic* availability (A_i):

$$A_i = \frac{UT}{UT + DT_i} \tag{2.3}$$

If we define *MDT* as mean downtime, *MTBF* as mean time between failures, and *MTTR* as mean time to repair, availability can be calculated from the steady-state formula:

$$A_o = \frac{MTBF}{MTBF + MDT} \tag{2.4}$$

$$A_i = \frac{MTBF}{MTBF + MTTR} \tag{2.5}$$

This formula is known for its simplicity; however, it is based on several assumptions that are not always true in the real world. These are:

(1) The product is operating in the constant failure-rate (normal operating) phase.

(2) Downtime distribution is exponential.

(3) Efforts to locate product failures do not change the overall failure rate.

(4) No reliability growth occurs as, for instance, might result from design improvements or the repair of failing parts.

(5) Preventive maintenance is not part of the overall downtime.

The amount of time that a product is available for its intended use depends on its reliability and the ease with which operability can be restored after a failure—known as serviceability and maintainability.

SERVICEABILITY AND MAINTAINABILITY

The tools used during design to specify, analyze, and predict serviceability or maintainability fall in the same basic categories as those for reliability and availability.[7] These tools apply to both *preventive* maintenance (that which is aimed to reduce the number of future failures) and *corrective* maintenance (that which is aimed to restore a product to the operative state after a failure has occurred).

Serviceability can be specified in quantitative form. However, just as with reliability, there is no one serviceability parameter that applies to all work products. Some of the most common serviceability/maintainability parameters are shown in Table 2-4.

Table 2-4. MAINTAINABILITY/SERVICEABILITY PARAMETERS

Serviceability Parameter	Description
Mean time between maintenance (*MTBM*)	Mean elapsed time between successive occurrences of a specified type of maintenance (or service) action
Mean time to repair (*MTTR*)	Mean elapsed time to perform repair action (assuming availability of spare parts, supplies, and personnel)
Mean downtime	Mean elapsed time during which system or product is in inoperative state
Downtime probability	Probability that an inoperative product is restored to operational state within a specified (down) time
Mean time to preventive maintenance (*MTPM*)	Mean elapsed time to perform scheduled preventive maintenance action
Rate of preventive maintenance	Number of preventive maintenance actions per unit time

Just as with reliability, serviceability objectives for a given product can be allocated to the various components of that product. Also, serviceability can be predicted based on an analysis of the design. These methods establish the absolute value of repair or maintenance time:

(1) Extrapolate past experience on the serviceability of similar equipment to a new design.
(2) Break down the maintenance activity into elemental tasks which are not product- or design-dependent. Then collect data representing "standard

---

[7]The term *maintainability* is used more for manufactured products, instruments, and the like; *serviceability* relates to a wider range of work products and offerings. We prefer using the latter term.

times" to accomplish these elemental tasks. From these standards, a predicted total maintainability time can eventually be derived, in much the same way as total reliability is built up from elemental failure rates.

Relative measures of maintainability are sometimes used to evaluate the maintainability characteristics of a product design, such as by using a rating system to calculate a comparative rather than an absolute measure of maintainability, both for preventive and corrective maintenance. A scale of point values is applied to each of several predetermined categories of maintainability, such as frequency of maintenance operations, accessibility of the part to be repaired, and the like. The maintainability rating of the design is the sum of the point values for all categories. Because the rating has no absolute meaning, it is useful mainly in comparing design alternatives by changing some of the maintainability characteristics.

Serviceability must be an inherent part of product design. If the design does not give adequate consideration to serviceability, the result will be either a continuing high level of maintenance cost during the life of the product, or costly design changes in the product development cycle. Worse yet, there may be costly engineering changes after the product has been shipped or installed.

General approaches for improving the serviceability aspect of a design include these fundamental trade-off decisions:

- Reliability against serviceability: For a given availability requirement, should the solution be an improvement in reliability or in serviceability, or both?
- Repair against replacement: For certain products or components of complex products, the cost of repair in the field may exceed the factory cost of producing replacement units. In such cases, the concept of "field replaceable unit" (FRU) is an economic improvement in overall serviceability. FRUs may be returned to a service center or the factory for repair; in other cases, repair as such is uneconomical, which leads to the concept of "throwaway design."
- Maintenance automation: Should maintenance operations be automated with special instrumentation and repair equipment, or should they depend on the availability of skilled maintenance technicians with general-purpose equipment?

DESIGN FOR SAFETY

With increasing consciousness and focus on safety issues in the automotive, nuclear, and consumer goods (food, health, cosmetics) industries, safety in product design has received increased emphasis in American business and industry. As with reliability and serviceability, the evolution of modern approaches to safety followed similar patterns. With the increased complexity of today's products, the specification and prediction of safety is treated through quantitative techniques which also take into account the effects of component interaction on overall product performance.

For purposes of this discussion, the term *hazard* means an attribute or condition of a product that is capable of causing harm (damage, injury, and so on). *Risk* is the probability of a harmful result actually occurring, once a hazard exists and when the product is in actual use.

The general approach to safety analysis comprises:

(1) Review of available historical data on the safety record of similar or predecessor products—including complaints, claims, and the like.
(2) The study of actual or potential use or misuse of the product in question. Such studies are of particular value for products which find wide use in the consumer population (children, homeowners, drivers of automobiles, and the like).
(3) Assessment of the risk that damage will actually occur. This, in turn, may be the result of several possibilities, each having a certain probability:
   (a) The product will fail such that it will create a hazard.
   (b) Despite no failures in the design or the product, it will be misused so as to cause a hazard.
   (c) The hazard will cause damage.
   The exposure (length of time, frequency of use, etc.) of the product and its users to hazardous conditions must be expressed in quantitative terms so that the probability of resulting damage can be calculated.
(4) Determine the severity of the damage, as related to the product or its user.

2.3.2 Specifications

In modern industrial or business processes, quality cannot be achieved by simple collaboration. For any one product, the activities of design, manufacturing, production, marketing, and operations are carried out by numerous people employed in various organizations and perhaps even widely dispersed geographically. In complex products or systems, thousands of individuals may contribute to the final result. Consequently, it is necessary to provide these people with precise and detailed instructions to carry out their individual roles in the process, that is, *specifications*. Subsets of specifications (for example, bills of materials, manufacturing and test procedures, operating and maintenance instructions) are available for every activity which ultimately contributes to quality.

Specifications are the result of the product design effort and represent the provider's approach to meeting user requirements. For the industrial organizations of today, with material sources, factories, vendors, and markets located in multiple countries and with products and systems operating interchangeably on a global scale, the written specification has become an indispensable document for ready communication of product characteristics and operations. Contents of material and the structure of product specifications have become highly formalized and standardized.

In the context of quality management, specifications represent the base against which a work product is developed and implemented. Although most of the text to follow will concern itself with measurements, methods, management techniques, tools and aids aimed at ensuring that a work product conforms to specifications, the overall quality management process must equally focus on conformance or agreement between specifications and the original stated user requirements, for only the combination of the two will ensure ultimate work product quality—that is, conformance to requirements. This distinction is not always made, with the sad result of either ignoring or "descoping" aspects of the user requirements. This in turn will lead to user dissatisfaction and a consequent *increase of work* related to redefinition of specifications, rework, adjustments and corrections, and retesting with a resulting loss of productivity—which may lead to loss of competitiveness and market share as well.

2.3.3 Design of the Process

Planning for quality includes process design activities that lead to the specification of procedures, work activities, and other components of the process that yields the final work product. This portion of the specifications is also known as the implementation plan, manufacturing plan, build plan, or simply *process plan*. The process plan in turn must include the controls which will ensure adherence to applicable standards, legal and technical guidelines, and measurements against the documented specifications. (For more detail on process design, see Section 4.1.)

Control is the set of activities through which we detect deviation and restore a desired state. The control process operates through a mechanism universally known as the *feedback loop* (see Figure 2-6). At the center of this loop is the control variable which we are trying to regulate. In the operation of the feedback loop, the specifications set the *intended* state of the control variable; the *actual* value is measured by agreed-upon means. When the actual deviates from the specified by a margin greater than a predetermined limit or tolerance, the loop is "closed," setting into motion the means for correcting the error, and restoring the status quo.

At this level, the control process may take any one of several forms:

- Automated control: The loop is closed without human intervention (used in manufacturing processes and information and communication systems, for example).
- Worker self-control: The individual at the work station level observes and measures deviation and then takes action in light of the information.
- Inspection feedback: Measurements made by inspectors are given to the workers at the work station level who then close the loop.

At the technological level there are enormous numbers of control variables: subsystems and systems, elements of documentation, scheduled tasks, and a multitude of measurements. Control over this huge number of variables can

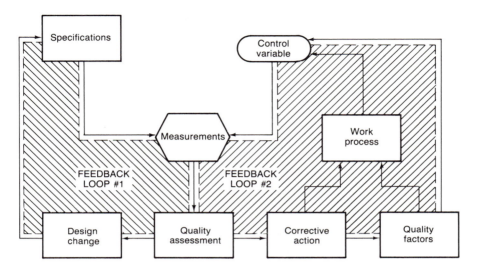

Fig. 2-6. Control based on the feedback loop.

nevertheless be accomplished by technical means, relatively straightforward procedures, and a few human beings. At the managerial level, the control variables are few in number, but each becomes quite important in terms of the cost of quality. As the principle of the feedback loop is applied to the two basic components of control, detection and correction, managers get a handle on some well-known tools, including *statistical process control* and *control charts.*

Most process control activities take place at the subprocess (departmental) level and are planned to meet the needs of specific operations. Some of these controls are designed to be carried out at individual work stations.

Any well-designed process plan must include provisions for reviewing results to see whether implementation follows the plan. Sometimes these provisions are written into the plans themselves; more usually there is a separate "plan" for review or audit.

Applied to quality management, audit has two vital applications:

(1) To judge whether the process plan is adequate to achieve quality objectives, and
(2) To assess whether implementation follows the plan.

Responsibility for process planning activities varies widely and depends, among other things, on:

• Complexity of the work product
• Process configuration (e.g., is it highly concentrated within one functional organization or department, or is it dispersed across the company?)
• Education and training level of supervisors and workers

- Extent of managerial commitment to the concept of separation between planning and implementation

The people responsible for implementing the process plan have the responsibility to meet multiple goals: conformance to requirements, cost, delivery schedule, safety, personnel relations, environmental guidelines, and so on. Some of these factors are so critical that businesses set up special safeguards to assure that compliance in some areas does not affect efforts in other areas. In the case of quality, managers are concerned with the parameter of conformance to specifications; to safeguard this compliance, inspection and test departments have been established and, more recently, staff quality functions added (quality control engineering and quality assurance, among others). These in turn often play a leading role in planning the process controls and in quantifying and measuring process capability.

> An important aspect of process planning is participation in the product design reviews. A major reason for this is to assure—especially in the manufacturing processes—that product tolerances and process capabilities are compatible. If the process is unable to hold the product tolerances, the consequences can be severe. There will be many defects, with associated scrap, rework, and increase in the cost of quality. There will be an increasing number of inspections and beyond them, some nonconforming units which may escape detection altogether, will get out to users—all of which is very costly in real terms. For most work products, the number of conformance characteristics is very large. As a result, the number of measurements, as well as tolerances, is also very large. Such large numbers make it uneconomic and even unrealistic in terms of time to review all measurements and tolerances individually. Instead the reviews concentrate on the relatively few factors which are potentially the biggest source of trouble—or, in other words, which dominate the work process.

The design of quality controls is really equivalent to applying the *defect elimination cycle* (see Figure 3-10). It also deals with such matters as standardization of inspection and test methodology; choice of measurements, instrumentation, and test equipment; schedules and frequency of tests; data recording, reduction, and analysis systems for process control and work product evaluation.

A further need in process planning is to provide *traceability* so that the product and its origins can be mutually identified. This is needed for many reasons: to assure lot uniformity in such manufactured products as pharmaceuticals; to aid in proper sequential usage of perishables; to simplify investigation of product failures; and to expedite the application of corrections or adjustments, and as a result, to minimize the extent of product recalls. Attaining complete traceability for complex work products or systems can be a formidable job, involving extensive documentation, record keeping, data processing support, and the like. Yet this is actually one of the requirements for many products in the chemical, pharmaceutical, or nuclear industries.

In planning the quality aspects of a process, nothing is more important than advance assurance that it will be able to hold to prescribed limits or tolerances against stated requirements. *Process capability* provides a quantified prediction of this ability—which is a major element of both quality planning and control.

Process capability is defined as the measure of the inherent uniformity of the process, that is, its ability to consistently meet specifications.

It is possible, through process capability measurement, to discover:

(1) The *natural* or *inherent* variability of the process—that is, the "instantaneous reproducibility" of its product
(2) The *time-to-time* variability of the process

Both of these measures of variability can be quantified in statistical terms, a topic we will discuss in more detail in Chapter 3.

In some businesses the transfer of responsibility from planning and development to implementation is formalized through a *release document* (in the world of manufacturing, *release to manufacture*). Completion of this formality is usually made contingent on the results of prototyping, experimentation, or simulation—acts of appraisal, along with follow-through to make the indicated and needed changes or adjustments.

2.3.4 Statistical Aids for Design

Quality planners have evolved numerous tools through which planning becomes economical as well as effective.

Statistical tools can be used prior to process implementation to analyze data in order to quantify process variation and compare the variation to engineering tolerance limits (also known as process capability study). In addition, they can be used to evaluate proposed tolerance limits on several interacting characteristics to assure that the manufacturing function is permitted the maximum possible variation consistent with overall work product requirements.

There are also some universal planning tools which have wide application in various areas of quality planning:

- Pareto analysis to identify the "vital few" causes of potential nonconformance, dominant variables, and the like
- Return on investment analysis (see Section 6.2.4) to compare the cost of solving the problem with the value of the solution
- Tools for establishing and controlling schedules and timetables, such as Gantt charts, CPM, and PERT diagrams[8]

---

[8]The Gantt chart, named after Henry L. Gantt, is a series of bars plotted against a calendar scale. Each bar represents the beginning, duration, and completion time of some activity or subprocess; together, the bars make up a schedule for the entire process. Critical Path Method (CPM) and Project Evaluation and Review Technique (PERT) are network techniques for project scheduling and control. A PERT diagram comprises a number of arrows, each representing an activity or subprocess, with its estimated duration and cost. For more detail on network methods for project scheduling and control, the reader is referred to the literature, especially [25] in the Bibliography.

The area of design for which statistical aids were first developed is related to quantifying, designing, and predicting the reliability, availability, and service-ability characteristics of complex products. These characteristics in turn are closely related to the analysis and predictability of failures and failure rates, which leads to *frequency and probability distributions*, in particular the *exponential* and *Weibull* distributions (see Appendix A.)

2.4 Appraisal

Appraisal is defined as the act of judging as to quality, status, or value.[9]

Its overall purpose is to identify existing or potential variations or nonconformances. The activities and techniques which comprise appraisal fall into two categories: *prediction* and *detection*. By definition, prediction is before the fact and is future oriented; its objective is to assess the outcome of a process before it actually happens. Detection, on the other hand, is past oriented and based on established results; its objective is to assess the outcome of a process after the fact—to ascertain real status or real value. Detection takes the form of *inspection* if it is related to exterior or observable characteristics; it becomes *evaluation* or *analysis* if it is related to measurements, and it is termed a *test* if it is aimed at establishing operating characteristics or performance. Detection is related to the management of outcome, and it will be discussed in more detail in Chapter 3.

> In some cases, *test of process* is also a future-oriented activity, since it is conducted before the process is put into operation, and certainly before any output is produced. However, test of process can take place while the process is already running and producing output; therefore, in process terms, the terminology *prediction* versus *detection* is appropriate.

The predictive techniques of appraisal are again divided into two groups: first, those which focus on the *process* and its capabilities to predict outcome, such as simulation and experimentation; second, those which are aimed at assessing the *work product* by reviewing and testing its design and specifications.

2.4.1 Simulation and Experimentation

The technique called *simulation* comes from the field of operations research; it can be useful in analyzing quality problems before a process is implemented. Simulation provides a method of studying the effect of a number of variables on a final characteristic, but all of this is done "on paper" using analytical methods

---

[9]*Webster's New Collegiate Dictionary*, 2nd ed.

without actually conducting an experiment. A simulation study requires the following inputs:

- Definition of the output variables
- Definition of the input variables
- Description of the complete process relating the input and output variables, usually in mathematical terms, such as a mathematical model
- Data on the distribution of each input variable—which implies that variability is accepted as inherent to the process

In simulation, a process model is usually developed and translated into a computer model or program. This program not only defines the relationship between input and output variables, but also makes provision for storing the distribution of each input variable. The computer then selects values at random from each input distribution and combines these values, using the relationship defined, to generate a simulated value of the output variable. Each repetition of this process results in a simulated output result. This can then be described in statistical terms, using a frequency distribution, for example. The clear advantage to simulation is the ability to make changes in the input variables or the relationships, to run another simulation, and to observe the effect of various changes. Thus the significance of variables can be evaluated on a model, providing one more way of evaluating theories on causes of problems. Simulation has been applied to many quality problems, including those related to interacting tolerances, reliability, manufacturability, and the like.

Simulation, then, is the technique of observing and manipulating an *abstract* mechanism (model) that represents a real-world process which, for technical or economical reasons, is not suitable or available for direct experimentation. The simulation model ideally represents the essential characteristics and behavior of the actual process under study. The model may be used to derive information about process performance by following the change of state of the process resulting from the succession of events affecting it.

Simulation is a *synthetic* tool which offers a combination of advantages of both the analytical and experimental approaches.[10] Synthesis allows the exploration, in a trial-and-error manner, of the relationships between the inputs and the outputs of a complex process that is composed of many definable subprocesses. If the characteristics and behavior of individual subprocesses (tasks) are known and if relationships among them can be defined in analytical terms, simulation can be used to predict the net outcome of all interactions—that is, the behavior of the total synthesized process.

The advantages of simulation are:

---

[10]Analytical methods, when applicable, are most efficient in describing the characteristics of a real-world process in terms of a logical set of rules (algorithm). The derivation and solution of such algorithms is known as *analysis*.

(1) It permits the realistic representation of complex processes, the analytical formulation of which would require generally difficult-to-solve mathematical functions.
(2) It can be used to determine optimality.
(3) In simulating probabilistic processes, random events can be reproduced by appropriate mathematical techniques (random number generators) which can be built directly into the simulation model.
(4) Simulation makes it possible to analyze multi-variable problems by holding every variable constant except the one under consideration—a condition which can otherwise be approximated only under laboratory conditions.

In view of its many advantages, simulation was quickly recognized by scientists and engineers, who began using it as a valuable tool in research and development activities. In fact, the rapid growth of certain specialized areas of industry and technology, such as aeronautical and nuclear engineering, can be partly attributed to the availability of simulation as a design aid.

Based on the role of uncertainty, a simulation model may be deterministic or probabilistic. A *deterministic* model is an algorithmic representation of an actual situation, with single-valued solutions for a given set of input parameters. There are many engineering applications that can be adequately simulated by deterministic models. A *probabilistic* model is one in which the relationships among variables are represented by chance parameters or probability distributions; the results for a given set of input parameters can be predicted only in terms of probabilities.

The validity of simulation results depends largely on complete and accurate data. Data are usually hard to come by, and it should be recognized that a large part of the time and cost of simulation is directly devoted to the gathering, handling, and organization of data.

The simulation model should have the same variables, constraints, and objectives as the real-world process it represents. Ideas and plans are expressed as assumptions or alternatives and are introduced into the model as such. The interactions among the variables, their attributes, and the constraints which limit performance are described in terms of logical procedures or mathematical relationships. The model may represent the special behavior of a single element of the process, involving few variables but many proposed alternatives, or it may represent a complex operation in which a single change affects hundreds of variables.

In constructing a process model, its deterministic or probabilistic characteristics are determined from data related to the process being simulated. Such characteristics may be:

- Reliability or availability
- Process effectiveness; that is, the capability of operating at a certain defined level to achieve conformance (see also the discussion on process capability later)

- Event occurrences within the process
- Functional operation time; that is, the duration not to be exceeded by a given process activity or task
- Tolerance of measurements

Whenever these data are available in the form of observations or measurements, functions describing the process can be derived by employing standard statistical techniques. Whenever these data are not available, *hypotheses* about the process are made and *a priori* functional relationships are established, based on initial assumptions.

A simulation model can be constructed and tested during any phase of process design or implementation. The model can be constructed *before* the process is designed in order to appraise the importance and role of certain parameters and variables, and determine their sensitivity to varying operating conditions. It can also be constructed *during* process design to experiment with various design alternatives, an approach often taken in the planning phase of the expansion of already existing complex processes—for example, a communications network, process control system, or complex business procedure. The model can also be constructed *after* the process is designed and during process implementation, in order to verify the results of process tests and to evaluate process performance. This approach is taken during startup phases of the operation of advanced, complex technological systems when individual components or subsystems have already been tested, but the entire system has not.

Experiments may be necessary to determine and analyze the dominant causes of a quality problem.[11] Experimentation is always aimed at the real-world process or a *physical* (laboratory) model of it. Three types of experiments are summarized in Table 2-5.

Experiments for evaluating one or two selected variables are sometimes called *directed* experiments.

Table 2-5. TYPES OF EXPERIMENTS

Experiment	*Description*
Directed	Values of a variable are evaluated by re-running process at different values of (assumed) dominant variable.
Exploratory	A number of variables are varied to provide data for quantifying potential dominant variables and their interactions.
Production	Small changes are made in selected variables; effect of changes is evaluated to find optimum combination of process values of selected variables.

[11]Direct experimentation on the actual process may be employed when the difficulty or cost of constructing a meaningful analytical model is prohibitive.

In the *exploratory* experiment, the dominant variables are not known but must be pursued by a formal experimental effort. A well-organized experiment of this type has a high probability of identifying the dominant causes of variability.

Experimentation is often regarded as an activity that can only be performed under laboratory conditions. To achieve maximum performance in some manufacturing process, however, it may be necessary to determine the effect of key process variables on process outcome or product properties under shop conditions. Laboratory experimentation to evaluate these variables does not always yield conclusions that are completely applicable to production conditions. In such cases, and when justified, a *pilot plant* or *production experiment* may be set up to evaluate process variables.

2.4.2 Review and Test of Product Design

Design review is used to evaluate a proposed product design to assure that the work product (1) will perform satisfactorily, (2) can be produced at acceptable cost, (3) is serviceable in the field, and (4) meets other requirements or guidelines related to quality.[12] Modern products require a more formal design review, which compensates for individual designers' lack of specialized knowledge in such areas as reliability, safety, and serviceability, which nevertheless are important in achieving overall quality. For modern work products, design reviews are integrated into the overall process management and have the following characteristics:

(1) Mandatory, primarily through top management policy.
(2) Formal, planned, and implemented like any other process activity. Review meetings produce formal reports and also generate formalized follow-up actions.
(3) Conducted by a team of specialists who are familiar with, but not directly associated with, the design effort—for reasons of objectivity. (The success of design reviews, of course, largely depends on the degree to which management supports the program by insisting that the best professionals are made available for review work.)
(4) Complete, covering all functional and performance-related parameters.
(5) Conducted at several phases of the design process itself, such as general design, detail design, and so on, as well as at several levels of the process hierarchy, such as subprocess and task.

Reliability prediction, design review, and test are valuable early warning techniques. But while the ultimate proof is the actual use of the work product by the customer, such experience may come too late for achieving optimum design.

---

[12]In IBM, a corporate instruction specifies that new products must have a reliability, availability, and serviceability (RAS) performance superior to that of the products they replace, and also better than that of competing products. Product developers are required to demonstrate, during the design review, that this instruction has been met.

This consideration led to the development of a substitute approach, which comprises various forms of testing the product design to anticipate field use.

Even before the advent of reliability technology, several types of tests were available for design evaluation, including performance and service life tests. Focus on reliability, serviceability, and other performance indicators has, however, necessitated additional types of tests (see Table 2-6). It is desirable to plan a test program so that one or two types of test can evaluate multiple functional, performance, and environmental capabilities.

Accelerated testing can provide reliability data in advance and at reduced cost. In this form of test, work products are driven to abnormally high levels of stress or other environmental conditions in order to make them fail sooner. The short life under severe test conditions is then converted, by using extrapolation, into expected life under normal operating conditions. Accelerated testing can be of substantial value, but its results can also be misleading. Therefore it is essential to use sound engineering judgment when calling for and conducting such tests.

Test of design and the pre-operational testing of the process are preventive measures, related to managing intent; test of process operation and of process performance are related to managing outcome.

Table 2-6. TYPES OF TESTS FOR DESIGN EVALUATION

Test	*Description*
Functional	Determine capabilities of work product to meet stated functional requirements.
Performance	Determine characteristics (e.g., speed, fuel consumption, response time, etc.) of the work product to meet stated performance requirements.
Environment	Determine capabilities of work product to meet functional and performance requirements under defined environmental conditions; determine ability of work product to withstand environmental effect.
Stress	Determine capabilities of work product to meet functional and performance requirements under excessively unfavorable operating or environmental conditions; determine non-time dependent modes of failure.
Reliability	Determine characteristics of work product to meet stated reliability requirements; determine time-dependent modes of failure, such as wearout period.
Serviceability	Determine characteristics of work product to meet stated requirements for preventive and corrective maintenance.

2.4.3 Process Capability: Aid to Process Design

The concept of process capability provides a quantified prediction of process performance. This has resulted in widespread adoption of the process capability concept as a major element of quality management.

Process capability prediction is a part of process design, which in turn is part of the management of intent—so are actions on the process, whose objective is process capability improvement, which, in turn, results in continuing quality improvement.

As it is not practical to determine process capability by direct measurements on the process under operating conditions, it is calculated indirectly from measurement or simulation data on the process output. In certain situations, process capability can be analyzed with no statistical aids to draw conclusions; many times, however, statistical techniques are required. They include:.

(1) Frequency distribution
(2) Probability paper
(3) Control charts

These statistical techniques are covered in greater detail in Section 3.5.1 and in Appendices A and C.

2.5 Prevention Through Process Improvement

Process improvement is the managerial process to insure that the results of corrective actions and changes become *permanently* embedded in the process, with the overall objective that process output consistently and continuously meet user requirements. Process improvement is the second half of the defect elimination cycle, which falls in the area of prevention. To be successful, a continuous process improvement effort needs management commitment so that it is equally effective and pervasive in every part of the process. Only the process management approach makes this possible, as it is the process owner who has the responsibility for carrying out the improvement effort.

The problems causing unacceptable process capability—as indicated by nonconforming process output—are usually *common* (management controllable) causes. Consequently, corrective action must be directed toward the *process factors*, which are causes of process variability. Such corrective action requires management intervention to make basic process changes through process redesign or modification, and to provide coordination to implement these changes to improve the performance of the process.

Before any process-related action can be taken, however, management must ensure that the process is *stable*, that is, in statistical control. In other words, process improvement must be preceded by completed control actions: error detection and the elimination of *special* (worker controllable) causes of output variation. (It should be noted, however, that corrective actions to both process output and the process itself can be applied concurrently, not necessarily in chronological sequence.)

Since process capability represents the performance of a stable process with a predictable distribution of output, corrective action upon the process to improve process capability will result in an improved state of stability—which means the correction and changes applied will become permanently embedded in the process. Permanent process changes (as contrasted to process adjustments or modifications possible within an existing process design with a measurable capability), by definition, imply process redesign, resulting in a changed process plan. (This may or may not mean concurrent changes in work product requirements or specifications; in fact, changing specifications usually is a short cut to show *perceived* process performance improvement.) By definition, changes to the process which result in permanent process improvement are part of *prevention*.

The theoretical basis for process improvement is represented by three key concepts:

(1) As a result of effective *process control*, aimed at maintaining or restoring the state of stability through the identification and removal of special causes of variation, the process must be brought under control before any action to improve its capability.

(2) The *principle of equifinality* (see Section 4.2.1) makes it possible that the intended end state (state of conformance) may be reached through various alterations to the process, without changing its initial conditions (work product requirements and specifications). Alterations to the process are effected through process capability improvements.

(3) In business and industrial processes, a transition toward a state of improvement is only possible if an *import of information* to the process has taken place. This is the *concept of feedback* which means that processes can maintain and move themselves to improved levels of stability with the aid of feedback information. This, in turn, leads to the conclusion that prerequisite to continued process improvement is the availability of adequate and timely feedback information. Since, by definition, the capability for continuing process improvement is *process adaptability*, the latter is primarily determined by feedback information from the management of outcome.

Adaptability is a characteristic that must be carefully designed into the process by means of (a) flexibility in the process plan to absorb known and potential change and (b) appropriate and effective mechanisms for allowing the flow of feedback information from control to prevention.

Summary

The success of continuing and consistent quality improvement depends on the following:

- The quality of requirements
- The quality of product design (specifications)
- Completeness and flexibility of the process plan, that is, the quality of process design
- Process adaptability—the capability for continuing process improvement: to absorb and make permanent, dynamic changes to the process, in response to new conditions and changed customer requirements

Statistical control provides a base for further management actions to improve the process; the effect of proposed changes to the process can be anticipated and the actual effect identified in advance through the use of more advanced methods of process analysis, including statistical techniques such as statistical inference, design of experiments, and the related techniques of analysis of variance, simulation, and experimentation.

The primary reason for using statistically *designed experiments* prior to implementing permanent process changes is to obtain maximum amount of information on the future behavior of the process, for a minimum expenditure. The fundamental purpose of a designed experiment, therefore, is to determine the course of future action. Similar to simulation, such action results from conclusions drawn from the experiment.

The steps to be taken in designing any experiment:

(1) Objective statement: Defect causes to be eliminated, process areas and components proposed for change.

(2) Formulation of hypothesis: Assume effect of proposed process changes.

(3) Planning the experiment:

  - Choosing the appropriate statistical technique

  - Examination of possible outcomes to ensure that the experiment will yield the required information

(4) Data collection for the experiment.

(5) Statistical analysis of the data, according to the choice of statistical technique made under 3.

(6) Evaluation of results (drawing conclusion with appropriate significance levels).

(7) Recommendations (for alternate experiments or implementation of proposed changes).

  These seven steps are present in any statistically designed experiment, indicating the logical framework for the experimental process. A detailed discussion of designed experiments is beyond the scope of this book. For further study, the reader is referred to [7], [14], [19], [23], and [35] in the Bibliography.

Many aspects of redesigning and improving a process require efficient and accurate experiments because as process changes are implemented—whether to improve effectiveness or efficiency—the change can be disruptive to operations, potentially causing new control problems that could negate the effect of process improvement. After any instabilities of the change have been resolved, the new process capability should be used as the basis of control, and decisions for further improvement.

DISCUSSION QUESTIONS

1. Define the term *prevention*. Discuss how it contributes to conformance to requirements.

2. Define the terms *goal, objective, strategy,* and *policy*. Explain the difference between goal and objective, policy and strategy. What is the difference between strategy and plan?

3. Explain how quality contributes to competitiveness.

4. Describe the three major steps of the requirements process.

5. Define the term *reliability*. What are the requirements for its quantification?

6. Describe the product design process. What does quality planning involve? What is optimum design? What are the five essential parts of the design process?

7. Describe process design. How does it differ from product design?

8. Explain the role of design reviews. Are they part of prevention or control?

9. Define the term *appraisal*. Name the two major categories which comprise appraisal activities.

10. Discuss simulation and experimentation. Explain the difference between them and their respective uses in managing intent. Describe the three major types of experiments: directed, exploratory, and production.

11. What are the key characteristics of design reviews, applied to high-technology work products?

12. Describe at least three forms of testing product design. Which forms of test are preventive and which are related to control (managing outcome)?

13. What two steps of qualification are carried out before actually building a product?

14. What does the "bathtub curve" represent? Describe its three distinct phases and their meaning.

15. Describe the three basics steps of reliability quantification for complex products. How does predicted reliability differ from that experienced in operational use?

16. Define *availability*. How is it measured?

17. Name and describe at least four serviceability parameters. What are some of the fundamental trade-off decisions related to improving serviceability?

18. Explain how process capability can provide a quantified prediction of process performance.

3

CONTROL: MANAGING THE OUTCOME

The basic concepts of prevention and detection are well enough understood and easy to distinguish. However, as we have already seen, the success of a preventive strategy assumes (1) sound control over the plans, procedures, and designs developed; and (2) reliable, timely, and complete feedback on both the process and its output. Assurance that both assumptions become reality is through appropriate *management of the outcome* or, in other words, through the activities of *quality control*. (In this text the terms *management of outcome* and *control* are synonymous.) Control comprises *detection* and *correction;* the latter, in turn, includes action on the work product and action on the process itself (see Figure 3-1).

Detection, the outcome-related component of appraisal, comprises such activities as inspection, measurements, and test. *The purpose of detection is to identify nonconformances; its result is the identification of defects and their causes.*

Correction is the totality of actions taken, both upon the process and its output, including the generation of feedback information, to achieve conformance to specifications, as well as to requirements. When permanently embedded in the process (through, for example, process redesign), corrective action on the process becomes part of prevention, or the management of intent.

Process management comprises quality management and process optimization. Quality management, also known as *quality improvement*, is the totality of management actions aimed at achieving conformance of the work product to

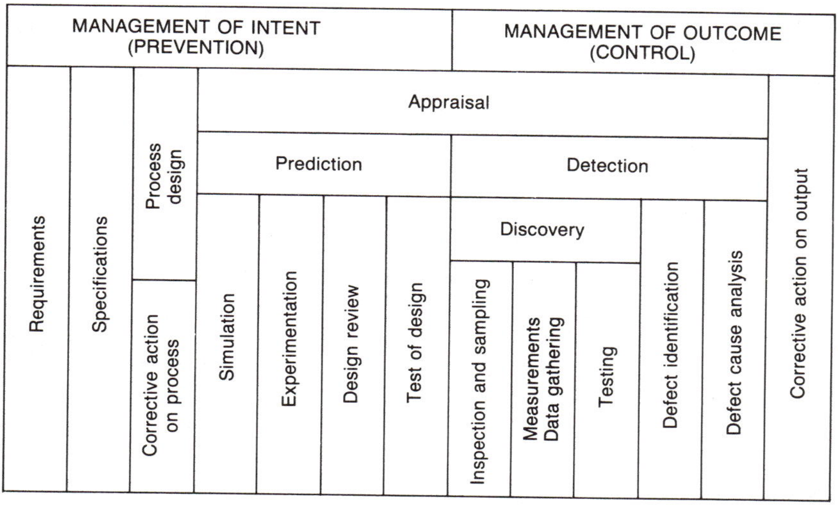

MANAGEMENT OF INTENT (PREVENTION)				MANAGEMENT OF OUTCOME (CONTROL)									
				Appraisal									
				Prediction				Detection					
								Discovery					
Requirements	Specifications	Process design	Corrective action on process	Simulation	Experimentation	Design review	Test of design	Inspection and sampling	Measurements Data gathering	Testing	Defect identification	Defect cause analysis	Corrective action on output

Fig. 3-1. The management of quality.

requirements. It includes both the management of intent and the management of outcome.

The other major aspect of process management is *process optimization*, which concerns itself with the efficiency and productivity of the process—that is, the economic factors. The key management tool which ties process control and process optimization into a single management package is the *cost of quality*. It can be used both as an indicator and a signal for variation (more often, patterns of variation), as well as a measure of productivity and efficiency. Although this chapter is mainly about managing outcome, it will be shown that the cost of quality, which is a key tool in quality management, can also contribute to overall process optimization.

3.1 Theory of Quality Control

A traditional approach in manufacturing has been to depend on production to make the product and on quality control to inspect it and screen out items not meeting specifications. In nonproduct (administrative) situations, the role of quality control is carried out by supervisors and managers who check and recheck the work product to catch errors. Both cases involve a strategy of control, that is, a method of managing outcome. By itself, this after-the-fact method is a wasteful approach to quality improvement because it allows time and materials to be invested in products or services that do not always meet specifications, let alone requirements. After-the-fact inspection is uneconomical: It is expensive and at times unreliable, not to mention the fact that the wasteful production has already taken place.

It is much more effective to avoid waste by not producing defective output in the first place—that is, to employ a strategy of prevention, or managing intent. It sounds sensible, even obvious, to most people; but beyond capturing it under such slogans as "Do it right the first time," or terms like "defect-free," what is required is an understanding of the elements, balance, and interrelationships between the two strategies: control and prevention. The remaining sections of this chapter cover aspects of control and show their purposefully managed contribution to the overall management of quality (refer again to Figure 3-1).

Quality control means primarily managing outcome, and one of its main purposes is to reduce or eliminate overall variation in the work product. Beyond this, it also affects the management of intent in the form of feedback and resulting changes to the preventive aspects of the process (Figure 3-2).

Before going into more detail on quality control, the definition of a few critical terms is in order:

- A *defect* is any state of nonconformance to requirements.
- A *variance* is any nonconformance to specifications; a *deviation* is any nonconformance to a standard or other accepted true value.
- A *divergence* is a difference between specifications and requirements.
- A *problem* is a question or situation proposed for solution; it is the *result* of not conforming to requirements or, in other words, it is a potential task resulting from the existence of defects. A problem is not a defect; it is the result of defects. Conversely, several problems may result from a single defect.
- A *symptom* is a phenomenon that signals or points to a problem. It can be described or represented by data and other descriptive parameters. Because a symptom is an observable condition arising from a problem, sometimes the same description is used to identify both a problem and its symptoms. More often, however, a problem will have multiple symptoms; for example, "insufficient torque" may include the symptoms of vibration, overheating, erratic functional variations, and so on.
- A *cause* is an established reason for the existence of a defect. When there are multiple causes, they are assumed to follow the Pareto principle; that is, a few causes will dominate the rest. The relationship between problems and their symptoms, defects, and defect causes is illustrated in Figure 3-3.
- A *remedy* is a change that can successfully remove or neutralize a defect. Usually, there are multiple possibilities for remedy, and the remedial process must choose from the alternatives. In many cases, a remedy is effected without knowledge of causes, such as a repair or replacement. In other cases, the cause is known but its removal may take a nontrivial amount of time or resources and, therefore, the direct removal of the defect itself is preferable.

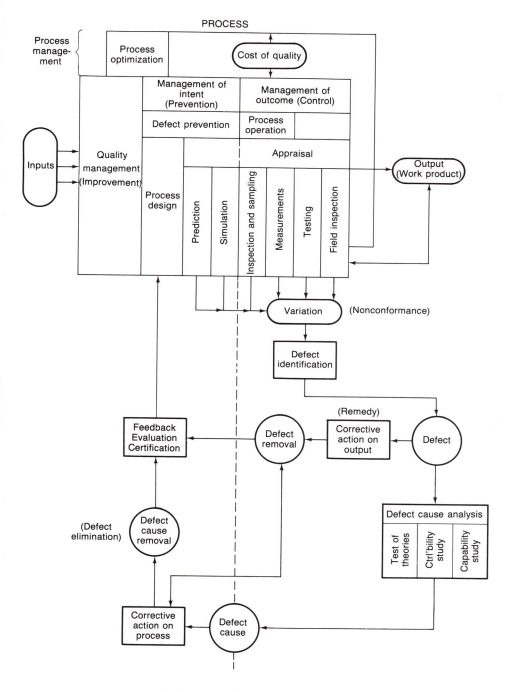

Fig. 3-2. Process management model.

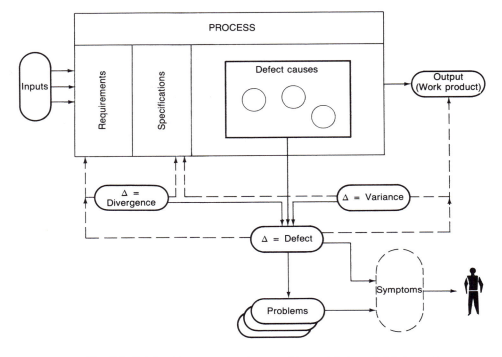

Fig. 3-3. Relationship among symptoms, problems, defects, and defect causes.

The solution to the problems caused by defects involves two lines of action: *detective* and *corrective*. Of these two, detection is the more difficult concept for management to understand and implement. One of the main reasons for this has to do with concepts and terminology, as many managers tend to confuse:

- *Problem* with *defect*
- *Common* cause with *special* cause (management-controlled defects with worker-controlled ones)[1]
- *Correction* with *remedy*

The detection line of action consists of:

- A study of the symptoms surrounding nonconformances to serve as a basis for separating problems and defects: *discovery*
- An analysis of the problems and defects causing these symptoms: *defect identification*
- An effort to establish the true causes of defects: *defect-cause analysis*

---

[1]The term *worker* in this context includes humans performing every conceivable type of nonmanagerial task, individually or in groups; for example, operators, administrators, professionals, and so on.

At this point, a decisive action in detection is to conduct one or both of these studies:

(1) *Controllability*: To determine whether defects are primarily the result of special (worker-controllable) or common (management-controllable) causes. A defect and its causes are worker-controllable, if the following three criteria of *worker self-control* have been met:
(a) Workers know what they are expected to do.
(b) Workers know what they are actually doing.
(c) Workers have the means for adjusting their own performance, to get from what they are actually doing to what they are expected to do.

(2) *Distribution*: For the management-controllable causes, to determine distribution over the various contributing functions (such as design, manufacturing, marketing, and the like) or performance factors (such as reliability, serviceability, and so on). Management-controllable causes are also known as *root causes*.

The principle of the "vital few and the trivial many"—a universal rule which is sometimes called the "80–20 rule" or known to many quality managers as the "Pareto principle"—is one of the many powerful quality management tools. It illustrates the fact that quality costs are almost always distributed with a bias toward a relatively few contributing functions (plants, products, procedures, and so on). It is widely used as a means of attacking the bulk of the costs with a relatively small amount of analytical study.

Knowing whether defects are caused by special or common causes is important because the approach to eliminating management-controllable causes is very different from that used for worker-controllable ones.

As only management can provide the means for meeting the criteria for worker self-control, any failure to meet them is a failure of management, and the resulting defects are not controllable by workers.

The only safe method to detect the existence of a special cause of variation is the use of statistical techniques. The discovery of a special cause and its removal are usually the responsibility of those persons who are connected directly with some operation. Thus it is the workers' job to find the defect and its cause, and to remove both, through the application of self-control. This concept is the basis of the many forms of *participative management* and other group problem-solving activities (such as quality circles and quality teams)—aimed at the elimination of worker-controllable defects.

Corrective action taken by workers may be aimed at either the product or the process itself. In the latter case, the worker must know what kind of process adjustment to introduce in response to a product variation.

As performance is measured and corrective action is taken by workers, management can respond with short-term feedback summaries and analyses. These take several forms, the most important and effective of which is the Pareto analysis. This approach allows a minimum of detail to be given to managers; however, they do receive valuable information on the total variations for a given time period, plus a list and a number of the few key (one to three) variations encountered during that same period. (This concept is similar to "management by exception," the logic of which is that management should not be dealing with more than a few key problems at any given time.)

One of the key contemporary questions of control is whether workers should make *conformance decisions* about the products they produce. Clearly, workers are already a part of the product flow, are familiar with product characteristics, and, in most cases, carry out performance measurements. Thus the requirement for a second person (inspector or supervisor) to make another set of measurements and then judge conformance is at least a partial duplication of the measurement process; it incurs additional effort and therefore added cost. Thus, work product acceptance (conformance decisions) by workers—along with the implied decision whether or not to stop the process when a nonconformance condition occurs—has significant cost reduction opportunities. Furthermore, a delegated inspection process is viewed as one that will certainly increase the workers' sense of responsibility for the work products they make.[2]

During the 1984 U.S. presidential election campaign, much public attention was directed to the "$400 hammer" and "$511 light bulb." The sad thing is that these items did indeed cost the taxpayers the amounts quoted—not necessarily because the producers chose to charge such absurd prices but because the bureaucratic requirements for inspection, checks and balances, and other control mechanisms inflated the cost beyond any reasonable proportion. An extreme case of overinspection is quoted by Deming, where the acceptance criterion for a certain circuit board was signed by four different inspectors for each circuit on the card—a total of 4400 signatures for a 1,100-circuit board![3]

The nuclear power industry is another good example of overinspection and overcontrol to the point of virtual paralysis, and the interference of essentially nonexpert outsiders (community groups, lawyers, politicians, and the like) in what is essentially a technological and management process. For example, the American Society for Testing Materials (ASTM) specifies a maximum of 300 revolutions of a concrete mixer drum, needed to provide quality concrete for a nuclear power plant—when the only relevant test should be whether the concrete meets strength requirements. On this basis contractors are being reported as deficient for failing to record the number of revolutions, which is counterproductive to say the least. This troubled industry is also an example where in many cases, engineers have ceased to act as

---

[2]Delegation of work product acceptance to workers, which allows them to stop the manufacturing process upon the detection of a defect, is a key rule of *continuous-flow manufacturing* (CFM).

[3]W. Edwards Deming, *Quality, Productivity, and Competitive Position* (Boston, MA: MIT Center for Advanced Engineering Study, 1982), p. 80.

professionals—writing specifications and implementing them in such a way that any political activist or other outsider can make an accusation that these specifications have not been met. The nuclear power industry is now in an adversarial situation where codes and specifications are routinely being interpreted and debated in the courts by lawyers, instead of qualified technical experts. In one case, a court hearing was held up for one week for discussion over the difference between 1/32 of an inch and 0.037 inch in the code. (*Civil Engineering*, February 1985, page 64.) Yet another part of the overcontrol problem in the nuclear industry is that there are up to seven levels of inspections. No inspector wants the next level above him to fault his work. Consequently, if four inspection levels say something is in order, the fifth is naturally reluctant to override the previous finding. Everyone becomes overcautious—yet neither safety nor quality is served in essence. The cost of this overcontrol is extremely high and may lead to the ultimate demise of this key industry. Each nonconformance report can cost thousands of dollars in paperwork for the owner, regardless whether indeed it was a major design error or just the fact that the inspector signed a report with his initials rather than with his full name.

Another cost-effective approach to product acceptance is known as the *decision audit*. Under this concept the audit verifies the conformance-related *decision process* used by workers to accept or reject a work product. As a result, resources devoted to inspection, except for audits, are largely eliminated. The decision audit procedure, however, works only if most variations are worker-controllable, the workers are both trained and well motivated to comply with specifications, and the cost of variations or defects is low. In the case of complex processes or high-technology products, these criteria cannot always be met and therefore the elimination of nonconformance requires management intervention and control.

Worker response to self-control and the delegation of conformance-related decisions, where applicable, is generally favorable—especially where job enrichment is perceived as a significant factor. However, continued motivation and incentive are important, with an attendant assurance of some form of continued improvement in compensation, career advancement, and the like. Since the economics of delegating conformance decisions are favorable, many businesses have been responsive to these worker expectations.[4]

In service industries, where the ratio of the human element (labor) to inanimate components (equipment, materials) ranges over a wide spectrum, the approach to quality control is heavily dependent on the specific mix in any given industry.

As these industries are becoming increasingly more technological, their key incentives for the adoption of technology are to provide service (1) at a low cost, (2) in minimum time, and (3) in a consistent manner. While cost is a universal business parameter, time is a particularly important quality parameter in service industries

---

[4]Refer to the Sterling Forest case study in Chapter 7.

(for example, response time or turnaround time). The concept of self-control can help bring further focus to the process management approach in these industries, which will also lead to much-needed productivity improvements. While the task of defining what is meant by quality is more of a challenge in service industries, they do have the benefit of clear and immediate feedback on performance, because service is in many cases offered directly to the end user (consumer). Taking corrective action on the process is particularly applicable to equipment-intensive service industries, but with proper planning and integration of manual tasks, it is equally effective in labor-intensive service industries as well.

In contrast to worker-controllable causes, there are underlying *common* causes of defects—low rates of productivity, frequent accidents, customer complaints, and the general lack of quality, which are all the responsibility of management. While workers are responsible only for the special causes assignable to them, they cannot do anything about raw materials, supervision and training, pricing policies, or problems common to most equipment used in the process. Common causes, or faults in the process, stay until corrected. Elimination or reduction of common causes can only be effected by management action.[5]

A defect falls into the common, or management-controllable, category if any one or more of the criteria for worker self-control have not been met. Here are some causes of variation that fall into this category:

- Incomplete or unclear requirements statement
- Poor product specifications
- Poor instruction and job training
- Poor supervision
- Lack of detection system to identify common causes
- Vendor supplies not meeting specifications
- Procedures which are incomplete or do not meet the process plan
- Equipment of low availability
- Chronically inaccurate settings of machine tools
- Poor or unsuitable work conditions (poor lighting, high humidity, unsuitable temperatures)
- Breakdown in management communications or lack of management direction

3.1.1 Process Control

As stated above, the term *control* is used in this text to refer to the activities employed to detect and correct deviations from specifications. These activities

---

[5]Herein lies the fundamental reason for the limited effectiveness of quality circles and other group problem-solving activities. While they can successfully deal with worker-controllable defects and their causes, by definition they cannot bring about continued, permanent quality improvement.

represent a subset of the overall process producing the work product against stated requirements. Control is synonymous to managing outcome, as related to output.

Control is a process universally observed in nature and the functioning of most biological mechanisms; it essentially represents a *feedback loop* and involves a well-established and accepted sequence of steps:

(1) Detection:
   - Choosing the measurement system (units of measure, instruments, and so on)
   - Establishing actual performance through measurements
   - Comparing actual performance against a previously established specification to detect variation
   - Interpretation of the variation between actual performance and objective (statistical process control)
(2) Correction:
   - Action to minimize or remove the variation (remedy)
   - Action to remove the causes of variation (defect-cause removal)

This sequence of steps is universal and applicable to the control of almost any process, for example, inventory, production, distribution, cost accounting, order entry, or office administration.

The goal of *quality control* is to arrive at sound decisions about actions affecting the process and its output. This means balancing the risks of taking action when action is not necessary (overcontrol, or error of the first kind), as opposed to failing to take action when action is necessary (undercontrol, or error of the second kind). These risks must be handled in the context of the two sources of variation—special and common.

A process is said to be *stable* when the only source of variation is common causes. Such a process (with no indication of a special cause of variation) is also said to be *in statistical control*. The initial function of *process control*, therefore, is to provide a signal when special causes of variation occur and to avoid giving false signals when they do not. This will enable appropriate action that will eliminate special causes and prevent their recurrence.

In addition, the management of outcome concentrates on evaluating process performance data so that identical problems can be prevented from arising in the future.

3.1.2 Statistical Process Control

Given the well-known fact that variability exists everywhere in nature and in virtually every process, probability and statistics are at the heart of process control technology. They are tools which help summarize data, understand variations, apply the concept of tolerance, use and interpret the results of measurements, assess risk, and therefore make sounder decisions.

Among students of quality control, Deming describes recognition of "statistical quality technology"[6] by top management as a key element to quality and productivity improvement. Among Juran's three steps needed in creating a "quality revolution," the first is quality related and it includes statistical control.[7]

Statistics can be defined as that branch of applied mathematics which describes and analyzes empirical observations for the purpose of predicting certain events as a basis for decision making in the face of uncertainty.

Statistics, in turn, is based on the *theory of probability*—the two together provide the abstraction for the mathematical model underlying the study of problems involving uncertainties. The application of statistics to manufacturing and engineering problems has led to the recognition that statistics is a complete field in itself. However, people should not become so involved in statistics that they ignore other problem-solving tools at the disposal of management. Statistical methods may or may not be the best tool for the solution of a given problem, and in the management of quality, the key objective is to solve the problem of variations and not to promote statistical process control as an end in itself.

Accordingly, the treatment of statistical process control in this text is not a rigorous exposition of the theory of statistics; rather it is a review of fundamental quality management-related situations, where statistical methods will help in making a particular decision. In the main text, little statistical theory will be discussed; the reader is referred to Appendix A for some of the fundamentals of frequency and probability distributions. (Appendix B contains some of the most frequently used statistical tables for these distributions.)

However, sound understanding of the *value* of statistical control techniques is essential to quality management. The existence of a stable process is seldom a natural state. It is an achievement, the result of eliminating all special causes on statistical signal, leaving only the random variation, which by definition will also be the minimum level of variation. Such a process is a *random* process; its future behavior is predictable. A stable process also has a definable *capability*.

Statistical control does not imply the absence of variation or defects; it does imply, however, a *minimum* level of these. Statistical control is a state of random variation; the process is stable in the sense that the limits of variation are predictable and therefore can be held to a predetermined level; *yet it may produce defective output*. In fact, it could produce a high rate of defective output—which in turn will require intervention to change the process itself.

The performance of a process that is in statistical control is predictable, and so are its work output and costs. Without statistical methods, attempts to improve a process are "hit and miss," with results that are usually unpredictable and which

[6]Deming, *Quality, Productivity, and Competitive Position*, p. 80.

[7]J. M. Juran, *Managerial Breakthough* (New York: McGraw-Hill Book Co., 1964); and J. M. Juran, "Product Quality—A Prescription for the West," *Management Review* (New York: American Management Associations, June-July, 1981).

may make matters worse. *Only a process that is in statistical control can be further and systematically improved.*

The following definitions will be helpful in any discussion of statistical concepts and methods:

- A *population* is a large collection of items (product observations, data) about certain characteristics of which conclusions and decisions are to be made for purposes of process assessment and quality improvement.

- A *sample* is a finite number of items taken from a population. Given a set of data known as a sample, any parameter which can be determined on the basis of the quantitative characteristics of the sample is called a *statistic.*

- A *descriptive statistic* is a computed measure of some property of a set of data, making possible a definitive statement about their meaning.

- An *inferential statistic* indicates the confidence which can be placed in any statement regarding the expected accuracy and the range of applicability of the statement and the probability of that statement being true; consequently, decisions can be based on inferential statistics.

There exist a large number of statistics that may be computed for a given set of data and there also exist a great number of statistical methods to compute them. Also, data may arise in an infinite number of forms, quantities, and frequencies.

A *variable* is a data item which takes on values within some range with a certain frequency or pattern. Variables may be *discrete,* that is, *limited in value to integer quantities*, in which case they relate to *attribute data*, for example, the number of bolts produced in a manufacturing process. Variables may also be *continuous,* that is, *measured to any desired degree of accuracy*, in which case they are known as *variables data*, for example, the diameter of a shaft.

In making decisions, interest may center on (1) the measurability of a single variable such as the expected life of a brake shoe under test, or (2) the interrelation of several variables, as in the study of factors determining the quality of a manufactured product—dimensions, weight, material properties, reliability, serviceability, and the like.

The more common methods of statistical control and the type of results desired fall naturally into a pattern that progresses from simple to more complex techniques:

(1) *Descriptive analysis* of a set of sample values to compute such statistics as *central tendency* (mean, median) and *dispersion* (variance and standard deviation) for a given variable.

(2) *Probability analysis* of a variable, useful in quality control and in the testing of operational performance of products. No cause-and-effect relationship is considered.

(3) *Statistical inference,* which includes problems of estimation and testing hypotheses in order to arrive at conclusions regarding certain characteristics of populations. This technique is based on information contained in a set of sample values drawn from that population.

(4) *Analysis of variance* to determine the significance of differences between grouped data, such as the differences caused by variations in the manufacturing process of a product. Analysis of variance represents a test for the existence of a cause-and-effect relationship.

More complex statistical methods, such as regression analysis and correlation analysis, lie beyond the scope of this book.[8]

The management of quality really centers on the elimination of variations (defects). These in turn are described by various forms of data, derived mostly from observations and measurements. What statistics helps do is to analyze data properly and draw certain conclusions based on the existence or predicted occurrence of variation.

VARIATION

In the industrial and business world no two things are ever exactly alike. The concept that no two work products are exactly identical is known as *variability.* Any process can contain many sources of variability; the differences among repeated outcomes of the process may be large or they may be almost unmeasurably small, but they are always present. (This is one reason why designers include tolerances in their specifications.)

Recognizing that variations exist in our processes, and that the eventual outcome is naturally influenced by those variations, we need to establish ways to measure variation, understand its causes, predict its occurrences, and arrive at appropriate decisions to eliminate it.

There are two types of variation: *random* and *nonrandom.* Random variation, often called the "natural" or "basic" behavior of the process, is said to be caused by *common (root) causes*, because it potentially affects all components of the process. As a group random variations tend to form a pattern that can be described by such statistical tools as a *frequency distribution* (see Figure 3-4). Such a distribution in turn can be characterized by:

- Central tendency (location where most of the values are centered)
- Spread or dispersion (amount by which the smaller values differ from the larger ones)
- Shape (the pattern of variation—whether symmetrical, peaked, or skewed)

Nonrandom variation, also called "unnatural" or "sporadic" behavior, is said to be caused by *special (assignable) causes*. These refer to any factors

---

[8]The interested reader is referred to standard statistical texts dealing with the subject, particularly [11], [19], [25], and [35] in the Bibliography.

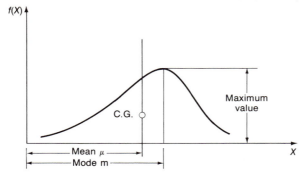

a. Geometric interpretation of central tendency.

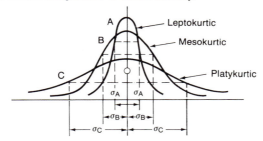

b. Spread (σ^2 = variance) and kurtosis (peakedness).

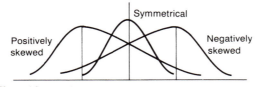

c. Shape (skewness).

Fig. 3-4. Characteristics of a typical probability distribution curve.

Source: Reprinted, with permission of the publisher, from *Introduction to Scientific Computing* by G. A. Pall (New York: Appleton-Century-Crofts/Plenum Publishing, 1971).

causing variation that cannot be adequately explained by a single distribution of the process output. Unless all these special causes of variation are identified and eliminated, they will continue to affect the process output in unpredictable ways—that is, the process will stay unstable.

> The causes of variation can be further broken down into categories which tend to correspond to the key components of the process—people, equipment, materials, procedures, and so on. Each of these components may contribute some degree of variability to the process.

Some sources of variation in the process cause very short-run differences, such as backlash and clearances within a machine and its fixtures, or the accuracy of a bookkeeper's work. Other sources of variation tend to cause changes in the output only over a longer period of time, either gradually as with tool or machine wear, stepwise as with procedural change, or irregularly as with environmental changes such as power surges or outages. Therefore, the time period and conditions over which measurements of variation are made will affect the amount of the total variation that will be present. In any case, *the fundamental purpose of process control is to reduce variation to a minimum.*

To accomplish this, variation must first be traced back to its sources. There is an important connection between the two types of variation and the types of action necessary to reduce or eliminate them.

The extent of common causes of variation can be indicated by statistical techniques, but in order to isolate the particular causes more detailed analysis is needed. Common causes of variation are usually the responsibility of management to correct (management-controllable), although workers directly connected with the process sometimes are in a better position to identify causes and pass them on to management for correction. Overall, *the removal of common causes of variation usually necessitates changes in the process;* as such, it falls under the management of intent.

Special (assignable) causes of variation can be detected by simple statistical techniques. However, these causes are not common to all the components of the process. The discovery of a special cause of variation and its removal are usually the responsibility of someone directly connected with the process (worker), although management sometimes is in a better position to undertake overall corrections. *The removal of a special cause of variation usually requires action upon the output, also known as local or limited action;* as such, it falls under the management of outcome.

> Only a relatively small portion of all causes of variation (about 15 to 20 percent) is worker-controllable; the majority (the remaining 80 to 85 percent) is controllable only by management, through action on the process.

One of the prime problems of quality management is caused by confusing common and special causes of variation, and therefore, the type of action to be taken. This is very costly to the organization in terms of wasted effort, false starts, and delayed resolution of problems.

> Quality requirements vary with the task but the need for requirements and direction is the same in almost any industry or process. Because lack of management direction is so often the common cause, it is probable that a quality problem in one area will uncover problems in other areas of the business as well. While this in itself is bad news, the good news is that fixing responsibility for the lack of quality where it belongs—namely, management—will lead to improvements which will have a positive effect on the entire process or business. The assertion that management is responsible for quality is not always well received in all quarters, and understand-

ably so. This is because it contradicts the popular view that workers are to blame for quality problems and therefore, any solution must start there. While this is a comfortable position for management to take, it does not represent reality. The true picture can be seen by analyzing defects through the causes of variation, suggested by such students of quality control as Deming.[9]

DATA ANALYSIS

In the industrial and business environment, data derived from direct observation or measurements often form the basis for decisions and management action. There are two basic kinds of data: *measured* (referred to as *variables* data) and *counted* (also known as *attribute* data).

Once raw data are collected, they are analyzed and converted to more meaningful information through the use of statistical techniques and other analytical methods, for process control and capability studies.

The first step in analyzing data is *data summarization*, which may take several forms: *tabulation, graphs* and numerical parameters, or *statistics*. Sometimes, one form of data summarization will suffice and will provide a complete summary for the purposes of decision making. In other, more complex cases, and especially where larger amounts of data must be dealt with, two or even three forms of summarization are needed to create a clear base for analysis.

TABULAR SUMMARIZATION: FREQUENCY DISTRIBUTION

The frequency distribution of a discrete variable is defined as the count of the number of occurrences of individual values over a given range.

The frequency distribution of a continuous variable is defined as the count of cases which lie between certain predetermined limits over the range of values the variable may assume.

Simply put, a frequency distribution is a tabulation of data arranged according to value. Table 3-1 shows the tabulation of measurement data for the tensile strength of 140 steel rods, measured in a materials testing laboratory, along with the frequency distribution and cumulative frequency of these data. (For example, there were 6 rods, each having a strength of 44.2 tons per square inch, etc.) While the conventional frequency distribution highlights where most of the measurements are grouped (the values are centered about a tensile strength of 44.7) and how much variation there is in the measurement data (values run from 43.5 to 46.0), the *cumulative frequency distribution,* in which the conventional frequency values are accumulated, shows the number of rods with tensile strength equal to or less than a specified value. Each of these distributions is helpful in different aspects of the analysis of a problem.[10]

---

[9]Deming, *Quality, Productivity, and Competitive Position*, pp. 68-69.
[10]Frequency distributions are not to be confused with probability distributions!

Table 3-1. TABULATION OF TENSILE STRENGTH
OF 140 STEEL RODS

Tensile Strength T, 1000 lbs per in²	Frequency Distribution	Cumulative Frequency
43.5	1	1
43.6	1	2
43.7	2	4
43.8	2	6
43.9	3	9
44.0	4	13
44.1	5	18
44.2	6	24
44.3	7	31
44.4	9	40
44.5	9	49
44.6	10	59
44.7	10	69
44.8	10	79
44.9	9	88
45.0	9	97
45.1	7	104
45.2	7	111
45.3	7	118
45.4	6	124
45.5	6	130
45.6	4	134
45.7	2	136
45.8	2	138
45.9	1	139
46.0	1	140
TOTAL	140	140

GRAPHIC SUMMARIZATION: THE HISTOGRAM AND SCATTER DIAGRAM

A *histogram* is a frequency distribution represented in the form of a vertical bar chart. (Figure 3-5 shows the histogram which corresponds to the tensile strength data shown in Table 3-1.) The ease of its construction and interpretation make it a very effective tool in the initial display and analysis of data.

The *scatter diagram* is another useful data analysis tool. It can be used to determine if a cause-and-effect relationship exists (see Figure 3-6).

When plotting paired data, the horizontal axis of a scatter diagram usually denotes the measurement values; the vertical axis reflects the process element values, such as temperature, pressure, or current. The diagram is then interpreted for levels of positive or negative correlation, no correlation, or nonlinear correlation.

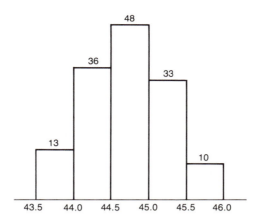

Fig. 3-5. Histogram of tensile strength.

Graphical methods are useful in presenting a summary or general description of collected data. These techniques, however, have limitations for analyzing data, limitations which can be overcome by the numerical methods of calculating parameters (generally computed from population measurements) or statistics (typically computed from sample measurements).

QUANTITATIVE SUMMARIZATION: STATISTICS

Measurement data can also be summarized by calculating (1) a measure of *central tendency* to indicate where most of the values are centered and (2) the measure of *dispersion* to indicate the amount of scatter (variation) in the data. These numerical parameters represent a statistical model of the tabular or graphical summaries discussed earlier and, in many cases, provide a more than adequate summary.[11]

The key measures of central tendency are the *mean* (average), the *median*, and the *mode*. The two basic measures of dispersion are *standard deviation* and *variance*. In some cases, especially when the number of observations is small (ten or fewer), the *range* over which values are considered becomes important.[12]

These methods of data summarization usually represent the first but most important step in the statistical analysis of a variation. The better known types of problems whose resolution can benefit from statistical analysis are:

(1) Usefulness of a limited number of test results in estimating the true value of a work product parameter

---

[11]The aim here is to show where numerical techniques fit into the education of management for the improvement of quality through data analysis. The reader wishing to pursue the study of data analysis techniques is advised to consult the literature, particularly [4], [7], [11], [14], [19], and [35] in the Bibliography.

[12]The definitions for mean, median, mode, standard deviation, variance, and range are given in Appendix A.

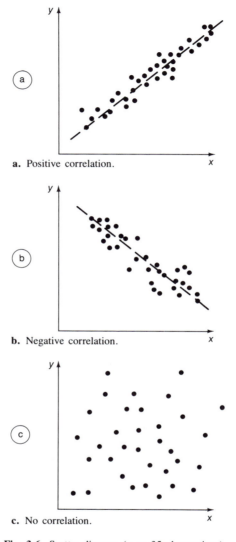

a. Positive correlation.

b. Negative correlation.

c. No correlation.

Fig. 3-6. Scatter diagram ($n = 35$ observations).

(2) The number of tests required to provide adequate data for analysis

(3) Comparison of test data between two alternative designs

(4) Comparison of test data from a single design against specifications

(5) Planning of experiments to determine the significant (dominant) variable influencing a performance parameter

Identifying the dominant subprocess usually has value in both process control and process improvement because it directs attention to the variables which will provide the highest return on an investment in quality management efforts. A further development of this logic, incidentally, will lead to the conclusion that the cost of quality, as a process management tool, should ultimately be used as an investment tool.

(6) The quantitative relationship between two or more variables

STATISTICAL INFERENCE

Statistical inference is defined as a process leading to conclusions about a population parameter based on sample data.
Its two major fields are:

- Estimation (applications: confidence limits, sample size for accuracy)
- Testing of hypotheses (applications: sample size, acceptance or rejection of a hypothesis)

Since statistical inference is based on results derived from samples, its conclusions will be susceptible to variations among those samples.

The concept of *sampling variation* means that if multiple samples of *equal size* are repeatedly drawn from the same population, different results would be obtained in most samples in that the *sample means* (sample averages) will very likely differ from each other. This is significant because all the samples were drawn from the same population.

In many situations—because of time or cost limitations—only a limited number of samples can be drawn from a population. Given that samples vary, the question is how reliable those samples are as the basis of a decision about the population itself. The extreme case is where only *one* sample can be drawn; statistical approaches have been devised to analyze the data in this sample, taking into account the possible sampling variation that could occur. There exist formulas which help define the expected amount of sampling variation; once this is known, a valid decision about the population from which the sample was drawn can be reached, based on only that one sample.

The concept of sampling distribution is fundamental to the two major areas of statistical inference—estimation and tests of hypotheses.

Statistical estimation is defined as the analysis of a sample parameter in order to predict the values of the corresponding population parameter.
An estimation statement comprises two parts:

(1) The *point estimate*, which is a single value for estimating the population parameter in question, such as average, median, standard deviation, and so on.

(2) The *confidence interval,* which is a range of values that includes the true value of the population parameter with a preassigned probability known as the *confidence level.* The latter is the probability that an assertion about the value of the population parameter is correct. *Confidence limits* are the two values representing the upper and lower boundaries of the confidence interval.

A hypothesis is defined as an assertion made about the value of some parameter of a population.

This assertion may or may not be correct, and a *test of hypothesis* is used to test its validity by analyzing a sample drawn from the population. When testing a hypothesis, there are two possible choices: the hypothesis is either accepted or rejected. In making one of these choices, there is always the risk of making the wrong decision, either

(1) Rejecting the hypothesis when it is true (the probability of committing this *error of the first kind* is denoted by α and is also referred to as the *level of significance* of the test), or

(2) Accepting the hypothesis when it is false (the probability of committing this *error of the second kind* is denoted by β).[13]

The possible results of testing a hypothesis *H* are summarized in Table 3-2.

Table 3-2. TESTING HYPOTHESIS *H*: ERRORS OF THE FIRST AND SECOND KIND

	Reject H	*Accept H*
H : True	Wrong decision (error of the first kind) Probability $= \alpha$	Right decision Probability $= (1 - \alpha)$
H : False	Right decision Probability $= (1 - \beta)$	Wrong decision (error of the second kind) Probability $= \beta$

Reaching useful conclusions about a population is the ultimate objective of tests of hypotheses. Normally, the desired or allowable values for α and β, respectively, are defined in advance and the sample size *n* required to satisfy these values is calculated. However, in practice—because of cost or time limitations—the sample size is often fixed in advance. In such cases, a decision to accept or reject the hypothesis is made, and the appropriate conclusion about the population itself is drawn in a specific sequence of steps.[14]

When a hypothesis is rejected, the conclusion is that the value specified in the hypothesis for the parameter is wrong. This conclusion is made at a confidence level of $1 - \alpha$.

When a hypothesis is accepted, the value specified in the hypothesis for the parameter has been neither proved nor disproved.

---

[13]Adapted, with permission of the publisher from *Introduction to Scientific Computing* by G. A. Pall (New York, NY: Appleton-Century-Croft/Plenum Publishing, 1971), p. 221.

[14]See also J. M. Juran and F. M. Gryna, Jr., *Quality Planning and Analysis* (New York: McGraw-Hill Book Co., New York, 1980), p. 73.

In other words, a hypothesis is tested to see if there is a statistically significant difference between the sample characteristic and the value of the population parameter specified in the hypothesis. "Reject the hypothesis" means that there is a statistically significant difference; "accept the hypothesis" means that a statistically significant difference was not found—but this may have been due, for example, to a small sample size.

REGRESSION ANALYSIS

In quality control, it is sometimes required to study the relationship between two or more variables in the process. The statistical approach to such a study is called *regression analysis;* its uses include forecasting, determination of important variables affecting a certain result, and calculation of optimum operating conditions.[15]

QUALITY IN END USE

User complaints are generally a poor measure of product or service quality. They are merely an indicator of "customer satisfaction," which may or may not be an accurate measure of conformance to requirements. While a low complaint rate is not necessarily proof of customer satisfaction, a high complaint rate certainly signals dissatisfaction. Therefore, complaint rates should be measured and recorded closely, even though several extraneous factors will determine whether or not customers will take some type of complaint action:

- Demographics such as age, education, income, and social position
- Price of the product or service
- Impact of defects as perceived by the user
- Economic conditions

An ideal user feedback system should report not just customer satisfaction or the lack of it, but also the number of actual defects experienced by users during and after the warranty period. Also, the information must be detailed enough to determine defect causes from the problems reported by consumers. Lastly, the information must show the quantified effect of defects on customer use or operations—in terms of time lost, economic impact, value of lost production or sales, etc.

User feedback data may be applied to problem identification, problem cause analysis, prediction of future failure rates, and so on.

An example of a defect control system is the Applied Programming Analysis and Review (APAR) technique, used by several major software providers, including IBM. Software errors detected by users are categorized by the severity of their impact on user (customer) operations, and corrective action is taken in direct proportion to the severity category indicated.

---

[15]Further discussion of regression analysis and its more advanced forms, such as multiple regression and nonlinear regression, is beyond the scope of this text; the literature should provide more detail to the reader, especially [11] and [20] in the Bibliography.

In summary, statistical process control provides powerful tools to detect and analyze variations and their causes in the process. As will be seen in Section 3.5, it also contributes to the use of the two most important tools in managing outcome: process capability and the cost of quality. Their use in turn will lead to actions, both upon the work product and the process itself, which will result in overall quality improvement (see Table 3-3).

3.1.3 Measurement System

As discussed before, the control of a process depends to a large extent on the feedback loop, which in turn involves a specific sequence of steps, from detection to correction. Measurements represent that part of detection which is aimed at discovering the existence of a finite, measurable variation in either the process or its output. In more complex processes, the measurement-related aspects of the process taken together comprise a *measurement system*. The following items are part of such a measurement system:

(1) Units of measurement, facilitating conversion of properties (such as mass, conductivity, dimensions) into quantified, measurable forms (kilograms, ohms, millimeters)
(2) Measuring instruments, calibrated in terms of units of measurement
(3) The actual use of measurement instruments to quantify observations—the act of establishing actual performance
(4) Comparison of actual performance against a previously established standard in order to detect variation

The objective of a measurement system is clearly detection—as it affects the overall assessment of process outcome, it is planned and designed as part of the process design. Measurements are needed to verify compliance, identify defect sources, identify process trends, provide input for common cause analysis and defect prevention, and to determine process efficiency and productivity. In other words, *measurements are needed both for quality management and process optimization.*

Interpreting the difference between observed actual performance and the specifications (or requirements, as the case may be) is not part of the measurement system; rather it belongs to problem analysis or defect-cause analysis, aided by statistical control tools and other quality management techniques.

The choice of control subjects also lies outside the measurement system; that choice is made usually during process design and can be based on several prioritization and cost analysis techniques, such as Pareto analysis, cost of quality studies, and so on. The chosen control subjects usually represent dominant factors or variables in the process; in terms of achieving quality objectives, they are also known as "critical success factors" (CSF). In fact, they are the few key areas of activity in which favorable outcome is absolutely necessary for a particular pro-

Table 3-3. AIDS TO QUALITY MANAGEMENT AND THEIR APPLICATION

Aids to Quality Management	Activity Supported		Business Function Supported		
Statistical Tools	Prevention	Control	Design	Mfg.	Field
DATA DESCRIPTION					
Frequency distributions			X	X	
Histograms (Graphs)				X	X
Control charts		Process control Process capability		X	X
DATA ANALYSIS					
Probability Distributions (Probability Paper)					
Poisson		Inspection and sampling	X	X	X
Normal		Process control	X	X	
Exponential	Process design		X		
Weibull	Product specifications		X	X	
STATISTICAL INFERENCE					
Estimation		Inspection and sampling	X		
Testing Hypotheses		Process control Process capability	X	X	

Special Tools	Prevention	Control	Design	Mfg.	Field
PROCESS CAPABILITY	Process design Process improvement	Process control	X	X	
SIMULATION			X		
GAUGE CAPABILITY		Process control	X	X	
EXPERIMENTATION			X	X	
PARETO ANALYSIS			X		
COST OF QUALITY			X	X	X

cess to reach its objectives. Measuring and monitoring them, therefore, is also critical to overall process outcome.

The discipline of measurement, also called *metrology,* has evolved gradually over the history of civilization to become an essential part of quality control. Even during the days of early manufacturing—before the onset of the industrial revolution—correct observations and measurements were considered important in establishing conformance to requirements. The more recent emphasis on prevention in quality management, however, has broadened the purpose of measurements to include information not only on the work product, but also on the process and measuring instruments themselves. Technological developments led to ever-decreasing tolerances and units of measurement, in turn requiring measuring equipment and instrumentation of the highest accuracy and precision.

The three systems of measurement used today in technology and commerce are (1) the *English* ("avoirdupois," "troy," or "apothecary's"), (2) the *metric*, and (3) the *SI system*, for "système international d'unités." The original metric system, developed in France toward the end of the eighteenth century, was primarily concerned with quantifying the then observable physical properties (dimensions, volume, mass, temperature, and the like.) The metric system is used by most of the world today. With technological development, the original metric system was modified into what is now known as the SI system. In the latter, most of the fundamental units of measure are defined in terms of natural phenomena that are unchangeable. For example, the unit measurement of length is the *meter*, defined as the 1,650,763.73 wavelengths of the red-orange light emitted by *krypton-86* under certain conditions. This recognized true value in turn is called the standard of measurement for length. Most countries are now committed to the adoption of the full SI system. The English system, which has no such features, is only used in the United Kingdom, parts of the British Commonwealth and the United States—primarily for historical and convenience reasons. However, both countries are now committed to change to the SI system and are in the process of gradual conversion. Considerations of history and tradition aside, there is no valid technological or commercial reason for these two leading industrialized nations to have stayed on an archaic system of measurement for so long. The only valid consideration—the cost of conversion—increases exponentially with time; therefore, the conversion process should be accelerated rather than delayed.

MEASUREMENT ERROR

The determination of conformance depends on meaningful and valid data. Such data are the result of the measurement system in place. When measurement results are reported, it is useful to state an estimate of accuracy as well. Such an estimate includes an assessment of the measuring instrument, as well as the variation being measured.

There is some degree of error in all measurements, even at the highest levels of accuracy. Therefore, it is important to understand the magnitude of the measurement error and to hold it within reasonable and predictable limits, consistent with the specific requirements of the process at hand. In fact, the results of repeated observations will almost always disagree among themselves to some degree, dependent upon such factors as the calibration of the instrument, its inherent precision, and the inspector's ability to use the measuring device consistently. Since we cannot arrive at a completely true value of a measured parameter, the truth must be approximated by the best value that can reasonably be derived from the measurements. In doing this, the existence of both random and nonrandom measurement errors must be taken into account. Accordingly, the measured and recorded deviation of a given variable from the true value always includes the actual deviation plus the measurement error.

    To determine the magnitude of the measurement error, a *gauge capability study* is performed.

    Gauge capability is the accuracy, repeatability, reproducibility, and stability of measurements combined into a single parameter.

    The elements of gauge capability are defined as follows:

- *Repeatability* is the variation of repeat measurements, carried out by one inspector on the same work product, using the same measuring device.
- *Reproducibility* is the variation in measurement averages when multiple inspectors each carry out repeat measurements on the same work product using the same measuring device.
- *Stability* is the variation in measurement averages when repeat measurements are carried out over a specified time period.

A schematic to illustrate the concept of gauge capability is shown in Figure 3-7. On the left of the schematic is shown the repeatability (the expected variation in one inspector's readings). The averages for two different inspectors A and B are shown as $\overline{X}_a$ and $\overline{X}_b$; the reproducibility distribution represents the average variation. Accuracy is calculated by averaging $\overline{X}_a$ and $\overline{X}_b$ and determining the difference between this and the true value. Stability appears as a distribution in the second time period and is again represented as a variation in average values. Finally, gauge capability is represented as the difference between the extremes encountered over the time periods.

    Considering the measurement system as a subprocess of the overall process in question, *gauge capability* can be defined as the process capability of that subprocess.

    The difference between the true value and the measured value can be caused by problems of inherent characteristics of the measurement system:

- *Accuracy*: The closeness of the average of a series of repeat measurements, made on a work product, to the accepted true value. The smaller the

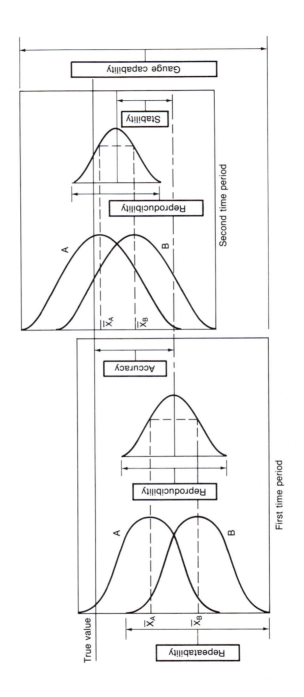

Fig. 3-7. Schematic of gauge capability.

difference between measurements and the true value, the more accurate the measuring device. If the difference is due to a systematic error in the measurement process, the measuring instrument is said to be "out of cali- bration."[16]

- *Precision*: The closeness of a group of repeat measurements, made on the same work product, to a mean value. The smaller the difference between the group of measurements and the mean value, the more precise the instru- ment. Precision is an indicator of the repeatibility or consistency of the measurement.

The term *bias* is sometimes used to indicate systematic error, resulting in change to the inherent accuracy or precision of an instrument.

The conceptual difference between accuracy and precision is illustrated in Figure 3-8.[17]

In case the measurement error is found to represent a large proportion of the total variation from the true value, the measurement process itself must be ana- lyzed and evaluated before implementing a quality improvement program on the overall process. (A large measurement error can lead to incorrect decisions about the acceptance or rejection of work products.)[18]

Through appropriate steps, systematic errors in both accuracy and precision can be reduced and controlled. Errors that affect accuracy can be handled by applying numerical corrections to the measurement data. Another approach is the recalibration of the measurement instrument. (The measurements made by the device are compared to a reference standard of known accuracy; if the instrument is out of calibration, an adjustment is made.)

Precision of measurement can be improved by multiple measurements and statistical techniques to determine and control the error of measurement. (The use of multiple measurements is based on the known rule, which states that to halve the measurement error, a quadrupling of the number of measurements is re- quired.) Another basic approach is the discovery and systematic removal of the causes of variation affecting precision.

---

[16]*Calibration* is the process to establish and transfer the accuracy of instruments by comparing one standard against a higher-order standard of greater accuracy. Accuracy is an indicator of the measured value's approach to the true value.

[17]More often than not, the terms *accuracy* and *precision* are used interchangeably, which is obviously incorrect.

[18]A discussion of the methods of determining the probability of accepting a nonconforming unit, or of rejecting a conforming unit, as a function of measurement error goes beyond the scope of this book. For further treatment of the concept of measurement error, the reader is referred to the literature, in particular: A. R. Eagle, "A Method for Handling Errors in Testing and Measuring," *Industrial Quality Control* (March 1954), pp. 10-14; and J. A. McCaslin and G. F. Gruska, "Analysis of Attribute Gage Systems," *1976 ASQC Annual Technical Conference Transactions*, pp. 392-399.

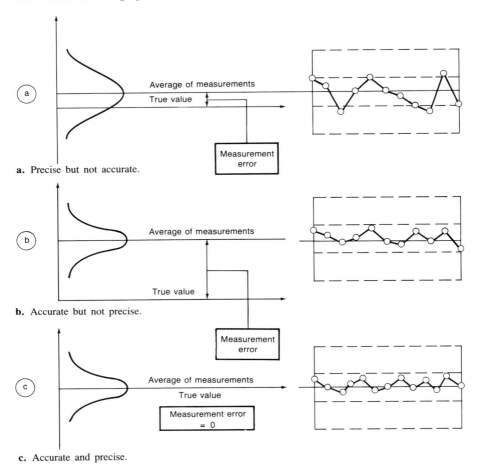

a. Precise but not accurate.

b. Accurate but not precise.

c. Accurate and precise.

Fig. 3-8. Conceptual difference between accuracy and precision.

3.2 Detection

Detection can also be looked upon as that part of *appraisal* which falls within the management of outcome; *examination* is the component of appraisal in the management of intent. Detection, in turn, comprises *discovery* (inspection and sampling, measurements, testing, problem analysis), *defect identification*, and *defect-cause analysis*.

Defect identification and defect-cause analysis are two steps of the "defect elimination cycle" (DEC) which fall in the area of detection; defect removal and defect-cause removal (defect elimination) are two further steps of the same cycle which, however, fall in the area of *correction* (see Figure 3-2).

Detection includes the discovery of *defects* (variations) as well as their *causes*. This section, and the rest of this book, focuses primarily on management-controllable defects—because they have been shown to be by far the dominant group and, also, because taking corrective action on them means action upon the process, which is a management responsibility. This, by definition, includes all the cases where corrective action upon the process is achieved through changes in managing intent, such as process design, change of specifications, and the like.

Worker-controllable defects, on the other hand, are those whose correction and elimination require worker self-control. Although the elimination of worker-controllable defects in itself will not lead to permanent and continuing quality improvement, worker control and decisions for acceptance are a key ingredient of the overall quality improvement program for reasons of efficiency, effectiveness, and, most importantly, employee commitment. From a chronological standpoint, most quality improvement efforts start with the elimination of worker-controllable defects.[19]

Starting quality improvement with the detection and elimination of worker-controllable defects also makes sense from a statistical control viewpoint, for a process must first be brought under statistical control before it can be improved. This in turn means that the elimination of special causes—which are mostly worker-controllable—can be effected by local action (see Table 3-4).

Table 3-4. COMPARATIVE OVERVIEW OF QUALITY CONTROL
TERMINOLOGY

Statistical Quality Control	*Quality Management*
Variation	Nonconformance; defect
Common cause	Management-controllable cause
Special cause	Worker-controllable cause
Control (stability)	Predictable rate of defects
Removal of special causes of variation	Removal of worker-controllable defects
Elimination of common causes of variation	Elimination of management-controllable defects

3.2.1 Discovery: Inspection, Sampling, Test

A subset of detection is *discovery*, which means determining the existence of a defect. It comprises such methods as inspection, sampling, and problem analysis, and it leads to *defect identification*. Discovery does not concern itself with the cause of the variation, that being the subject of *defect-cause analysis*.

Inspection, sampling, and other related techniques of discovery are usually discussed in the context of populations and samples.

---

[19]This approach was taken at Sterling Forest; see Chapter 7.

The data related to a sample are usually the result of measurements made on the items contained in the sample. Based on statistical analysis of the sample data, conclusions can be drawn and predictions made about certain parameters of the population from which the sample was drawn. (Random sampling is normally assumed; that is, each possible sample has an equal chance of being selected or, alternatively, items are selected systematically from material that is itself random on account of prior mixing.)

INSPECTION

In any given industrial or business process, there are usually deficiencies in some, if not most, of the subprocesses that make up that process. There are deficiencies in market research and forecasting, engineering design and specifications, purchasing, manufacturing planning and production, order entry, shipments, billing, and service—just to name a few typical activities related to an "average" manufactured product. In addition, there are deficiencies in procedures, communications, and organization—that is, in the management system itself. As a result there is always some tangible nonconformance present with regard to both specifications and requirements. If intent could be managed perfectly—the process design formulated without error, specifications established in total conformance to requirements, and all possible causes of variations foreseen and provided for—*prevention alone* would guarantee quality. For simple processes, this is possible and it has been done; however, for more complex and especially highly technological processes, such a perfect system of prevention, with its elaborate planning and design activities, would be too time-consuming and too costly.

This is a key philosophical point because it seems to contradict earlier statements in this book about the "economics of quality," as well as the statement that quality cannot be inspected into a work product. The question, however, is not prevention versus detection but rather how much prudent and planned inspection can best help a quality management approach based primarily on prevention, and also contribute to process optimization? Also, there are certain work product performance characteristics, such as reliability, availability, and the like which are extremely difficult to model and predict by either analytical or statistical methods; it is more practical and cost efficient to measure them in a prototype or test environment and then take appropriate corrective or preventive action, as necessary. Therefore, the concept of inspection and test has evolved as an important step in the process, to contribute to the management of *both* intent and outcome.

All inspection and test involves some form of assessment of work product to determine whether there is conformance. This decision about conformance is made up of two components: conformance to specifications (the input to *product acceptance*) and conformance to requirements (that is, establishing if there is a variance between specifications and requirements—the key input to *product disposition*). There are, however, other reasons for carrying out inspection that relate to the process or its component subprocesses. The major types and purposes of inspection are shown in Table 3-5.

Table 3-5. TYPES AND PURPOSES OF INSPECTION

Inspection	Purpose	Description
Acceptance sampling	Identification of bad lots of work product	Results of sampling used to classify product lots as acceptable or unacceptable
Full inspection	Identification of bad units (pieces) of work product	Work product is sorted between good and bad pieces
Control sampling	Determine if process is changing	Detects appearance of special causes of variation; usually implemented through use of control charts
Accuracy inspection	Rate accuracy of the inspection(s)	Accuracy of inspection(s) is the ratio of defects found to defects which should have been found
Qualification test	Rate service capability of work product	Helps secure product design information
Process capability assessment	Measure process capability	Quantifies inherent variability of process; its ability to consistently meet specifications

Of all the purposes of inspection, the most important and most extensively used is product acceptance.

Product acceptance should not be confused with product disposition, which involves a further decision—namely, conformance of specifications to requirements. The question arises whether a product that has been accepted against specification is also a quality product—one that meets user requirements.

Product disposition is really a separate decision usually made after completion of the inspection activity. In many cases inspectors do not even have access to user requirements, as their specific job is to establish conformance to specifications (aside from a fairly limited number of special cases where the inspector can make both the product acceptance and the product disposition decision).

Work product can mean a *discrete* unit or a collection of units—called a *batch* or a *lot*. In still more complex forms, it may be a *system*—a computer installation, a communication network, or an automated manufacturing plant. For each of these forms of work product, a corresponding set of specifications exists comprising all the product and performance characteristics which have to be achieved. Similarly, the inspection and test programs for these products will range from the very simple to the extremely elaborate, based on a planned series of tests at successive steps of the work process (raw materials, components, subassemblies and assemblies, subsystem interfaces) and consisting of both system-level tests and functional and environmental tests. Planning the inspection and test program for any given work product requires not only familiarity with the applicable specifications but also much advanced knowledge about actual conditions of end use, as well as a clear understanding of the underlying work process and relevant technologies.

A key question to be answered in establishing inspection and test programs is the amount of inspection needed to decide *lot acceptability*—a pervasive problem in the management of supplier quality. There are two levels of inspection:

- Random sampling (small or large samples)
- Full inspection (100 percent sampling)

In random sampling, small samples usually suffice for (1) inherently uniform processes with the order of production preserved and (2) homogeneous products (gases, liquids, or uniformly mixed substances). Large samples, which are used in the absence of prior knowledge about product or lot quality, require a relatively large number of items to be inspected. Random sampling is also used to determine certain process characteristics, such as process capability.

Full inspection is used when the results of previous sampling show an excessively high level of defects or reveal other critical circumstances, as for instance inspector incompetence or negligence.

> This approach is prevalent in publicly funded projects or processes where several levels of inspection are needed to control the inspectors themselves. Construction of the 63rd Street subway tunnel in New York City is a glaring example of successive levels of ineffective inspection and reinspection, independent reviews and subsequent audits of the independent reviewers, which cost the City—but more sadly, the taxpayers—untold millions of dollars in waste and years upon years lost in construction delays, litigation, and so on.

A special case of drawing conclusions about populations is the acceptance or rejection of product lots (raw materials or bulk shipments, for example) based on the inspection and testing of a *single* random sample from the lot. This is facilitated by *acceptance sampling* which can be used if lot quality requirements are defined in numerical, quantitative terms.

In addition to the two basic forms of inspection, the inspection of incoming lots of products can also be accomplished using vendors' outgoing inspection and test data. The histogram is a useful tool for learning about a vendor's process and comparing the work products of several vendors against the same specification. A random sample is drawn from a lot and measurements are made on the selected quality parameters. The data are then charted as frequency histograms and compared by way of analysis to the specification limits.

Another tool to detect vendor quality problems is Pareto analysis, which can be used to identify a problem by analyzing a few key defects:

- Part number
- Product family
- Subprocess
- Vendor
- Cost of parts

In many high-technology manufacturing situations, a few part numbers account for a major proportion of the cost and, therefore, defects in these are "the vital few."

ACCEPTANCE SAMPLING

The process of evaluating a portion of a lot for the purpose of accepting or rejecting the entire lot (as either conforming or not conforming) is called *acceptance sampling.*[20] Acceptance sampling is used when (1) the cost of inspection is high relative to the risk resulting from passing defective units to the user; (2) inspection is destructive; or (3) full inspection may lead to inspection errors because of monotony. In fact, acceptance sampling is most effective when it is preceded by a working prevention program and appropriate process design.

The main advantage of sampling lies in the overall cost reduction realized by inspecting only part of the product lot. However, these savings are usually not offset by the higher process design and administrative costs related to the preparation and implementation of sampling and test plans.

As compared to full inspection, disadvantages are sampling risk, administrative cost, and inherently less information about the entire product lot. While acceptance sampling provides, with stated risks, an acceptance or rejection decision on each lot, it does not provide a judgment whether or not a rejected lot conforms to specifications. In summary, *acceptance sampling is not statistical inference, and it does not lead to statistically valid conclusions about the lot itself.*

ECONOMICS OF INSPECTION

The economic comparison of the two basic forms of inspection for the evaluation of lots, as just described, is based on the total costs associated with each of the alternatives. Inspection (appraisal) costs represent an important component of the

---

[20]In statistical terms, the lot is the population from which samples are drawn.

total cost of quality and can contribute to important trade-off decisions. In most cases, economic evaluations are done in support of the decision between sampling or full inspection.[21]

Neither sampling nor full inspection will guarantee the discovery of every defective item in a lot, because (1) the sample may not reflect the true conditions in the lot, and (2) monotony and other factors may result in inspectors' errors. These *sampling risks* can be quantified:

(1) Conforming lots can be rejected (producer's risk). This risk corresponds to the error of the first kind, denoted by α.
(2) Nonconforming lots can be accepted (consumer's risk). This risk corresponds to the error of the second kind, denoted by β.

The *operating characteristics (OC) curve* is used to quantify these risks for a given sampling plan. (The OC curve is covered in greater detail in Appendix A.)

There are two types of sampling plans: *(1) attribute plans,* in which each unit within a random sample taken from the lot is classified as acceptable or defective; and *(2) variables plans,* in which the measurements of a specified characteristic of each unit within a sample are summarized into sample statistics and compared with an allowable value defined in the plan; based on this comparison, a decision is made to accept or reject the lot.

Because a variables sampling plan provides additional statistical information on each sample, it requires smaller sample sizes in comparison with an attribute plan of the same level of risk.

An example for a variables sampling plan is MIL-STD-414 which includes the concepts of acceptable quality level, inspection levels, and OC curves. It is a codification of the concept of "permissible levels of defect" and the result of the inspection-oriented approach to quality management.

3.2.2 Problem Analysis

In quality management a problem arises as a result of nonconformance. Problems manifest themselves through symptoms, which can be described or represented by observations or data. A problem may or may not be related to the process subject to quality improvement.

The solution to a problem usually, but not always, relates to the elimination of one or more defects causing it, including the removal of defect causes as well (see Figure 3-3). Problem solution is not the direct objective of quality management; rather it is the *path* to the real purpose: defect-free work products. The

---

[21]Examples of such an evaluation are given in the literature, notably the work by Juran and Gryna, *Quality Planning and Analysis*, pp. 408–410.

outcome of problem analysis, in turn, is the discovery and definition of nonconformances to requirements, that is, defect identification. However, it should be pointed out that problem analysis is not the only way to discover defects; in fact, one of the major errors committed in quality management is confusing problems with defects.

The severity of a series of problems can be quantified and placed in a relative order of importance. When this is done and graphically presented in the form of a Pareto diagram, we can recognize what are popularly referred to as the "vital few and trivial many"—thus providing graphic guidance for prioritized problem solving.

When a problem has been defined, the next logical step is to determine the possible causes. The cause-and-effect diagram, also referred to as the fishbone or Ishikawa diagram, assists in identifying potential process elements or typical causes, such as materials, equipment, method/procedure, operator, measurement, or environment (see Figure 3-9).

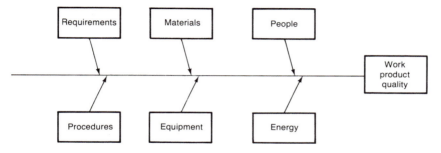

Fig. 3-9. Cause-and-effect (Ishikawa) diagram representing major process components affecting quality.

"Managerial breakthrough" is a term coined by J. M. Juran in the 1960s[22] to designate a management-initiated change to a higher level of quality performance. A breakthrough generally involves a set of five management steps common to problem solving:

(1) Recognize and accept the problem

(2) Make a commitment to improvement

(3) Organize and manage the analysis

(4) Take action

(5) Monitor results

This view of quality management emphasizes the need for on-going, committed management participation in the improvement effort.

---

[22]J. M. Juran, *Managerial Breakthrough* (New York: McGraw-Hill Book Co., 1964).

3.2.3 Defect Identification

Once the existence of nonconformances to requirements (or possibly incompleteness or inconsistencies in the requirement statement) has been discovered, we enter the phase of *defect identification*. Here we attempt to identify the defects as definable and measurable nonconformances. A specific nonconformance to requirements can be identified as a single defect. In many cases, such a nonconformance may be made up of two elements: (1) nonconformance to specifications (variance), and (2) nonconformance of the specifications to requirements (divergence).

A key conceptual point, in many cases easily overlooked even by professionals or students of quality management, has to do with levels of nonconformance. Just as it is important to understand the distinction and relationship between problems and defects, it is equally important to understand and trace the various levels of nonconformances in arriving at a correct quality assessment.

A defect (default or failure) is always viewed *in the context of requirements*. Accordingly, a defect is visible to end users and contributes to their perception of quality—or the lack of it.

When a nonconformance is viewed *in the context of specifications*, it is always related to control, or the management of outcome. When the specification is a standard, the nonconformance is a *deviation*—a special category of variances. (For purposes of process management and control, this book treats specifications and standards as equivalent concepts: Their source and method of development may be different but their role and end effect on the process is identical. Hence, the terms *variance* and *deviation* will be treated as having the same meaning.)

The objective of defect identification is to define all of these nonconformances—defects, variances, and divergences—which contribute to the total condition of nonconformance to requirements and the resulting quality problems. Key steps of defect identification are:

(1) Define the nonconformance as a defect, variation, or divergence, for example, by establishing the relationship of the nonconformance with a specific part of the process (subprocess or activity). The supporting methodology is to select the appropriate process variables, parameters, or indicators which are affected by the nonconformance. (*Failure mechanism analysis* can be a helpful tool in this particular step.)

(2) Determine the *measurability* of the nonconformance based on the process variables already defined. (Tools supporting this activity include tally sheets and histograms, control charts, and frequency distributions.)

(3) Establish the relationship or interaction, if any, with other nonconformances, which is an important input to defect-cause analysis, as well as the corrective actions to be undertaken. (Supporting this activity are such tools as scatter and fishbone diagrams, Pareto analysis, departmental activity

analysis [DAA], and in some cases regression analysis to establish correlation [cause-and-effect relationship] between two or more process variables.)

The net result of defect identification is a list of (one or more) defects, including their component nonconformances (such as variances and divergences), the exact location of their occurrences in the process, and any relationships or interactions that can be identified among them.

In today's complex processes, it is often impractical or even impossible to implement a single defect elimination cycle for the entire process. In such cases the process is broken down into component subprocesses or activities, and the cycle is implemented at these levels on a repeated basis. As will be seen later (Chapters 6 and 7), the defect elimination cycle is most effective when implemented at an activity level managed by a single function or even a single individual. Accordingly, when reference is made in this book to detection and correction activities related to the "process," the term will usually mean a subprocess of a size determined as the lowest rather than the highest level of manageability.

3.2.4 Defect-Cause Analysis

Defect-cause analysis is the second and completing step of the detection phase in the defect elimination cycle (see Figure 3-10).

The main focus of this section is on the *causes* of nonconformances to specifications, because these are the main contributors to quality problems and they also lend themselves to most of the available statistical control methods and tools. In those cases where a single *variance* represents nonconformance to requirements, its causes will be the same as the causes of the *defect*, and no further analysis will be needed. In other cases where there is a *divergence* between the specifications and the requirement statement, the causes for defects can be arrived at by determining the causes of variance (usually the dominant component) plus the causes of divergence. This second aspect of the problem is helped by looking at management techniques such as specification review, department activity analysis, and the like. The discussion which follows will be in the context of "variance-cause analysis," but the reader may mentally substitute "defect-cause analysis" in its place, subject to the assumptions just stated.

Key objectives of this analysis are:

(1) Separation of common (root) causes from special (assignable) causes
(2) Identification of specific parts of the process (subprocess, activity) for corrective action

The key activities, undertaken to achieve the first objective, are:

- *Cause-effect determination*, where the variation is the effect, and one or more of its causes are sought. (Supporting statistical control techniques include scatter diagrams, control charts, and Ishikawa diagrams.)
- *Identification of cause alternatives*, resulting in a list of alternative causes of

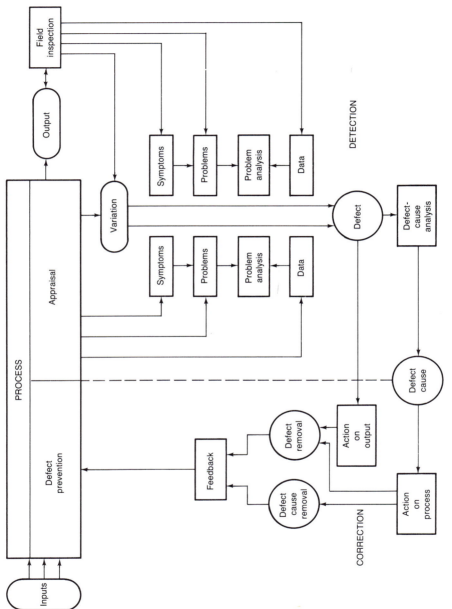

Fig. 3-10. Defect elimination cycle (DEC).

122

varying significance and weight, in priority sequence. (Supporting tools and techniques include histograms and Pareto analysis.)

- *Definition and selection of relevant causes* from the list established in the previous activity. (Supporting statistical techniques here include sampling, statistical inference, and regression analysis.)

At this point, both special causes (if they exist) and common causes of the variation have been identified.

The next key activity of the analysis is carried out to achieve the second objective—that is, identify specific subprocesses or activities for corrective action:

- *Cause location identification* within the process, that is, to a specific activity or individual task level. In some cases this is followed by:
- *Correctability analysis* to establish the feasibility of removing the causes of variations from the various parts and components of the process just identified.[23]

The net result of defect-cause analysis is a list of special causes and another list of common causes contributing to the nonconformance in question, along with the identified locations where the causes exist in the process (not necessarily the same as the location where the nonconformance occurred or was observed) and an assessment of the feasibility of their removal. At this point the process manager has sufficient information to decide what actions on the output and what actions on the process are needed to remove both the variations and their causes.

At this point the analysis can be augmented to establish whether or not the variances are the sole contributors to nonconformance with requirements or whether there might be divergences (differences between specifications and requirements) further contributing to defects. The result of divergence-cause analysis will invariably lead to management action on the process, primarily in the form of adjusting specifications or the requirement statement or changing to the design of the work product and potentially the process itself.

3.3 Correction

The defect elimination cycle is a structured, stepwise implementation of the classic control feedback loop adapted for the purposes of quality management. The first half of the cycle falls into the area of detection, while the second falls within correction (see Figure 3-10.) The key objectives of correction are:

(1) Removal of defects, in many cases, worker-controllable.
(2) Removal of defect causes (i.e., elimination of defects) whether worker- or management-controllable, dependent upon the defect cause.

---

[23]The same kind of correctability analysis should also be carried out at the end of defect identification, for the removability of the defect itself.

(3) Attainment of a new state of process which will prevent defects from happening.

(4) Maintenance or enhancement of the efficiency and productivity of the process, an essential condition for continuing process optimization and ultimately increasing the competitiveness and profitability of the business itself. The removal of defects and defect causes at the expense of productivity or efficiency is inherently self-defeating.

Correction comprises a number of key activities which are carried out to achieve one or more of the these objectives as follows:

- *Action on the output* will result in the removal of defects but not their causes. It is a necessary but not always sufficient condition to achieving the first objective (removal of defects).
- *Action on the process*, undertaken primarily by management (and at times by workers as well), will result in the removal of both defects and their causes. It will therefore contribute to the achievement of the first and second objectives, being both a necessary and sufficient condition for it.
- *Feedback*, comprising test, evaluation, and certification of changes, is a necessary followup to the removal of defects and their causes.

3.3.1 Defect Removal

In many situations, total elimination of a defect (extending to the removal of its causes) may involve complex and time-consuming actions upon the process, such as testing, evaluation, change of process design or product specifications, and the like. In such cases, the removal of the defect itself (usually within the worker's control or based on management-organized action) provides temporary and immediate quality improvement, also known as a *remedy*. Such remedial actions include, among other things, repair and rework, adjustments to the task (changes in instructions or time-and-motion relationships, for example), changes to tolerances or tool settings.

Defect removal is primarily the result of action on the output, but occasionally of action on the process as well. In most cases, both of these actions are worker-controllable, but on occasion action on the process by management is required to remove a specific defect such as, for instance, a change to certain task parameters or such inputs as raw materials, vendor parts, and the like. (Task parameters that management can change, in many cases upon worker request, are such things as working conditions, lighting, ventilation, power, lubricants, and the like.)

3.3.2 Defect-Cause Removal

Defect-cause removal, or *defect elimination is the necessary and sufficient condition of preventing the same defect from occurring again*. Defect-cause removal always requires action upon the process, which may be carried out by workers, but more likely by management. In terms of statistical process control, special (assignable) causes are mostly worker-controllable and, therefore, may be removed by them; common (root) causes, however, are always management-controllable and require management action upon the process.

As we have already seen, defect causes may lie in any part or component of the process which, in turn, will determine the type of corrective action to be taken. Process changes related to people may involve additional training, changes in skills, or a reduction in the people dependency or labor intensity of a particular subprocess or activity. Equipment or machines causing defects may require upgrading or redesign. Procedures contributing to nonconformances must be corrected or changed. If the defect is a nonconformance to schedule commitments such as shipment dates or service turnaround, resource and capacity enhancements may be in order—more personnel, better equipment, and more efficient, streamlined procedures.

The prime result of the sum total of these corrective actions should be the removal of all identified causes of defects. Another, equally important result is an *improved* or a *new* process which has to be tested, evaluated, and certified, both in terms of its output meeting requirements and its continued and enhanced efficiency and productivity. This is part of the *feedback action* which completes the defect elimination cycle and facilitates the tracking of the results of change and the re-examination of targets; it *reinitiates the process.*

3.4 Special Quality Characteristics

In managing outcome and making the necessary adjustments to the process, three key quality characteristics whose conformance to requirements is usually most visible—or critical to the user—deserve special attention:

- Availability
- Reliability
- Serviceability and maintainability

The first three quality characteristics exhibit a remarkable level of interrelation—vitally important from a quality management standpoint. The characteristics of availability, reliability, and maintainability come into play primarily for long-life products, such as manufactured durable goods, complex systems, and products intended for frequent and repeated use (vehicles, airplanes, and the like), which over their lifetime may display inherent changes in performance or other characteristics.

Safety is another characteristic receiving increased attention, especially in today's era of nuclear technology, high-speed mass transportation (in particular, air traffic and its control), and increasing levels of pollution affecting personal safety and health. Furthermore, as traditional manufacturing technologies give way to growing levels of automation in a continuing drive for quality and increased productivity, the *manufacturability* of a given product or system is becoming still another, progressively important quality characteristic.[24]

3.4.1 Availability and Reliability

The lives of individuals and of organizations in today's highly developed industrial society depend fundamentally on the continuity of service from the providers of energy, communications, transportation, financial resources, and the like. In attempting to ensure this continuity, the "utility" concept of service has evolved with the attending assurance that failure rates in offerings and services are kept to a very minimum, and the restoration of service in case of failure is as prompt as possible. One key element in implementing this concept of service is the recognition that continuity of service—also known as *availability* for use—is a quality parameter which can be specified both in terms of requirements and measurable value. Availability is time-related and it is measured by the extent to which the end user can secure the related service when it is wanted—that is, *on demand.*

Availability assumes a failure-free state; however, since products do occasionally fail, the *reliability* parameter is introduced to describe time-dependent behavior with respect to the occurrence of failures. In simple terms, reliability can be described as *time-dependent quality.*

The calculation of reliability for today's complex products and systems can be very involved. Because reliability is extremely difficult to predict, it is important to undertake every possible measure and management action to ensure that the reliability called for by specification (product design), is (1) attainable (design qualification) and (2) achievable by the final work product (process qualification). In many cases, reliability cannot be readily tested until the work product is in actual use over a period of time, and until appropriate observations and data have been collected and interpreted. Consequently, for products and services for which reliability is an important quality characteristic, the overall quality assessment may not readily be available for some period of time, perhaps months and years after installation or the beginning of operational use.

> This is one of the reasons why reliability improvements for complex systems—for example, digital computers and communications networks—are achieved over generations of such systems, as reliability measurements and assessments become known and fundamental technological improvements become available over longer periods of time.

The general approach to quality improvement is widely applicable to reliability improvement, as far as the cost analysis and managerial tools are concerned. The differences are in the technological approaches and tools used for

---

[24]Manufacturability and safety are beyond the scope of this text; the reader is advised to refer to the growing and increasingly rich literature on these subjects, especially [7], [13], [20], and [32] in the Bibliography.

diagnosis and correction. Areas for improvement are identified mainly through use of prioritization techniques, such as the Pareto principle.

The continuing efforts to reduce failure rates result in continuing increases in reliability—known as "reliability growth." Some of this takes place during the design phase, but additional improvement can be attained after field performance data become available and, in turn, trigger further action upon the process such as changes to design or requirements. Reliability growth, just as reliability itself, can be measured, and reliability objectives are set with an awareness that growth can and will take place. (There have been a number of efforts to predict reliability growth as an aid to establishing reliability objectives; see also Section 2.4.)

3.4.2 Serviceability and Maintainability

Dependence on continuity of service has also focused on the improvement of the maintenance of long-life products and systems. Maintenance comprises two major types of activities:

(1) Preventive or *scheduled* maintenance, which consists of tests and diagnostic activities to detect potential failures or deteriorating conditions, planned servicing (cleaning, lubrication), and overhauls (replacement of worn parts plus scheduled replacement of failure-prone components)

(2) *Unscheduled* maintenance, aimed at restoring operations or service after failure through repair or replacement action

The terms *serviceability* and *maintainability* are both used to express the ease with which the above types of activities can be conducted. The term *serviceability* is given preference in this text, especially when used in the generic sense; *maintainability* relates more to manufactured products such as machinery, vehicles, and so forth.

Quantification of maintainability has to take into account that maintenance activities require both time and also a variety of resources (human resources, parts, supplies, energy, money, and so on). Of these, the time-oriented aspects of maintenance are considered the most important, because they are the most visible to the end user and also because disruptions and their economic effects can grow to disaster proportions unless service is promptly restored.

Effectiveness of maintenance is strongly influenced by *product design* (easy access, replaceability of modules, technical information, among other factors) and *maintenance technology,* including diagnostic instruments and special repair tools. Also, effectiveness of maintenance depends heavily on the availability of necessary skills and parts, also called *logistics support.*

The user's ability to secure continuity of service further depends on clear and adequate administrative and procedural arrangements (unequivocal contracts, responsive service dispatching system, and so on). In some industries, maintenance technology and logistics support are offered not by the provider of the product but rather by separate service contractors, also known as *field service industries,* which have an extensive range of contacts directly with the end user. In today's world of evolving complex and decentralized systems and services, the quality of service includes the appropriate measurements and controls over *all* related service industries, which then become part of the overall process to both produce and maintain the work product.

Some of the major areas in which the extent and importance of maintenance have grown during the twentieth century, especially in the last 25 years are:

- Centralized services such as utilities, communications, or on-line information systems.
- Mechanized and automated factories in which maintenance is a major force in maintaining productivity.
- New high-technology consumer products, including electronic entertainment devices, personal computers, and the like; for these the cost of maintenance over the life of the product may exceed the original price. (Included in this category are new military equipment such as weapons systems for which maintenance costs have soared to unprecedented levels.)

As mentioned before, serviceability is a key parameter which contributes to product availability. (Figure 2-5 shows in greater detail the elements which make up total availability.)

3.5 Aids for Quality Control

Of the three powerful concepts which can aid in the management of outcome, *process control, process capability*, and *the cost of quality*, this section focuses on the latter two.

In managing outcome, the cost of quality is used mainly as a *reporting, tracking, and analytical tool.* Since it is also a general process management tool that contributes to process optimization, a further detailed discussion of its use will follow in Chapter 6.

3.5.1 Process Capability Analysis

Capability, in plain language, means the degree to which the process produces uniform output within its specified limits. In statistical terms, process capability can be defined as the spread within which almost all of the values within a data distribution (describing some output of the process) will fall. In quantitative terms, process capability is generally described as within ± 3 standard deviations ($\pm 3\sigma$), or six absolute standard deviations. This definition conveniently enables us to compare the process capability with the *process tolerance*.

> One of the frequent mistakes made by the uninitiated is to confuse process capability with process tolerance. The former is an inherent, measurable characteristic of

the *process in operation*; the latter is a parameter specified *in advance* by the process design.

The *process capability index* is frequently used to make this comparison which, for bilateral tolerances, is defined as the relationship:

$$I_c = \text{Capability Index} = \frac{\text{Process Tolerance}}{\text{Process Capability}} \qquad (3.1)$$

A graphic representation of this relationship is shown in Figure 3-11a. In practical terms, a capability index greater than 1 indicates that the process is capable of

a. Basic concept.

b. Noncapable process ($Ic < 1$).

c. Capable process ($Ic = 1$).

d. Capable processes ($Ic > 1$).

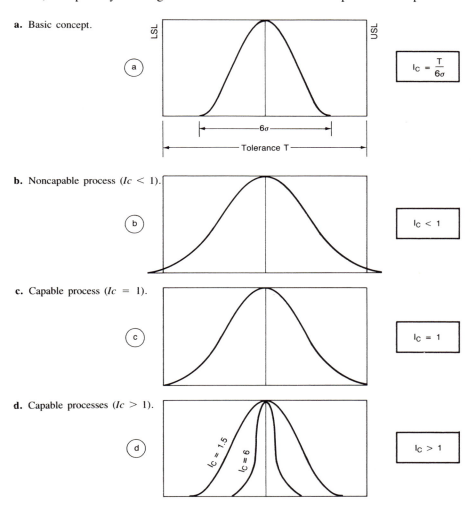

Fig. 3-11. Graphic interpretation of capability index.

producing all of its output within the limits specified for it, for example, within the process tolerance.

> Several industrial organizations have established required capability index objectives of 1.33 or greater. Figure 3-11 illustrates examples of the relationships of process capabilities to process tolerances for index values of less than, equal to, or greater than 1. Note that in all three examples the process is centered on the *tolerance mean* (the average of *USL* and *LSL*—which means that it produces output which will most likely assume values equidistant between the upper and lower specification limits). If a process is not centered, that is, if it favors one or the other specification limit (e.g., the median of the distribution is off center in one or the other direction), its capability index will be lower than that of a centered process of equal spread (Figure 3-12a and b).

Capability reflects variation from common causes, and management action on the process is almost always required for capability improvement. However, assessment of process capability (the question, Does the process output meet specifications?) can begin only after special causes have been identified, analyzed, removed, and prevented from recurring—that is, only after the process has been

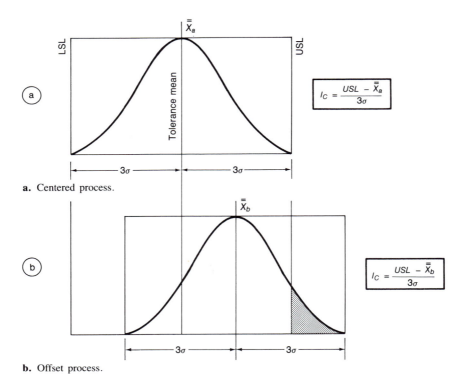

a. Centered process.

b. Offset process.

Fig. 3-12. Capability index.

brought under statistical control.[25] In general, process capability assessment means comparing the distribution of process output with process tolerance to see whether the latter can consistently, and with equal chance, be satisfied.

There are many techniques for assessing the capability of a process that is in statistical control. Most assume that the process output follows the bell-shaped normal distribution (as shown in Figure 3-11).[26]

> The calculation of the process capability is based on data from the control chart. The process average $\overline{\overline{X}}$ is used as the location of the distribution; a measure of spread is calculated from the simple formula
>
> $$\hat{\sigma} = \overline{R}/d \qquad (3.2)$$
>
> where $\overline{R}$ is the average of the subgroup ranges and d is a constant that varies with sample size, as shown in Appendix A. The value $\hat{\sigma}$ ("sigma hat") is known as the *estimate of the process standard deviation*, which can be used in calculating the process capability, as long as both the ranges and averages are in statistical control.

Once process capability has been calculated for a process in statistical control, the next step is to evaluate the process capability in terms of meeting specifications. The problems causing unacceptable process capability are usually common causes. The fundamental goal is never-ending improvement to the *total* process performance which means (1) process capability improvements and (2) process optimization (improvement in efficiency and productivity).

Improvement in process capability means reducing the variation that comes from common causes. This means taking management action to improve the process itself. Therefore, actions must be directed toward the process—that is, toward such underlying process factors as equipment performance, training, consistency of input, materials, and the like. As a general rule, these process-related causes of "noncapability" require management intervention for basic changes, reallocation of resources, and the like. Attempts to improve the process by short-range, local actions—such as altering specifications, sorting output and scrap, and the like—will be ineffective in the long run.

> When systematic process actions have been taken, their effects should be apparent in the control chart, especially in terms of reduced ranges. The chart becomes a way of verifying the effectiveness of management action. As process changes are implemented, the control chart should be monitored carefully. After any instabilities of the change period have been resolved, the new process capability should be assessed and used as the basis of new control limits for future operations.

---

[25]Using control chart terminology, achievement of statistical control means the resolution of control issues in both the $\overline{X}$ and R charts.

[26]If it is not known whether the distribution is normal, a *test for normalcy* should be made. For further study on this subject, the reader is referred to the literature, particularly [11] in the Bibliography.

From a statistical viewpoint, process capability is a measure of the inherent variability of the process. For purposes of analysis, the capability is related to process tolerance. This is done either by the capability index, discussed earlier, or its reciprocal, called the *capability ratio*:

$$R_c = \text{Capability Ratio} = \frac{\text{Process Capability}}{\text{Process Tolerance}} \qquad (3.3)$$

A rule of thumb for acceptable initial variability is that the capability ratio not exceed 0.75 for bilateral tolerance and 0.88 for unilateral tolerance (meaning that process variation is less than 75 percent, or 88 percent, respectively, of the tolerance range).

FREQUENCY DISTRIBUTION

Process capability refers to the variation in a process about some *aim*, as illustrated in Figure 3-12. The two processes shown have equal capabilities, as indicated by the spreads of the distribution curves. The process in Figure 3-12b is producing defectives because the aim is off center (of the tolerance range), not because of the inherent variation about the aim (e.g., the capability).

The use of a statistical distribution to describe process variation is far superior to nonstatistical methods, subject to these assumptions:

(1) The process is operating at its best potential; that is, it is in statistical control.
(2) The measured characteristic follows a *normal probability distribution*. (Should this not be true, specially designed probability tables can be used to arrive at a measure of process capability.)
(3) The effect of time-dependent factors on process capability (such as fatigue, wear) is not considered.

A *probability distribution function* is a mathematical formula that relates the values of the characteristic being observed with their probability of occurrence in the population. The collection of these probabilities is called a *probability distribution*. Probability distributions are discussed in more detail, and the more frequently used distributions are summarized in Appendix A.[27]

PROBABILITY PAPER

The use of probability paper is another approach to determine process capability. Figure 3-13 shows the use of probability paper in process capability analysis.

The probability paper method has certain advantages. Calculation of the standard deviation is avoided; for small samples the plot on probability paper may

---

[27]Probability distribution should not be confused with frequency distribution: The former is a mathematical formula or function; the latter is a count or tabulation of occurrences.

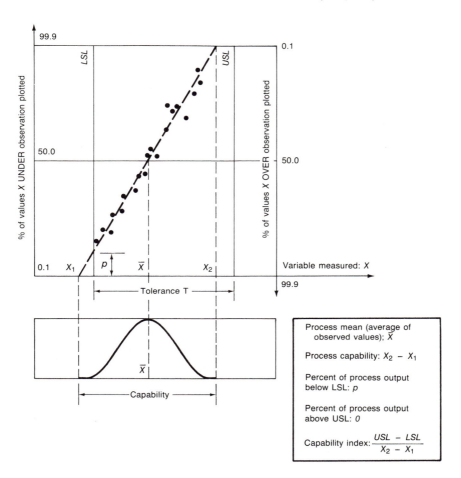

Fig. 3-13. Use of probability paper for normal distribution in process capability analysis.

Source: Adapted, with permission of the publisher, from *Quality Planning and Analysis* by J. M. Juran and F. M. Gryna, Jr. (New York: McGraw-Hill Book Co., ´)80).

be more illustrative than comparing histograms to the theoretical bell-shape curve. Furthermore, for skewed or other unusual distributions, for which it is difficult to construct histograms, Weibull probability paper provides a more practical approach.

STATISTICAL CONTROL CHARTS

The management of outcome means to assess and correct: If the work product of a process does not conform to requirements, corrective action has to be taken, both on the work product and on the process, to eliminate the nonconformance and to restore the process to its intended state.

In most cases, nonconformance is established by comparing the process output to requirements through observations and measurements; from data related to the output, conclusions are also drawn about the process. In some cases, however, nonconformance can be established from observations related to the process itself—although, as discussed before, variations observed in the process do not always cause variations in the output.

Process capability derived from a histogram or probability paper analysis represents the performance of the process, but not necessarily its best potential. This can occur if the data represent observations from several populations (readings made at different machine settings or measuring a process with different personnel assigned). Another situation may arise when there is no prior evidence for the stability of the process. In such cases, a more powerful analytical tool, the *control chart*, should be used. Ideally, only common causes should be present in a process because by definition it is a state of minimum variation, or statistical control. Thus, a control chart analysis should be made and special causes eliminated from the process before establishing process capability as six standard deviations, representing the true inherent process capability.

It was Shewhart who first made the distinction between controlled and uncontrolled variation, as a result of what is now termed common and special causes, respectively. He recognized the need for distinguishing and separating the two and developed the tool for doing so—the control chart.[28] Since then, experience has shown that control charts (1) effectively signal the *existence* of special causes when these appear, and (2) indicate the *extent* of variation resulting from common causes that must be reduced or eliminated by management action on the process.

A *control chart* is a graphic representation of measured process performance data relative to computed *control limits* shown as limiting lines on the chart. *The prime purpose of the control chart is to detect special causes of variation in the process.*[29] Table 3-6 presents an overview of basic forms of control charts and the corresponding control limit formulas for the underlying statistics.

A *control chart* is designed to detect the *existence* of a cause of variation that lies outside the process, also known as a *special cause*. It will also detect a change in the system and a shrinkage in spread (shift to greater uniformity in the process).

Courses in statistics often commence with a study and comparison of distributions. Students are not warned that for analytic purposes (namely, to improve a process) distributions and calculations of such statistics as mean, mode, or standard deviation serve no useful purpose unless the data were produced in a state of statistical

---

[28]See W. A. Shewhart, *The Economics of Control of Quality of Manufactured Products* (New York: D. Van Nostrand Company, Inc., 1931).

[29]For a summary of the construction and use of statistical control charts, see Appendix C.

Table 3-6. CONTROL CHART OVERVIEW

a. Comparison of Basic Forms of Control Charts

	Average $\bar{X}$	Range R	Percent defective p	Number of defects $\bar{c}$
Statistic observed				
Type of data	Variables		Attributes	
Data	Measured values of parameter		Number of defective units	Number of defects per unit (of product)
Applicability	Control of individual parameters		Control of overall percentage defective	Control of number of defects per unit
Advantages	Good detailed information on process average and variation		Good overall measure of quality	Ease of use, ease of understanding, data often available directly from inspection
Disadvantages	Extensive training required. Control limits and tolerance limits may be confused		No detailed information for control of individual parameters. No recognition of different degrees of defectiveness in units	

b. Control Limit Formulas

	Average $\bar{X}$	Range R	Percent defective p	Number of defects $\bar{c}$
Central Line	$\bar{\bar{X}}$	$\bar{R}$	$\bar{p}$	$\bar{c}$
Lower Control Limit	$\bar{\bar{X}} - a_2\bar{R}$	$d_3\bar{R}$	$\bar{p} - 3\sqrt{\bar{p}\dfrac{1-\bar{p}}{n}}$	$\bar{c} - 3\sqrt{\bar{c}}$
Upper Control Limit	$\bar{\bar{X}} + a_2\bar{R}$	$d_4\bar{R}$	$\bar{p} + 3\sqrt{\bar{p}\dfrac{1-\bar{p}}{n}}$	$\bar{c} + 3\sqrt{\bar{c}}$

control. Accordingly, the first step in the examination of any data is to question the state of the process that produced that data. Statistical control of the process is vital; otherwise there are no valid measurement data.

The control chart in fact represents the actual process, not its design or desired state. Several types of control charts exist to analyze both variables and attributes data; these will be discussed in greater detail in the material that follows, and their construction is described in Appendix C. However, all control charts have the same two fundamental uses:

- Control: To signal the presence of special causes of variation and provide evidence whether a process has been operating in a state of statistical control.
- Capability: For a process in a state of statistical control, to assess process capability by determining the extent of variation due to common causes. If this is excessive, the process cannot consistently produce output that meets requirements. This in turn requires management action to improve the process, which is the fundamental approach to continued quality improvement.

The control chart distinguishes between common and special causes of variation through its *choice of the control limits*. These are computed such that random variations of low probability are presumed to be the results of special causes. When the actual variation exceeds the control limits, it is a sign that special causes have been introduced into the process and the process itself should be investigated for stability. Variation within the control limits means that only common causes are present and the process itself is in statistical control.

Control charts are usually classified by the parameter being observed:

- The *average* or mean of the measurements in the sample, known as an $\overline{X}$-chart. (The mean measures the aim, or centering, of the process.)
- The *range* of the measurements in the sample, known as an R-chart. (The range measures variability about the aim of the process.)

The foregoing two measurements are most frequently used in calculating process capability. Other charts used in data analysis, related to defect detection are:

- The p-chart, which measures the percent defective in the sample.
- The c-chart, which measures the number of defects in the sample.[30]

Figure 3-14 shows some of the many possible observation patterns and their control chart interpretations.[31]

---

[30]Examples for establishing an X and R control chart and a more detailed discussion of p- and c-charts are included in Appendix C.

[31]The fact that all observation points are within control limits (Figure 3-14c, d, and e) does not necessarily mean the absence of special causes of variation.

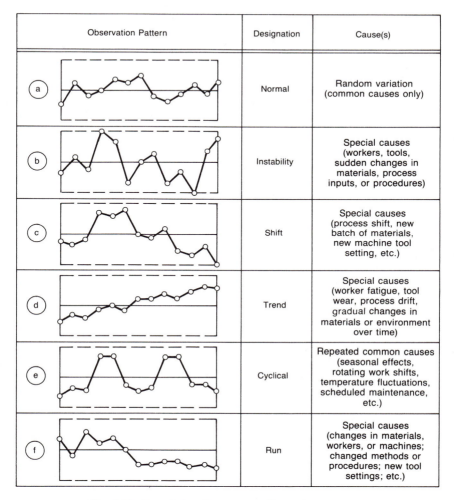

Observation Pattern	Designation	Cause(s)
a	Normal	Random variation (common causes only)
b	Instability	Special causes (workers, tools, sudden changes in materials, process inputs, or procedures)
c	Shift	Special causes (process shift, new batch of materials, new machine tool setting, etc.)
d	Trend	Special causes (worker fatigue, tool wear, process drift, gradual changes in materials or environment over time)
e	Cyclical	Repeated common causes (seasonal effects, rotating work shifts, temperature fluctuations, scheduled maintenance, etc.)
f	Run	Special causes (changes in materials, workers, or machines; changed methods or procedures; new tool settings; etc.)

Fig. 3-14. Control chart for averages: Observation patterns.

Source: Adapted, with permission of the publisher, from *Quality Planning and Analysis* by J. M. Juran and F. M. Gryna, Jr. (New York: McGraw-Hill Book Co., 1980).

A *normal pattern* (Figure 3-14a) indicates a stable process with no trend, shift, or other noticeable pattern. Such a process is said to be in statistical control over a period of time, with only common causes of variation present.

Indications of the presence of special causes of variation are:

- Points outside control limits (Figure 3-14b), indicating *instability,* or unnaturally large fluctuations. They may be caused by erratic test equipment, introduction of new procedures, overadjusted equipment, and the like.

- A *shift* (Figure 3-14c): A sudden change in process level, caused by a new tool setting, a new machine operator, or perhaps a new lot of raw materials.
- A *trend* (Figure 3-14d): The process is drifting, possibly caused by equipment wear, gradual environmental (temperature) change, or operator fatigue. A trend is usually represented by a gradual rise or fall of data values (five or more consecutive points) in the same direction.

In process capability studies the order of output over time is a very important variable. Over time, certain patterns may reveal further characteristics of process behavior:

- *Cycles* (Figure 3-14e): A consistent pattern of repeated high or low values that recur periodically over time. They can be interpreted as short trends in replicated patterns, caused by circumstances similar to those of the trend phenomenon described above.
- *Runs* (Figure 3-14f): A shift in one or more process parameters. Runs are represented by the existence of a succession of observation points on one side of the center line on the control chart. *Runs almost always signal the appearance of a special cause of variation in the process;* therefore, their correct evaluation and interpretation can be critical to the use of control charts. A suggested approach to evaluate runs is shown in Appendix C.[32]

An important lesson of control chart analysis is that, if there is no stable process, the usual statistical measurements and techniques such as frequency distributions and the various central tendency and dispersion statistics would have no predictive value. Analysis of variance and other statistical techniques would be misleading.

If the special causes of variation cannot be economically eliminated, process capability can be computed with the out-of-control points included in the calculation. However, process capability limits will be overstated because the process will not be operating at its best potential and, furthermore, because of the instability of the process, the prediction will only be approximate.

As a process becomes more complex, so does the analysis to measure its capability. (More advanced methods of analysis, such as the *analysis of variance*, are beyond the scope of this text.[33])

Here are some of the important benefits of the proper utilization of control charts:

- Universal applicability refers to any technological, business, or administrative process structured around the basic concept of the feedback loop.

---

[32]For further reading on this topic, see Juran and Gryna, Jr., *Quality Planning and Analysis*, p. 341; also Western Electric Company, *Statistical Quality Control Handbook* (Easton, PA: Mack Printing Co., 1956).

[33]The reader is referred to the literature on the subject, in particular, J. M. Juran (ed.), *Quality Control Handbook*, 3rd ed. (New York: McGraw-Hill Book Co., 1974), p. 295.

- Control charts are simple but effective tools to achieve and maintain statistical control. They can be maintained at the work station, with little special training, by workers or operators; they give the people closest to the work product reliable information about when action should or should not be taken.
- Once a process is in statistical control, its performance will be predictable; both provider and user can rely on consistent conformance to requirements and on stable costs to achieve quality. This provides a base for further management decisions and actions to improve the process; the expected effects of proposed improvements in the process can be anticipated and the actual effects can be identified by means of the control charts. Such process improvements will (1) improve conformance (increase the portion of output that meets requirements); (2) decrease or eliminate defects and reduce the cost of quality, thereby improving process efficiency; and (3) increase the total yield of conforming output (improve productivity).
- By distinguishing special from common causes of variation, control charts give a good indication whether a given problem is correctable by action on the output or will require action on the process (management action). This helps minimize the excessive cost of misdirected efforts at defect elimination.

While the control chart is a powerful statistical tool, it should be used judiciously. Given the vast number of components and factors present in a modern business process—be it manufacturing, chemical, administrative, or other—which all contribute to conformance of the work product, control charts are justified for only a relatively small number of these. Also, once charts have served their purpose in identifying and interpreting variations, they should be discarded as efforts are shifted to the detection and correction of other defects.

Control charts are a very useful tool which frequently help us determine if and when a variation does exist. The technical resolution of that variation, discovered by the control chart, is accomplished by using other tools or methods. Appendix C introduces the basic types of control charts that have been developed for the analysis of both variables- and attribute-type process data.

3.5.2 Cost of Quality

The cost of quality is recognized as another important aid in measuring and reporting overall quality performance—by product, by process, or by organization. When applied to process management and specifically the management of outcome, the following components of this powerful indicator are of importance:

- *Appraisal costs*: Specifically, the costs incurred while conducting inspections, tests, and other planned evaluations to determine whether the work product conforms to specifications.
- *Internal failure costs*: Those costs associated with correcting nonconformances found prior to shipment, transfer or installation for end use.

- *External failure costs*: Those costs associated with correcting nonconformances found after shipment and the beginning of end use.

Effective process management will allocate resources and apply methods such as process control and process capability improvement in the most highly leveraged areas to minimize total cost of quality.

Total cost of quality is determined by the interplay among the various cost of quality components, as described above. This interplay can be shown to lead to an optimum level (minimum) of the total cost of quality (Figure 3-15).

In the traditional model, failure costs are shown to drop from infinity to zero while the sum of appraisal and prevention costs rises from zero to infinity as the *point of zero defects* is approached. In this model, the total cost of quality, by definition, has a minimum (optimum) between the two extremes (Figure 3-15a).

The traditional view is that the appropriate strategy for an organization is to aim production at the point associated with minimum total cost of quality. The scenario leads to such concepts as *acceptable quality level* (AQL) and the conclusion that striving for zero defects, with the cost of prevention and appraisal rising dramatically as the *point of zero defects* is approached, is not economical, nor is it good business practice. What should be done instead is to establish a level of allowable percent of defectives and then insure that it is not exceeded.

It has been shown that in many business and technological processes the traditional model does not fit, and for many products it leads to an incorrect conclusion.[34] For high-technology processes and products with low failure rates (reasonably close to zero defects), there are many examples which show that such products can be built at a cost of prevention plus appraisal that is finite and reasonable (Figure 3-15b). Consequently, the increase in cost is not prohibitive as the *point of zero defects* is approached. The key difference is the *finiteness* of the sum of the prevention and appraisal costs *at the point of zero defects*. With the cost of failure decreasing steadily as the point of zero defects is approached, the minimum total cost of quality is *at* the point of zero defects which therefore becomes the acceptable quality level as well. Hence, the two schools of thought, zero defects and AQL, need not necessarily be in conflict: it is the process view that helps overcome the perceived philosophical conflict between them. (In any case, the concept of acceptable quality level should be downplayed because it is too often used as an excuse for nonconformance.)

When the cost element is introduced—namely the cost of detection and correction in the case of each defect—another dimension is added to the set of tools available to the quality manager. Especially in conjunction with such techniques as Pareto analysis and the use of attribute control charts, cost analysis helps focus on critical leverage items and the relative value of removing defects and their causes, which in turn will also contribute to the efficiency and productivity of the overall process.

---

[34]See [6] and [15] in the Bibliography.

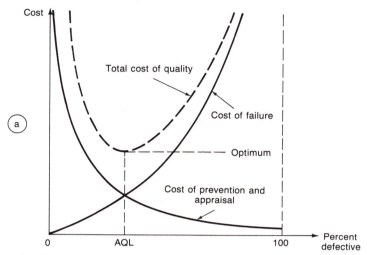

a. Traditional view.

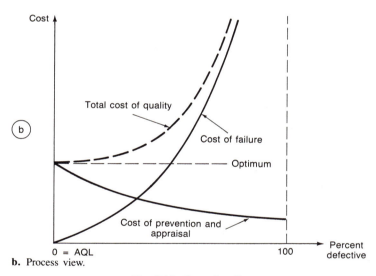

b. Process view.

Fig. 3-15. Cost of quality.

Because it is a powerful process management tool, the cost of quality will be further discussed in Chapter 6.

Summary

The management of outcome comprises all the activities which are necessary to detect and correct variations in the process output—without *permanently* changing or modifying the process itself. By definition, the management of outcome, also known as quality *control*, covers all the appraisal activities aimed at detection, including the traditional techniques of inspection and sampling; the measurement system with all the procedures and resources applied to it; analytical work related to problem analysis, defect identification, and defect-cause analysis; and all corrective actions applied to the output of the process.

These activities of control are "sandwiched" between the two major aspects of managing intent—also known as *prevention*: planning, design, and predictive appraisal on the one hand, and corrective feedback and action on the process, on the other.

In *traditional* quality management, the management of outcome used to represent the majority of actions and resources, as quality management was essentially synonymous with quality control. The cost categories associated with failure detection and correction (cost of appraisal and cost of failure) accounted for an overwhelming portion of the cost of quality. Accordingly, even today most of the literature and educational and training materials on quality management relate predominantly to quality control.

In *modern* process-oriented quality management, control finds a balanced application within the overall quality management cycle which, in fact, begins and ends with prevention, as it is repeated on a continuous, never-ending basis. As the quality management effort matures, control gives way more and more to prevention and, in the ultimate stage of maturity, the dominant portion of quality management activities and resources are preventive, rather than control-related (see also Sections 6.3 and 7.4).

DISCUSSION QUESTIONS

1. Draw a schematic representation of quality management. Identify the two key areas: management of intent (prevention) and management of outcome (control). Show the relationship of appraisal to both of these; establish the correct relative position of detection and correction.

2. Define *process management* in terms of its two major components. What is the key management tool that ties process management together?

3. Give the definition of these critical quality control terms: *defect, variance, deviation, problem, symptom,* and *cause.*

4. What is the objective of a controllability study?

5. Describe special and common causes of variation. Explain the difference between the two. How are they related to worker-controllable and management-controllable causes, respectively?

6. What are the three criteria of worker self-control?

7. Explain the Pareto principle. How does it relate to the distribution of quality costs?

8. What is the only safe method to detect the existence of special causes of variation? Whose responsibility is it? Should workers make conformance decisions? Discuss pros and cons.

9. What is the only way of eliminating or reducing common causes of variation?

10. When is a process said to be stable? Define *statistical control*.

11. Name and describe the four more common methods of statistical process control from simple to more complex techniques.

12. Name major forms of data summarization. Define *frequency distribution* of a discrete and a continuous variable. What is a histogram? How does it differ from a scatter diagram?

13. Name and describe the key measures of central tendency.

14. Name and describe the basic measures of dispersion.

15. Describe a statistical control chart. Name its prime purpose and explain its use. Name at lease three patterns which indicate the presence of special causes of variation in the observations.

16. Define the term *measurement system*. Name its four essential parts.

17. Define *gauge capability*. What are its three key elements?

18. Explain the difference between discovery and defect cause analysis. What are the respective results of these?

19. Describe at least four types of inspection and explain their respective purpose. What are the two levels of inspection?

20. Describe the operating characteristics (OC) curve. What is its prime application?

21. Describe the defect elimination cycle (DEC). What are its phases? Draw a schematic representation of the "defect elimination template."

22. What are the key objectives of correction?

23. Explain the difference between defect removal and defect elimination (defect cause removal).

24. Name the three powerful management tools of quality control. How is the cost of quality being used in managing outcome?

25. Define *statistical inference* and name its two major fields. What are some of their key applications?

26. What does improvement in process capability mean? Describe process tolerance and how it differs from process capability. What is the capability ratio?

27. Name the major classifications of control charts. What are their respective purposes and applications?

28. What are some of the important benefits of the proper utilization of control charts? What lessons can be learned from their use?

Part II MANAGEMENT FUNDAMENTALS

4

THE PROCESS

When it comes to the description, design, and control of a general industrial or business process, the classic approaches of process engineering and process control are useful but inadequate and limited, because they are based on the concept of closed technological processes.

Because managing quality pertains to the conformance of the work product to requirements, it essentially implies a way of managing the business process. Although this fact has been recognized recently by leading industrial and business organizations, in actuality very little is available to management in terms of structured disciplines or theoretical foundations for planning and organizing business process management.

The definition of a process given in Section 1.1.4 is very similar to that of a *system,* as used in general system theory. In fact, some of the fundamental principles established in general system theory can be extended and applied to industrial and business processes, which may be considered and treated as *open systems.* (A more detailed discussion of this concept will follow in Section 4.2.)

One of the most basic errors committed by management is to confuse process with organization. Quality management must concentrate on the *process,* not on organization. The traditional, organization-oriented approach is contrasted with the process view in Table 4-1.

A fundamental characteristic of a process is that it comprises a series of related activities which result in a work product, which in turn must conform to stated requirements. As will be seen later, such activities usually cut across

Table 4-1. PROCESS MANAGEMENT IN PERSPECTIVE

	Organizational View	*Process View*
Management Orientation	People	Process
Approach	Perpetuation	Initiation
Driver	Job	Customer
Progress	People motivation	Removal of barriers, process simplification
Control	Responsibility	Procedure
Business Measurement	Bottom line	Quality
Correction	Fix problem (Who is wrong?)	Reduce nonconformance (What is wrong?)
Motto	*Follow orders* ("Do your job.")	*Improve process* ("How can I help?")

organizations and even functional boundaries. The success of managing the process and controlling its output—and consequently controlling quality—will depend on management's ability to define and separate the components of the process from other organizational, political, and functional considerations and influences and to allow them to operate as a whole by removing barriers to process flow. One of the most frequent reasons why many quality management efforts fail is because *organizational and functional influences and priorities gradually erode the overall process objectives and controls.* This is frequently the case in large corporations where processes by definition must be task-oriented and often compete with established organizational and functional priorities.

These considerations must be reflected in both the design and the management of the process. The remainder of this chapter will take up these questions in greater detail.

4.1 Process Design

Every process—technological or administrative, complex or simple—must be designed around three fundamental concepts:

(1) The basic *feedback loop,* also known as the "command and control" concept. This means that to achieve satisfactory results—that is, conformance

to requirements—those responsible for managing the process must always be in a position to (a) know what is to be done (command or intent) and (b) know what is being done and take corrective action if and when necessary (control). Many processes, mostly administrative and political, break down because those responsible are not in a position to take such action for lack of authority—legal, political, or otherwise.

Without the basic feedback loop, no set of components, however well chosen and ordered, and no sophisticated management system will ensure effective operation and, as a result, conformance to requirements.

(2) *Independence of purpose,* coupled with a clearly defined relationship to other processes, and organizational and functional entities within the business. Such relationships are usually ensured through a properly implemented *management system,* which establishes the scope and relative position of a given process within the overall business environment.

The basic characteristics of an independent process include:

(a) The process must be *in control* and *capable* of producing defect-free output, which means it must be *effective.* Process effectiveness is ensured through continuing quality improvement.

Process effectiveness sometimes includes further desirable or prescribed attributes, dependent on the work product required and the environment in which the process is implemented:

- *Repeatability:* The process must be able to perform its operations (activities) in a specified, successive number of times, *in the same place.*
- Some processes must also be *reproducible*, which means the duplication or replication of the same set of process components and their interrelationships *in another place*—at the same or another time.
- Sometimes the need for process *portability* also exists—the need to transfer the *same* process, along with its components, to *another place* for repeated or continued operations.

(b) The process must be *efficient:* It has to operate at optimum cost (lowest possible cost of quality). Process efficiency is ensured through process optimization.

A process should always be designed for *continued quality improvement*, as well as *process optimization.* (Using Juran's terminology, process design should always be done for "managerial breakthrough," not just for controlling the "status quo.")

(c) The process must be *adaptable:* There has to be an effective and economical way of changing it over time as a result of corrections necessitated by variations in output, or by changing requirements. This means that changes to the process should be applicable without adverse impact on its effectiveness or efficiency. Process adaptability is ensured through appropriate design and process optimization.

The importance of *process adaptability* was recently pointed out by a senior Defense Department official, who equated the success of highly complex technological processes with the capability to absorb change and be self-corrective: "Finally, I came to realize that the common denominator was to be found in the programs that had failed or come in second best. An example was the German atomic bomb program of World War II, a program that was so highly structured and formal that it was unable to correct itself. By contrast, the Manhattan Project was dynamic, contentious, full of scientific give and take, and therefore capable of speedily correcting its own errors." (*New York Times Magazine*, August 24, 1986, page 22.)

(3) Clear and complete *definition of components*—people, procedures, information, equipment, materials, and energy. Procedures include the description of interrelationships of these components and of the activities they are expected to perform.

The definition of the process components must include:

* Inputs (materials, energy, information, and so on)
* Requirements (statement of customer/recipient needs and expectations)
* Specifications (description of output)
* Procedures (problem analysis, error elimination, corrective actions, process changes)
* Process hierarchy (subprocesses or activities)
* Organization (people, responsibilities, information flow)
* Measurement system
* Feedback (control points)

Incorporation of all three concepts is necessary for good process design and satisfactory operation. Whether the process is controlled by sophisticated methods, such as statistical techniques, or by simple visual observation and manual intervention, these three design concepts will determine its ultimate success or failure.

The process design must also provide for *traceability*, as described in Section 2.3.3.

The term *process design* as used in this text refers to the activities of planning the work process in order to achieve quality objectives. There is no such thing as process design in the abstract; the related planning is done to meet known objectives. The end result of this planning cycle is the *process plan:* a list of activities to be done, identification of the components needed to do them, a schedule, and other "elements of design" as appropriate (see also Section 2.3.3). Design is complete when all components of the process are in place and in a state of readiness for implementation.

4.1.1 Major Process Planning

Certain processes can be carried out by a few individuals in a department. Others require participation from multiple company departments or functions. For example, the order entry process requires varying degrees of participation from marketing, information systems, manufacturing, and service. For best results it is important to delineate—in terms of process components—the scope of every process which management intends to control as a separate entity. In the final analysis, a process thus defined can comprise a small number of business activities or the entire business itself.

In the case of major industrial undertakings, such as the design and production of a new and complex product, process definition and delineation become critical, as it would be risky to rely on traditional departmental planning. In some companies, the success of the enterprise may depend on the results attained in several major processes. For such key processes, companies create special management mechanisms to provide tailor-made process planning and management. As will be seen later, the process management mechanism usually comprises:

- A process owner.
- A committee or team of managers guiding and controlling the process and advising the owner (process management council).
- A process office to carry out the details of planning, measurements, reporting, feedback, and so on. In some cases, the process office is responsible for more than planning and coordination; it may also control funding as well as exercise "task-oriented control" over such line functions as product development or manufacturing. In such cases, personnel from the traditional organization are assigned to the process for the duration.

Making the process succeed requires that there be agreement among top management as to the assignment of responsibilities, authority, and accountability. This also requires that the activities comprising the process be subdivided into subprocesses small enough to be clearly identifiable and manageable.

The vast majority of industrial and business processes are constructed around one of three basic forms. Obviously, these forms affect the extent of process design and planning, as well as the choice of who does it.

- *Departmental process*: This process form receives its inputs and produces its output within an single, self-contained organization, usually a department (see Figure 4-1a). Well-known examples include programming departments in information systems organizations,[1] the tool room in a manufacturing facility, word processing centers, and libraries. In many cases, formal planning (process design) for such departmental processes is

---

[1]This process form was used in the Sterling Forest quality improvement effort.

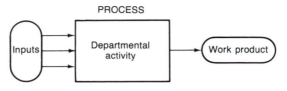

a. Departmental.

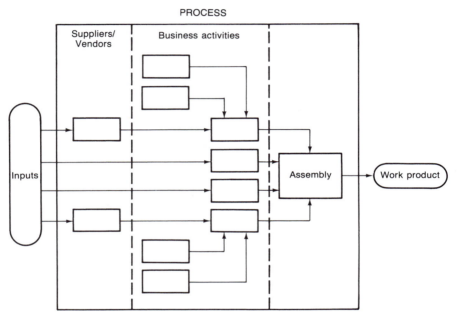

b. Tree.

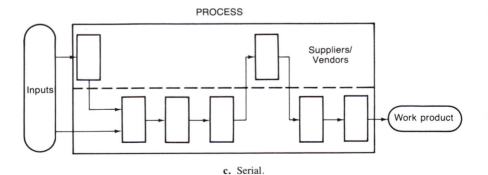

c. Serial.

Fig. 4-1. Process structures.

carried out by a member of the department or its manager. In very small departments, planning may be assigned to individual workers.

- *Tree process*: Widely used in manufacturing and electronic industries which build railroad equipment, heavy machinery, automobiles, household appliances, and electronic products (see Figure 4-1b). The base of the tree comprises vendors or in-house functions producing parts and components. These in turn are turned into subassemblies by still other functions and departments. Final assembly of the product completes the process. The tree process requires planning of two different kinds: traditional departmental and interdepartmental (or process-level). In complex processes, it becomes mandatory to use the process design staff to coordinate interdepartmental planning activites.

- *Serial process*: This process form may again comprise numerous vendors and in-house departments. However, all activities proceed sequentially through the participating functions and departments, each representing an operation which ultimately contributes to the final process result. This process form is found in the majority of "process industries," such as petroleum refineries, chemical plants, and the like. It is also exhibited in manufacturing industries that produce complex subassemblies or components on a repeated basis, for example, operator keyboards or engine blocks (see Figure 4-1c).

4.1.2 Process Effectiveness

Of the three basic characteristics of an independent process, effectiveness is the most critical because it, above all, ensures conformance to requirements.

The process owner should be able to assess *in advance* whether the process will be able to turn out defect-free products—that is, whether it will be effective. There are several ways of ensuring this: from direct measurements on the process, from product conformance to specifications, from data on product usage (conformance to requirements), or from process capability studies. Each of these methods has advantages and disadvantages, as we discuss now.

- Prediction from *direct process measurements*. One advantage is immediacy, that is, measurements are made without waiting for the work product to be available for processing; another is that defects in process facilities are detected, along with some causes. The disadvantage is that the process tested is not "under load." A typical example is the manufacture of machine tools, where machines are tested prior to shipment by placing various measuring devices in selected places and positions on the machine.

- Prediction from *successful usage*. The advantage of this is that actual use being the ultimate proof, it carries weight mostly with business management. Disadvantages include failure to provide quantitative performance measurements and the fact that usage feedback is not transferable to follow-on products still in design. Typical examples include the manufacture of drugs and complex chemical products.

- Prediction from product *conformance to specifications.* Its advantage is that it is still widely accepted in machine manufacturing as the traditional method. Disadvantages include failure to quantify capability with respect to the process variables involved and limited predictability in terms of ability to transfer available process knowledge to new product design.
- Prediction through measuring *process capability.* This is the most recent development in process management, and *it is the basis of quality management through process improvement.* Its advantage is the availability of quantitative data which can be used to predict the effectiveness of future designs. Its disadvantage is the added initial effort and resources needed for measurements, data analysis, and process capability assessment.

Process capability is determined by the total variation that comes from common causes—in other words, the minimum variation that can be achieved after all special causes of variation have been removed. Thus, process capability represents the performance of the process itself, as demonstrated when it is in a state of stability. Capability is often thought of in terms of the proportion of output that will be within stated (tolerance) limits. Since a stable process can be described by a predictable distribution of output, the proportion of out-of-specification work products can be estimated from this distribution. As long as the process remains stable, it will continue to produce the same proportion of out-of-specification products. Management action upon the process to reduce the variation from common causes is required to improve process capability—the ability to consistently meet specifications. This is known as *process improvement.* In short, the process must first be stabilized by identifying and removing special causes of variation. Only then will its performance become predictable and its capability to meet specifications assessable and improvable. *This is the theoretical basis for the concept of continuing quality improvement.*

In summary, the purpose of process control is to maintain or restore the state of stability (statistical control) by the prevention or elimination of special causes. Process improvement, on the other hand, enhances process capability by preventing or eliminating common causes. Process control and improvement together lead to total *quality management.*

The designer's greatest contribution to process effectiveness—and, therefore, to product quality—is most likely the concept of designing the process to be defect-free. Where this type of design is economically feasible, it provides excellent solution to some very difficult process management problems:

- Elimination of defects resulting from special causes, especially from inadvertent or willful human error such as a result of inattention, or indifference. A defect-free process, by definition, is also a process in control.
- Bypassing complex problem analyses and error-cause detection efforts by providing a solution even though the cause of variation remains unknown.

Some of the more usual forms of making the process defect-free are:

- Fail-safe mechanisms, which can consist of interlocking sequences, alarms and cutoffs, foolproof fixtures, tamper-free packaging and the like.

- Redundancy, including multiple approvals, checking procedures and audit reviews in administrative processes, multiple code identification to prevent product mix-ups (color codes for typing, various recognition patterns for labeling), design for verification (viewing holes, test coupons, eraser tags).

- Countdowns, which are prearranged sensing and information procedures parallel to the operation of the process to check operational steps against the prescribed sequence of events (procedure manual, space vehicle launch countdown).

4.1.3 Process Requirements

Any business operation can be characterized as a set of interrelated processes. In a large business enterprise, examples of such processes are:

- Order entry
- Billing
- Accounting
- Distribution
- Backlog management
- Procurement/Purchasing
- Product design
- Production control
- Materials management
- Product introduction
- Product service and maintenance
- Parts management

Each of these processes, in turn, is made up of subprocesses; for instance, in the case of billing, there is purchase billing, service billing, rental billing, and the like.

Beyond the basic external statement describing required *process output*, process design must also include the following process requirements:

- *Total process requirements*: In addition to user requirements, which shape the end product of the process, internal requirements may include such business requirements as productivity, and adherence to personnel policies and practices, legal guidelines, as well as prevailing standards for safety, security, etc.
- *Work activity requirements and specifications*: For each activity, its input, component tasks, output, and conformance criteria, as well as input-output linkages to other activities. These, in turn, require specification of the control activities, such as measurements, defect elimination cycle, and possible corrective actions. Work activity specifications include activity proce-

dures, which are the guidelines and operating instructions for people (in terms of requirements, specifications, or process criteria) and change control procedures in case work activities have to be modified to meet conformance requirements. Procedures for change control assure adequate review and approval of proposed changes prior to implementation, communicate proposed changes and their implementation plan to those affected, force accountability, and provide a record of change.

Using the general procurement process as an example, we illustrate process flow in Figure 4-2. Work activity specification is shown in Table 4-2.

Process controls, especially the defect elimination cycle, are the underlying elements of process design. Their purpose is to enable process management to operate and change the process, if necessary, so that requirements will be met.

Process design may be generalized into such concepts as "standard design." Several different enterprises have arrived at the concept of achieving better quality control through standardized design of subprocesses or even entire business processes.

4.1.4 Design for Worker Self-Control

In some processes, especially simple administrative and business situations, the end user requirement becomes the basis for both management's and workers' knowledge of what is to be done. This is especially true when workers are in direct contact with end users, for example, in such traditional trades as the electrician or plumber.

In larger enterprises and more complex industrial or business processes, work *product specifications* are widely used as a substitute for knowledge of end user requirements. In such cases management must have the means to assess and control the conformance of specifications to end user requirements. Also, other essential precautions must be observed, such as providing clear and consistent information through the various information sources reaching the workers (manuals, shop standards, verbal orders, inspection practices and the like); priority information ("vital few" characteristics of the product to be observed and controlled by workers); explanations of purpose supporting the specifications; standards in support of, or to enhance, specifications; and, last but not least, adequate training for workers, including special training for specific conditions, for example, safety, contingency plans, emergencies, and so on.

In many situations it is not even practical to provide product specifications to the workers. Identifiable characteristics may not appear within the particular subprocess, as the actual product may take shape only in a later operation. There may be no provisions for measuring the product until its final assembly. In such processes, workers involved in early-stage activities are provided with *process criteria* or variables (temperature and pressure gauge readings, valve settings, and so forth).

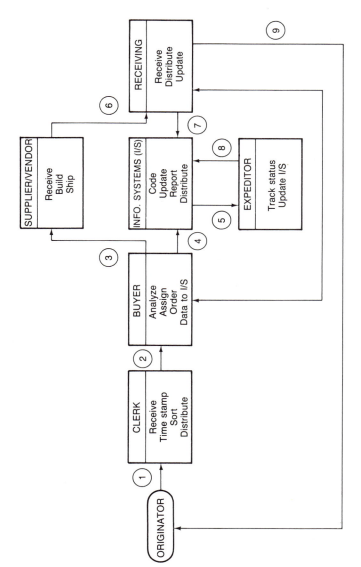

Fig. 4-2. General procurement process.

155

Table 4-2. GENERAL PROCUREMENT PROCESS ELEMENTS

Inputs	Function	Work Activity	Outputs
	CLERK:		
1. Purchase requisition		Receives Reviews for completeness Time stamps Assigns to buyer	2. Purchase requisition to buyer
	BUYER:		
2. Purchase requisition		Analyzes order Places order with vendor Assigns expeditor Sends data to I/S	3. Order to vendor 4. Data to I/S
	INFORMATION SYSTEMS:		
4. Data to I/S 8. Data to I/S		Receives data Codes data for system	5. Reports

3. Order to vendor

VENDOR:
Updates status
Generates reports
Distributes reports to buyer, expeditor, and receiving

6. Order to receiving

RECEIVING AND SHIPPING:
Receives order
Builds to order
Ships to receiving

6. Order to receiving

6. Order to receiving

Receives order
Updates I/S
Distributes order to originator

7. Data to I/S
9. Order to originator

EXPEDITOR:
Tracks status
Updates I/S

5. Report from I/S

8. Data to I/S

Workers in certain stages of a process need knowledge of what is happening in the process and what they are specifically doing. Only from such knowledge can it be determined whether or not a variation exists and corrective action is needed. Such knowledge is derived from multiple sources, such as personal observation, measurements inherent in the process (integrated instrumentation), measurements by the operator (prevalent in the manufacture of mechanical and electronic components), or measurement by supervisors or inspectors.

Knowledge can also be deduced from paper analysis, control chart assessments, and the like. In any case, based on the knowledge of what is being done (what is happening), corrective action (or confirmation of conformance in its stead) is taken to close the feedback loop.

4.2 The Work Process

An essential component of any industrial or business process is the human element: its *people*. In general terms, any process including humans is termed a *social process*, which includes all political, industrial, and business endeavors which require involvement, intervention, or supervision by humans and which are not purely technological or fully automated.

4.2.1 Process Theory [2]

General system theory classifies living organisms as *open systems*; by extension, any process that includes humans must also be classified as an open system—inherently capable of improvement and adaptation.

The modern industrial or business process is the result of the disciplined design and implementation, as well as the continuing enhancement of a complete range of activities performed by the interrelated components of the process. Their object is to assure quality to the user and optimum process performance to the enterprise. Just as the overall process can be viewed as a single open system, the many activities that must be brought together in proper relationship to provide the single major function of getting a quality work product to the end user can be regarded as subsystems.[3]

The overall process, then, is an integrated system, and the objectives of management are to (1) create within the process the most effective work pattern of people, equipment, materials, and information to ensure conformance to user requirements; and (2) optimize it in terms of efficiency and productivity at a minimum cost of quality. The system-theoretical approach simply provides the

---

[2]Adapted, by permission of the publisher, from *General System Theory* by Ludwig von Bertalanffy (New York: George Braziller, Inc., 1968), pp. 39-41, 141, and 150.

[3]The definition of a *system* is a collection of humans, methods, mechanisms, and automata organized to accomplish a specified objective.

conceptual framework for design implementation and process change: In system-theoretical terms, a process is defined as *a system put into operation to produce an output of higher value than that of the sum of its inputs.*

Thermodynamics expressly states that its laws apply only to *closed systems*, that is, systems which are considered to be isolated from their environment. Physical phenomena and most technological systems such as chemical processes or automated manufacturing tasks fall into this category, also known as irreversible processes.

We find, however, systems which by their very nature are not closed. *An open system is defined as a system in exchange of matter or energy with its environment.* For instance, every living organism is essentially an open system. It maintains itself in a continuous in- and outflow, a building up and breaking down of components, never being in a state of chemical or thermodynamic equilibrium, but maintained in a so-called steady state (which is quite different from equilibrium). Also, social processes, which include individuals or groups of humans, are in fact open systems. Only in recent decades have physicists been willing to expand theoretical physics to include open systems. This has led to important general conclusions:

(1) *The principle of equifinality.* While the final state of any closed system is unequivocally determined by its initial conditions, and if the initial conditions or the process is altered, the final state will also be changed, this is not the case for open systems. The principle of equifinality states that the same final state may be reached from different initial conditions and through various alterations of the process. This has a significant meaning for the phenomena of process regulation and management.

(2) *The principle of entropy.* Based on Lord Kelvin's law of dissipation in physics and the second principle of thermodynamics, the change of entropy in closed systems is always positive; order is continually destroyed and the system is headed for maximum disorder (and, ultimately, the "heat death" of the universe).

In open systems, however, a transition toward higher order and organization appears, along with an import (negative change) of entropy. This means that open systems such as living organisms can maintain themselves in a steady state (state of control).

The basic notion in communication theory is that of *information*; by extension, it can be viewed as negative entropy—or as a measure of order or of organization. Another central concept of communications theory is that of *feedback*. Feedback arrangements are widely used in modern technology for the stabilization of a certain condition or for the direction of actions toward a goal where the variation from that goal is fed back, as information, until the goal is reached. Mechanisms of a feedback nature—for example, processes—are the base of purposeful behavior in man-made machines or social systems. Feedback presupposes structural arrangements such as design, including arrangements and conditions of constraint, which render the process and its parts more efficient.

Characteristics of organization, whether of a living organism or a social process, include the concepts of growth, differentiation, hierarchical order, dominance, control, and competitiveness. Such notions do not appear in conventional physics or in closed systems, to which conventional physics apply. However, system theory—with the inclusion of open systems—is well capable of dealing with these matters. There are, however, many aspects of organizations which do not easily lend themselves to quantitative interpretation or description. Thus students of quality have to content themselves with an "explanation in principle"—a qualitative argument—which is the case in process management.

An open system may "actively" tend toward a state of higher organization; that is, it may pass from a lower to a higher state of order, as a result of conditions in or actions upon the system. *The notion of continuing quality improvement is based on this principle.*

A feedback mechanism can "reactively" reach a higher state of organization as a result of learning—that is, information fed into the system from external sources. Feedback systems are a significant, but special class of self-regulating systems capable of adaptation; they are "open" to incoming information, but "closed" to the exchange of matter and energy. A typical example is the defect elimination cycle in quality management, which is essentially a basic feedback loop. For purposes of process management theory, such feedback mechanisms, as "secondary regulators" are considered as embedded in the overall process, which is dynamic and can be considered as the "primary regulator."

As shown in Figure 4-3, the basic components of the process (people, equipment, materials, energy, procedures, and so on) are organized into a series of work activities whose purpose is to (1) change inputs (raw materials, information, and so on) into a specified output (work product) and (2) generate added value. There is dynamic interaction[4] among the process components as well as the work activities—in addition to the exchange of information, matter, and energy with the outside environment—which allows us to view the overall process as an open system.

For purposes of manageability and efficiency of individual work activities, the associated control mechanisms are organized into feedback loops, within which dynamic interaction no longer occurs. Causal trains, such as the relationship between and sequence of tasks, are linear and unidirectional (see Figure 4-3b). By definition, they transcend business organizations and functional lines (Figure 4-4).

Process control theory has traditionally focused on technological or production processes. However, the concept is eminently applicable, through the process management approach, to business and industrial processes as well—for example, purchasing, product assembly, orders and movements, people management, and the like.

---

[4]Dynamic interaction means that the relationship among components may be nonlinear and changing over time; the sequence of activities may be bidirectional.

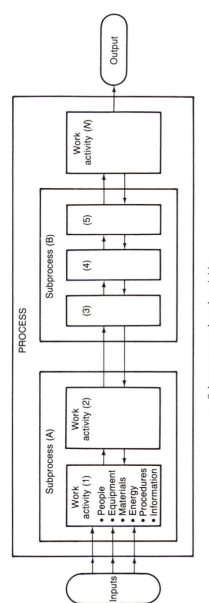

a. Subprocesses and work activities.

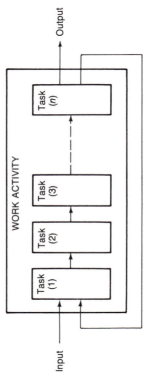

b. Tasks within work activity.

Fig. 4-3. Process definition and organization.

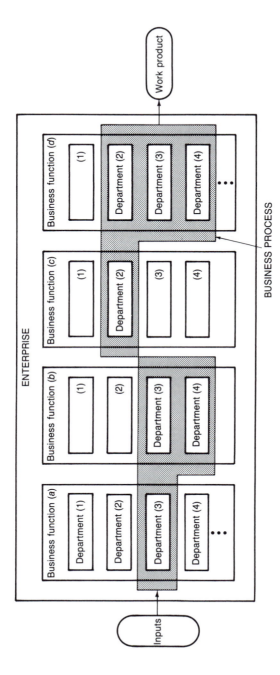

Fig. 4-4. Relationship between process, business functions, and organization.

4.2.2 Process Management

In the casually evolved quality management approaches that were characteristic of the past, the quality responsibility of management was equally casual. But experience indicates that the modern, structured business processes are so broad that they will downgrade and disintegrate unless, from their inception, they are managed on a systematic basis that is equally broad, to ensure that any given process will produce the intended results. Furthermore, the basic characteristics of the business process, which transcend established organizational and functional limits, make it necessary that the basic responsibility for the implementation of processes must rest in the hands of company general management rather than in the hands of its functional units.

> The management approach which characterized industrial operations for more than the first half of this century was based on what might be called *improvement through specialized division of effort*. This philosophy in turn led to the development of a wide variety of individual technical and managerial specialities. Indeed, specialization has brought significant advances to industrial development, especially during and immediately after World War II. It has been recognized since, however, that carried beyond a certain point, the theory of division of effort creates more problems than it solves, including narrowness of perspective, bureaucracy, duplication, diffusion of responsibility, and extremely complex and confusing lines of communication—hence the revived interest in *integration of effort* through prudent process management.

Because of the scope of process integration, which extends from initial requirements definition to assurance of actual end user satisfaction, the process can be thought of as "horizontal" in an organizational sense (Figure 4-4). This is in sharp contrast to the assignment of responsibilities in traditional quality control approaches, where quality control is assigned by function and can be thought of as organizationally vertical.

The organizational approach for total process management involves two parallel steps:

(1) Definition and establishment of the process.
(2) Addition of the horizontal organizational concept of process management, achieved from a general management viewpoint, through *process ownership*.[5]

---

[5]The activities which make up some of the very large and complex processes are logically related but organizationally, functionally, and physically dispersed. From an organizational and functional standpoint, this environment is vertically managed in a traditional manner—while processes flow horizontally. This may lead to diffusion of management focus on the process and costly suboptimization and undesirable trade-offs. "Process ownership" is the management mechanism which is designed to avoid this and to ensure continuing, coherent business focus on the entire process.

This approach requires that general management must become chief architect and designer of the process, just as it has the ultimate responsibility for structuring other business aspects for cost control, personnel management, financial planning, and so forth. In all these situations, the general manager will delegate the appropriate responsibilities to the process owner.

The key aspects of establishing process ownership are:

- *Selection:* The process owner must preferably be the line or functional manager with the most resources invested and the highest related workload. This person is most affected by nonconformance and also has the highest leverage on the overall process.
- *Organization:* Here a "quasi-line structure" is created to manage and control the key subprocesses (work activities) which normally cut across traditional business organization and functions (see Figure 4-5).
- *Responsibilities:* The process owner, among other things, is firstly responsible for *quality improvement* through
  (a) Process design, documentation, and quantifiable process improvement goals (process plan). In designing the process, its components are defined and assembled, bearing in mind that factors affecting quality can be divided into two major groupings: (1) *technological;* including equipment, materials, energy, procedures, standards, and the like; and (2) *human;* including workers, supervisors, managers, and other personnel. Of these factors the human is of greater importance in quality management by far. (Table 4-3 shows the relationship between human resource deployment and the hierarchy of other process components.)

Table 4-3. HIERARCHY OF PROCESS COMPONENTS

Process Component	Organizational Entity
Process	Multiple departments or functions
Subprocess	Department or function
Activity	Project team or task force
Task	Small team or individual

  (b) Process control: Defect detection and corrective action.
  (c) Process improvement by means of (1) definition of user requirements and specifications; (2) analysis of process capability measurements; and (3) corrective action on the process (process capability improvement and other preventive measures).
  (d) Reporting of progress in formal periodic reviews (rating and certification).

The process owner, within these responsibilities, sees to the establishment of a measurement system, control procedures, feedback on corrective actions, certification of process performance, and changes to the process for continued

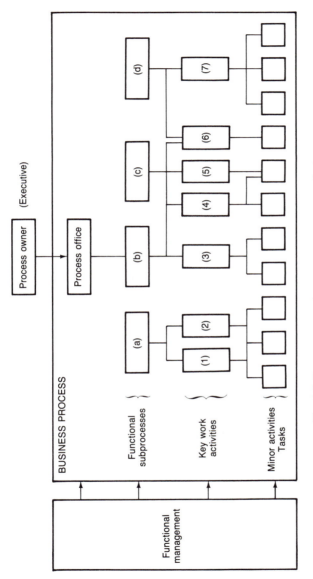

Fig. 4-5. Process owner and process management organization.

quality improvement. He or she also ensures that appropriate process management tools (planning aids, statistical process control, defect elimination, cost of quality) are made available, personnel are trained, and the necessary material and financial resources are committed. The allocation of resources, both financial and human, changes as process management matures over time. Resources previously put in place for classic quality control tasks such as inspection, quality control, and rework gradually diminish and partially give place to those devoted to process planning, defect prevention, and process control (Figure 4-6).

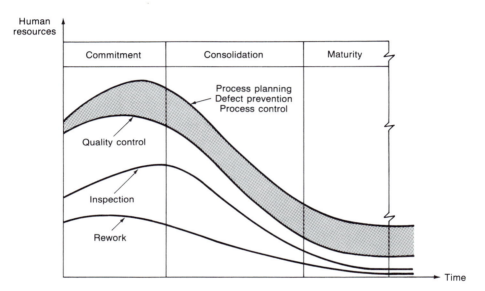

Fig. 4-6. Deployment of human resources and skills for quality management over time.

There exist several management tools for the structured and disciplined definition and analysis of a process. Among these are *business systems planning* (BSP), primarily an information-flow modeling tool; *department activity analysis* (DAA), a nonquantitative technique for establishing management priorities in departmental processes; *structured analysis* (SA), a portrayal methodology with limited problem analysis capability; and the *process analysis technique* (PAT), a tool for the analysis and improvement of time-dependent interfunctional processes.

Of the management responsibilities in this area, *process certification* and the *rating criteria* on which it is based deserve special attention. As the process moves through its stages toward maturity (see Section 1.3.3 and Chapters 6 and 7), it is the process owner's responsibility to assess and report on the overall performance of the process and certify it to top company management. (An example of a certification scheme, based on five rating levels, is shown in Table 4-4.)

Table 4-4. PROCESS ASSESSMENT CRITERIA FOR CERTIFICATION

Rating	Assessment Criteria	Process Identified	Process Owner	Basics of Process Management — Process Defined and Documented	Input/Output Relationships	Requirements	Measurements and Control Points	Quality Control Methodology (SPC)	Process Management Organization (Council)	Process Control	Process Improvement	Conformance to Requirements (Effectiveness)	Efficiency	Adaptability
5	Process identified and ownership assigned	X	X											
4	Process management in place; process stable	X	X	X	X	X	X	X	X					
3	Process effective; output meets requirements	X	X	X	X	X	X	X	X	X	X	X		
2	Process effective and efficient; competitive	X	X	X	X	X	X	X	X	X	X	X	X	
1	Process effective, lowest cost, adaptable; "best of breed"	X	X	X	X	X	X	X	X	X	X	X	X	X

Process optimization, which is the second major responsibility of the process owner, deals with maintaining and improving both the *productivity* and the *efficiency* of the process. (Productivity means more conforming output; efficiency means conforming output at a lower unit cost.)

Process adaptation, the process owner's third key responsibility, is the continuing modification of the current process to ensure its continued effectiveness and efficiency in the face of new requirements or other environmental and business changes anticipated in the future. Basic to process adaptation is the ability to anticipate and evaluate future user requirements (for example, through a strategic period) and to identify specific process or subprocess constraints and deficiencies in the light of these. The process adaptation or change plan would include means of eliminating or circumventing the constraints and deficiencies, as well as a schedule for implementing changes before overall business performance is impacted by the lack of them. The adaptation process is completed by evaluating and certifying the changes in terms of continuing quality, efficiency, and productivity improvements.

SUMMARY

Process management comprises: (1) *quality management,* to ensure conformance to requirements (it indirectly affects both the profitability and the productivity of the business, not the process itself) and (2) *process optimization,* to maintain and improve the efficiency and the productivity of the process itself (which directly contribute to the profitability and the competitiveness of the business) and to ensure process adaptability. Process optimization also focuses on people management, through the enhancement of professionalism, which in turn contributes to quality improvement in general.

> The four business goals set by the IBM Corporation for the 1980s—quality, efficiency, low cost, and profitability—can all be mapped into the objectives of process management.
>
> "We need a business process that is worthy of respect and is respected. This means a process that can handle today's volumes and complexities accurately and efficiently . . . one that is positioned for the future and, therefore, can move ahead with the business, not struggle along behind as it has been doing."[6]
>
> "We have focused increasingly on the work process, where the greatest gains can be made—improving the capabilities of the process."[7]

The process owner is responsible for implementing *both* quality management and process optimization. The interaction of various management disciplines with the individual components of the process is shown in Figure 4-7.

---

[6]John R. Opel, Chairman of the Board, IBM Corporation, October 5, 1984. (Internal communication.)

[7]John F. Akers, President, IBM Corporation; Presentation to the American Electronics Association, March 13, 1984.

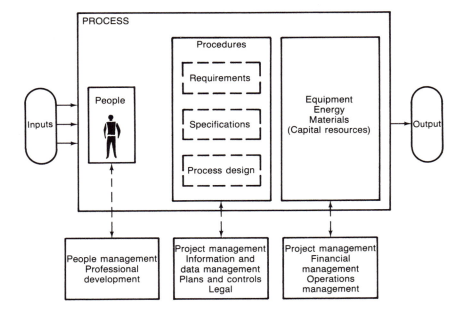

Fig. 4-7. Management interaction with process components.

DISCUSSION QUESTIONS

1. Define the terms *process* and *organization*. Explain the difference between the two and their relationship.
2. What are the three fundamental concepts of process design?
3. What are the basic characteristics of an independent process? Give a definition of each.
4. Describe process design and its end result.
5. Name and describe the major components of the process management mechanism.
6. Describe the three basic forms of industrial and business processes.
7. Describe at least two different ways of ensuring process effectiveness. Explain their advantages and disadvantages.
8. Explain the theoretical basis for the concept of continuing quality improvement.
9. What part of general system theory can process theory be considered part of? Give the system-theoretical definition of a *process*.
10. Define the terms *open system* and *closed system*. Explain the difference between the two.
11. Explain the principles of equifinality and entropy. How do they relate to open and closed systems, respectively?
12. Explain why process control theory is equally applicable to technological and business processes.

13. Discuss the concept of horizontal (process) and vertical (functional) organization. What are the managerial and organizational consequences of implementing the process management approach? What are the two key organizational steps for total process management?

14. Describe the key aspects of process ownership.

15. Identify and describe the key responsibilities of the process owner.

16. Name at least three management tools for process definition and analysis. Give a brief description of each.

17. Describe process certification and the related rating criteria for process assessment.

18. Define the terms *process optimization* and *process adaptation*. What are their respective objectives?

5

THE MANAGEMENT SYSTEM
FOR QUALITY

The starting point for effective process management is the establishment of a *management system*.

A management system can be defined as the method by which an enterprise, making use of available resources, directs and controls its business processes to meet established goals.

Simply put, a management system is the "managerial process" in support of business objectives. Separating *what* the organization does (processes) from *how* it does it (management system) is the key concept of management systems planning.

The *objectives* of a management system for quality are:

- To integrate processes into the overall business structure, and
- To ensure achievement of process management objectives (quality management and process optimization) across all processes.

The *components* of any management system are:

- Policies, procedures and standards, and support mechanisms (methodologies, tools, aids, education and the like), establishing direction and describing the *way* information and resources are used for decisions, actions and control.
- Organization, defined as a logical grouping of people, authority, and responsibility to accomplish a specific business objective.
- Communications, describing the information flow in the organization.

A management system is the framework for deploying resources and implementing work activities. The management system itself should not be confused with the process—*the management system does not have resources.*

The inherent responsibilities in a management system, and therefore the latter itself, may change over time, just as the business processes mature. In particular, the use of specific tools and aids through the phases of maturing will change and become more sophisticated and complex. The three stages of quality management development, defined in Chapter 1, are fundamental to the management system underlying the quality management effort. The relationship of the management system to process management is outlined in Figure 5-1.

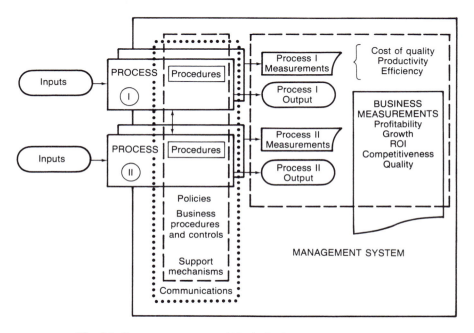

Fig. 5-1. Process management within the business management system.

The first fundamental purpose of a management system is to integrate the management of the various business processes engaged in producing output which conforms to user requirements, into the overall business structure of the enterprise. This is done by focusing on certain transition points between specific processes and the overall business—such as process measurements (cost of quality, productivity, efficiency) and overall business measurements (profitability, growth, competitiveness, and the like).

The second purpose of a management system is dynamic: It is to ensure progression of any given process from one stage to the next, as quality management matures and becomes more sophisticated *over time.*

Many enterprises and organizations, after several years of attempts at quality improvement, are still blocked at the beginning of the consolidation stage; for several large companies it has taken over a decade to progress to "readiness for stage three" or the "beginnings of maturity." Obviously, differences in the management approach and the management system employed will have a great influence.

There is clearly a discontinuity in the management experience and the ability to proceed in a steady and consistent fashion through continuing quality improvement. Such a discontinuity exists because progression from one stage to the next does involve stepwise improvements in both the process and in the use of techniques, management aids, and the like. Also, since conformance is a state rather than a degree of condition, its achievement in itself represents managerial breakthrough. In summary, the discontinuity results from shortcomings in both the management skills and methods used in process management, and the design and implementation of the process being managed.

To simplify our discussion, the three basic stages of quality management will be related to corresponding, basic issues in the management system:

- *Commitment:* The establishment and startup of the management system. Process design completed; initial implementation and basic methodologies of quality management in place.
- *Consolidation:* Growth of the management system; process control in place to ensure defect-free performance. Continuing quality improvement firmly established; management system ensures consistency of process indicators and general business measurements.
- *Maturity:* Management by return on investment; consistent, total conformance to changing requirements accomplished through process improvement. Increased process productivity and efficiency, contributing measurably to profitability, productivity, and competitive posture.

As we examine the management system evolution in each stage, we must constantly consider the view of both the outside world (marketplace and users, consumers, shareholders, stock market, government, and the like) and senior management of the company. Both groups can have a significant impact on this experience.

The stages-of-growth concept is quite adequate to show the natural maturing of the management system through time, and makes adaptation possible to the practical facts of the real world. With each stage slightly skewed, resources can be applied in the predecessor stage to install the necessary procedures (planning and control), required in the following stage. For example, many of the management aids, measurement approaches, and process optimization techniques required and used in the maturity stage can be planned for and even placed in readiness during consolidation. This concept accomplishes the following:

- Minimizes the time required for stage transition and, therefore, minimizes the effect of discontinuity

- Allows the natural flow, over time, of the cyclical activities of process control and improvement—with planning always aimed at the next time period
- Allows each stage to start smoothly and, conceivably, to be completed sooner
- Maximizes the productivity of human resources which are planning and implementing the management system itself

After requirements have been established and quality defined, it is still necessary to monitor work and observe that not only are requirements met (which is the purpose of quality management) but also that as it is done, the overall goals of the business, especially profitability and competitiveness, are also achieved. The management system is designed to ensure this happens.

Process control addresses the direct responsibility for quality through process management, but it does not answer all business-related questions. Among them the most important is to identify the key processes within the enterprise, for which the process management approach will be implemented. (Typical key processes in a large corporation include billing, accounting, order entry, inventory control, and purchasing—large sets of activities which cross functional lines.) Control of a complex work process is achieved through multiple levels of management whereby a manager at one level can give responsibility for a task to a subordinate; if anything goes wrong, however, both the manager and the subordinate are held accountable. This is why one of the fundamental principles of process organization is to subdivide the process into *manageable subprocesses* where individual *responsibility* and *accountability* can be identified. Because managers are responsible for all work produced in the subprocess under their jurisdiction, they must assess the quality of all their subordinates' work, as well as their own. Thus, each level of management is responsible for the self-assessment of its own work product and for making an independent assessment of the work product of all employees within the subprocess. At the process level, the process owner is responsible for this quality assessment—which is then verified through independent audit to the satisfaction of top management. Ensuring the achievement of process management objectives, then, includes the assessment and control of the hierarchy of processes and their contribution to overall business goals.

A business emphasizing self-assessment of work might still find it useful to have some staff organization for quality—that is, a structure which is *not responsible* for the quality of work (since that is an individual line responsibility), but rather provides guidance, applies specialized skills to planning (quality engineering), process design, and quality control, and makes independent assessments for management, including the senior management of the enterprise. Also, it promotes conformance by assisting in the adjustment of requirements, training and education, the application of quality management aids and specialized control tools, and the implementation of corrective actions.

5.1 Policy and Practices

In the past, quality tended to be something that was rarely defined or directed in formal policies for companies. Somehow it was felt that because quality was "approved" by nearly everybody, it did not really require documentation, policies, or formal direction. But it does, perhaps even more than other business activities, and a lot of problems can be avoided if a clear policy, covering the entire quality direction of an enterprise, is laid down by senior management.

5.1.1 Quality Policy and Guidelines

A policy is a broad guide to action, stating principles or beliefs.

A policy differs from a procedure which details *how* some set of activities shall be accomplished in order to implement a policy. Thus, a quality policy might state that quality parameters will be measured; the corresponding procedure would describe how this is to be done, for example, by means of cost of quality, product samples, customer satisfaction surveys, and the like. One can consider a policy the basis for consistent, predictable conduct on the part of an organization or enterprise. This is because as organizations grow, more and more people are engaged in making significant decisions; unless there is consistency in these decisions, there is no predictability.

Before a policy is published it is well to face realistically the question, "Does the company intend to adhere to this policy?" If there is doubt about this at all, the policy should not be published as there is no clear management commitment to quality. In fact, so important is the need for adherence to published policy that most enterprises establish audit procedures to provide feedback on how well a policy is being followed. Policy statements are usually formulated to answer the questions "What?" and "Why?" Based on such broad statements of policy, *procedures and practices* are developed for further implementation and administration in the normal course of doing business—to answer the question, "How?"

> Within IBM, as an example, *corporate instructions* provide the basic set of guidelines for answering this question. Specifically, Corporate Instruction 101 on the subject of quality (issued May 14, 1985) states: "A key requirement for the achievement of IBM's goals is the ability of our business processes to meet the changing needs of the business . . . the rate of change created by growth and diversity now calls for increased attention to the efficiency, effectiveness and adaptability of the business processes . . . this is to be accomplished through quality management."

> This corporate instruction essentially lays down the concept of achieving quality through process management throughout the corporation. Similar sweeping guidelines can be found in other business enterprises; from these originate a number of more detailed, division and location-level instructions for the implementation of the quality policy in their particular environments.

Thus, to be effective a quality policy must always be accompanied by more specific guidelines and instructions to both management and employees.

Such guidelines help the insiders understand not only what is expected of them, but also how they are to implement the stated policy. They also help outsiders understand what to expect from the company.

Choice of subject matter for quality guidelines and instructions varies with each company. However, certain topics have such general applicability that they should be considered by any enterprise which is about to document them. These include, among others, the following:

- Is the company's objective quality or technological leadership? or both?
- Should quality planning be done by the staff or line organization?
- Should vendors be covered by the quality policy, and should they be included in quality planning?
- Should top management actively and visibly participate in quality planning, or should it delegate this to lower-level line management?
- Should there be an independent quality staff?

The subject matter for quality guidelines also includes a ranking of quality against other business parameters, including schedule and cost; statements on whether it is the organization's policy to achieve quality through prevention versus control or both; and whether or not user requirements are part of the process management scheme.

As the company grows to the point where it is involved in multiple product lines and marketplaces, it becomes evident that no one set of quality guidelines and instructions can fit all company activities. This problem is solved by creating several levels of quality guidelines and instructions while maintaining overall company quality policy.

While general policy statements may be stable over a long period of time, companies and organizations must be sensitive to environmental, technological, and marketplace changes which may affect specific guidelines, instructions, and procedures. For example, just during the last two decades, the following truly massive phenomena have emerged:

- A "population explosion" of sophisticated consumer electronics products, with a resulting spectacle of tens of millions of consumers worldwide owning and depending for day-to-day use, convenience, information, and safety on products they are unable to fully understand, let alone repair.
- A growing public awareness of the problems of environmental risks such as pollution, many of which have their origin in the operation of modern industrial processes (chemical and nuclear industries).
- Entirely new attitudes toward matters of safety and product liability, a concern that applies especially to the health services industry and its liability to malpractice, and the chemical and pharmaceutical industries as to health hazards, cancer-causing agents, and the like.
- The emergence of very complex technological products, such as aerospace

and weapons systems, automated factories, sophisticated computer systems, and telecommunication networks.

- The growing imposition of government regulation and public legislation not only in the traditional fields of health and safety but also consumer economics, for example, integrity of guarantee, product labeling, product liability, and the like.

Most enterprises achieve their results through establishing specific, attainable goals and then meeting them. These goals, when defined and quantified, are known as *objectives*. The most important single decision facing senior management in setting quality objectives is whether to go for continued improvement toward zero defects (total conformance) or limited objectives on the journey toward quality (reduced levels of nonconformance).

As an alternative to the personal leadership of the chief executive—which is prevalent in smaller companies and businesses—a large enterprise can create an interfunctional and interdepartmental mechanism to identify potential objectives, estimate their impact in economic and other terms, and secure for them a priority in the overall program for action. The setting of objectives requires an organizational framework which gives managers the opportunity for participation in objective setting. To assist in this, quality professionals and other staff specialists are deployed throughout the organization to encourage the development of a formal set of specified and *measurable* objectives. An objective is unlikely to receive high priority unless it is quantified; as managers have multiple objectives for which they are accountable, quantified objectives usually receive preference and more attention since there is less room for debate about what constitutes the attainment of these objectives.

Contention among quality objectives is resolved by using analytical aids and techniques for setting priorities, such as return on investment, Pareto analysis, and the like.

At the upper levels of management, where quality objectives face competition from other fundamental business objectives, the prime criterion for setting priorities is *productivity growth* and *return on investment*. In addition, the climate of thinking in senior management is strongly biased in favor of total conformance (zero defects), business management versus technology (growth, share of market, competitiveness), and financial measurements (sales, profits, return on investment) as against other measurements such as training, technical excellence, reliability, and the like.

5.1.2 Laws, Regulations, and Standards[1]

In many cases, the procedures and practices which are developed in support of stated quality policies include references to applicable public laws, government

---

[1]Adapted, with permission of the publisher, from *Quality Data Processing* by C. W. Burrill and L. W. Ellsworth (Tenafly, NJ: Burrill-Ellsworth Associates, Inc., 1982), pp. 99-102, 104, and 113.

regulations, or industry standards. In some cases, it is more practical or convenient to incorporate appropriate sections of the law or regulations into the procedures and instructions themselves.

Quality means to meet the requirements of those who use the work product provided. Although most products are aimed at the end user, who is therefore the primary or *direct* user, there may be other people who are either exposed to, or will even inadvertently make use of, the work product even though they had little or no part in generating requirements for it. These are known as the secondary or *indirect* users. For example, a quality automobile must meet the requirements of potential purchasers who are the direct users. But it also must meet requirements of indirect users, namely, the public exposed to the operation of that particular vehicle—those who are impacted by its noise, who breathe the air polluted by exhaust fumes, and who may have the opportunity to test its brakes and other safety features as a result of accidental encounters.

The expectations and known requirements of indirect users must somehow be identified and incorporated into the overall requirement statement for the work product. To the extent this is done well, indirect users will derive the appropriate satisfaction or at least will not be adversely affected. But when indirect users—primarily the public at large—are ignored in the design process, or their requirements are given lower priorities, they will seek other remedies, usually through legislative or regulatory action. The outcome is *public law* or *government regulation*—which in turn will boost the requirements of indirect users from a lower to a high level of priority.

> Increased government regulation, especially in areas affecting safety, product liability, and health, is almost certain in our industrial societies, especially in the United States with its pluralistic legal and governmental system. It is beyond the scope of this book to even attempt exploring the body of law impacting various aspects of quality. Suffice it to say that there has been an onrush of legislation, executive decrees, court decisions, and government regulations, all related to some aspects of user requirements—which all affect quality. In addition, enterprises doing business overseas face a wide array of foreign legislation, primarily in such countries as the United Kingdom, West Germany, France, Italy, Sweden, and Japan.

The body of law has one definite bearing on conformance in that the various laws impose requirements which are often above and beyond those set by the users. If these legal requirements are not met, then the work product lacks quality just as surely as if the requirements of the end user were not met. Also, these laws add to the cost of failure to provide quality, thus strengthening the economic argument for conformance in the first place.

> An important consideration is that a law, a government regulation, or an industrial standard must have operational meaning if it is to be enforced. Compliance or conformance can only be judged in terms of a requirement and a test against it. In many cases, requirements and the corresponding tests are described in statistical

terms to have practical meaning. A corresponding law, regulation, or standard should similarly be expressed; otherwise, it cannot be legally enforced.

Aside from the direct cost of quality to the enterprise which results from legal or regulatory requirements, there are also costs to society and the economy that are real but sometimes not easy to measure. Regulations affect small and large businesses alike; however, the small ones cannot spread this regulatory burden over a sufficiently broad base, which means that increased regulation first drives small entrepreneurs out of business. In the long run this generates a need for still more legislative or regulatory action—without substantially changing economic dynamics. It is unfortunate that the cost of compliance is rarely considered by those making legislation or regulations. Many laws, regulations, and court decisions cost far more than most people realize; often the cost exceeds any reasonable estimate of the benefits.

As an example, the consent decree which resulted in the breaking up of AT&T and the creation of independent operating companies has cost the American public untold millions of dollars in increased administrative and procedural cost, complexity of service, uncertainty, and consumer confusion.

Some of the most publicized legal issues, having the biggest influence on quality, are:

- *Privacy*: This issue emerged during the late 1960s and early 1970s as part of changing social attitudes about equal employment opportunities and individual rights. It affects primarily the information systems and data processing industry in that it was nurtured by a suspicion of computers and integrated data banks, and has essentially resulted in a body of rules and legislative guidelines to ensure data privacy. Today, there is a whole set of federal privacy laws on the books, in addition to state and municipal legislation completed or in the process of being promulgated. Privacy legislation entails responsibilities for management, starting with the need to establish an organizational policy on privacy. Other responsibilities include the need to establish practices for the acquisition, use, and protection of data and procedures to examine existing systems and audit them for compliance. All these activities have an associated cost; conformance to the legal requirements will augment the cost of quality in data systems and applications programming.
- *Product warranty and liability* laws: In the United States, product liability litigation increased over three times between 1978 and 1985.
- *Patent laws* give protection to a whole host of manufactured and other work products and which have to be observed and satisfied in the process of establishing product specifications and designs.
- The *Foreign Corrupt Practices Act* of 1977 includes many provisions, in addition to the one designed to prevent the bribing of foreign officials to

procure business for American firms. Specifically, the act contains record-keeping provisions and internal control requirements that apply to any company doing business overseas which is also required to report to the Securities Exchange Commission whether it is engaged in foreign trade or not. These provisions, in the aggregate, give the government power to bring action against poorly managed companies through the authority of the SEC. (Although these provisions will probably cause little difficulty to most businesses with normal record-keeping practices, businesses with chaotic or poor accounting systems, or with illegal activities they wish to conceal, are likely to be affected.) An even greater impact is caused by the internal controls provision which has a direct bearing on the management system and its provisions for accountability of assets and access to them.

• Legislation and regulations related to *personal safety and health* are particularly applicable to such industries as the tobacco industry, automotive industry, chemical industry, and so on.

• *Taxes*: The area of greatest legal confusion in some cases is represented by tax law. Because so many tax jurisdictions can be involved, there is a bewildering array of contradictory definitions and provisions. Expert legal advice is often essential to unravel this complicated area of legislation.

In summary, we can observe that law has a clearly growing influence on quality, no matter how remote it seems to be from the particular product or service. Compliance with laws may be costly, both in terms of a violation for noncompliance and the cost of legal advice and planning for its prevention.

Regulations are made by government agencies, whereas *standards* are usually arrived at voluntarily and by agreement within a particular industry or a segment of an industry. The difference between a regulation and an industry standard lies essentially in the penalties associated with the failure to meet them.

A regulation is justifiable if it offers a greater advantage than the public risk or economic cost it entails. For example, the obligation of the driver of an automobile to halt at a STOP sign, even when there is no other traffic in sight, involves a waste of fuel, time, and possibly other consumables; however, if no such strict rule were imposed, the number of accidents at intersections—the public risk—would be considerably higher. In an orderly social system, checks and balances, rules and penalties are such that, in general, it is in nobody's interest to break a regulation. It goes without saying that government agencies or other authorities must not impose regulations that they are unprepared to enforce.

It is for the government to decide what activities can be regulated without at the same time giving rise to excessive waste, barriers to progress, or a general hardship to the public. In particular, the suppression of fraud, the protection of citizens against unscrupulous and misleading advertising, or the protection of the public against safety and health hazards do undeniably come within the province of protective regulation. On the other hand, government may or may not consider its obligation to protect individuals against the results of their own imprudence—as in connection with safety belts in cars, smoking, the consumption of alcohol, drugs, and the like—unless such actions result in antisocial behavior and thus endanger the health and safety of others.

Beyond regulations, there is the very broad area of voluntary industry standards, in which it is desirable for business and industry to reach agreements applicable in the majority of cases, but where enterprises or individuals are at liberty to exercise deviations from such standards in particular cases. This will help both the avoidance of economic waste and hindrances to technological progress.

One of the major advantages of standardization is that it enables public authorities to limit regulations to cases where compulsion is essential and enforcement is in the public interest. While reference in a regulation to an industrial standard provides a link that makes the regulation more effective and meaningful, standardization economizes on the making of regulations, because government agencies are relieved of a mass of detailed and unnecessary work. On the other hand, enterprises and individuals benefit from being subjected to fewer regulations and from enjoying greater freedom and flexibility than if standardization did not exist. This is an important reason why business and industry should push ahead for appropriate levels of standardization, thus avoiding the costly proliferation of mandatory government regulations intended to fill the gap left by a lack of voluntary standards. Standardization can contribute to quality because it results in more safety, greater availability, expedited exchange and repair service, interchangeability of parts and components, and all the other material advantages of organized mass production.

Electric appliances meet the same voltage, frequency, and current specifications wherever plugged in across the country; the convenience of uniform sockets for incandescent light bulbs, uniform wrench sizes, and the like would be difficult to be without. While American mass production, made possible by standardization, was one of our chief weapons in World War II, the Western powers and NATO in particular may suffer significant losses in equipment, materiel, human resources, and money in case of a future conflict because of the lack of complete standardization among the allies. It took long years of debate and arguments until the NATO partners finally agreed on standardized and interchangeable ammunition for infantry weapons; still, the NATO allies use a multiplicity of hand guns, rifles, submachine guns, and other infantry weapons. By contrast, the Soviet-led Warsaw Pact achieved equipment standardization at a very early stage with the result that today troops of any Communist-controlled country use the same ammunition and the same weapons—from North Korea to Cuba and from Afghanistan to Angola.

In the early days of standardization, the main objective was to permit mass production with the aim of reducing costs. Today, however, the importance of the product itself tends to fade into insignificance beside that of the service and use it provides. The user's choice nowadays is based not only on function and purchase price but also on working life, reliability, serviceability, and the like. This is why problems of compatibility and interchangeability are most important in standardization—especially in newly emerging industries such as consumer electronics or personal computers.

Safety, of course, remains an essential preoccupation, but its field is limited by the fact that only a relatively small proportion of products and services (or their characteristics) pertain to safety. Here again, changes are taking place and safety is gradually giving way to much more pressing health concerns, such as the consequences of air pollution, acid rain, nuclear waste, and chemical dumps—all essentially driven by the concern over cancer and cancer-causing agents.

> In managing quality it should be kept in mind that neither safety nor health are absolute and, therefore, the concept of probability must be introduced to ensure more consistency among the degrees of risk in different sectors of the economy. As a result of political, partisan, and media pressures, a tremendous imbalance exists in that a great deal more money is spent in some sectors of the economy than in others with the expectation of saving a human life. Yet it is possible to obtain better balance and therefore greater overall safety or health for the same economic cost by harmonizing costs and benefits among many of the sectors in the economy. For this reason standards and regulations related to safety and health should be increasingly based on probabilistic considerations, meaningful accident and health statistics, so that a sounder basis for investment decisions is developed than is the case today.

Although worldwide standardization reduces hindrances to trade, it may, in the short run, increase the possibility of barriers to technical advancement because the development and updating of international standards is a long, time-consuming, and tedious process requiring multilateral agreements that can sometimes constitute a brake on innovation.

5.2 Organization

This section will introduce organization, the second key component of a management system for quality. As previously stated, one of the most important components of any business process is the human element. But people will not come alive and become productive until they can operate in an organized manner, with responsibilities, authority, and accountability clearly established and proper motivation and supervision created. Organization as an *infrastructure* for the business process is the subject of this section.

Organization is defined as the logical grouping of people, responsibility, authority, and accountability to accomplish business objectives.

While this definition is applicable in most cases, establishing an organizational model requires further, detailed elaboration.

Organizing is part of the planning process and is an essential tool for getting work done *by people.* The word *organization* is used to denote two very different aspects of getting work done: the structure and the people who inhabit the structure. Structure is the subject of this section; the process of making human resources effective is discussed in Chapters 6 and 7.

One of the most important characteristics of any organization is *adaptability*: as the responsibilities within it change, so does the organization itself. Quality improvement requires special organizational structures if the process is interdepartmental or interfunctional. In such cases, means must be provided for interdepartmental steering of it. In addition, means must be provided for performing the detailed quality management work, again on an interdepartmental basis. The general approach to such organization is through process ownership, discussed in Chapter 4.

In this book, the terms *centralization* and *decentralization* will be applied to process management; that is, a centralized organization under a single line of management supports a single business process with a single owner identified. A decentralized organization will have the process and its associated resources either dispersed or distributed to several business units or divisions, under several lines of management, but still a single process owner. In both cases, the business process must optimize the efficiency and productivity of its human and material resources.

Building organizational structures requires a careful assessment and balancing of a set of managerial trade-offs, namely:

- Efficiency, productivity, or both
- Grouping by skills, functions, or both
- Delegation of responsibility and authority to the appropriate level of management so as to minimize building a bureaucracy
- Maintenance of educational and career opportunities and the motivation of the human element

The most frequently used organizational scheme is the *functional structure,* characterized by separate and independent functional entities aligned in a peer relationship, under a single managerial authority (Figure 5-2a).

Entrepreneurial structures tend to focus on productivity—that is, performing a given task in the shortest possible amount of time—by using temporary or alternate paths of responsibility and accountability with a specific objective to accomplish. Among entrepreneurial organizational structures are:

- *Project* or *task*: To accomplish a given work activity on a predetermined schedule and within resources.
- *Product*: To maximize return on investment over the life of a product.
- *Account*: To focus on the needs and requirements of a single user or customer.
- *Program*: To direct an overall effort comprising several projects, product programs, or accounts.
- *Geographic*: To coordinate multiple projects, product programs, or accounts for a defined geographic area.

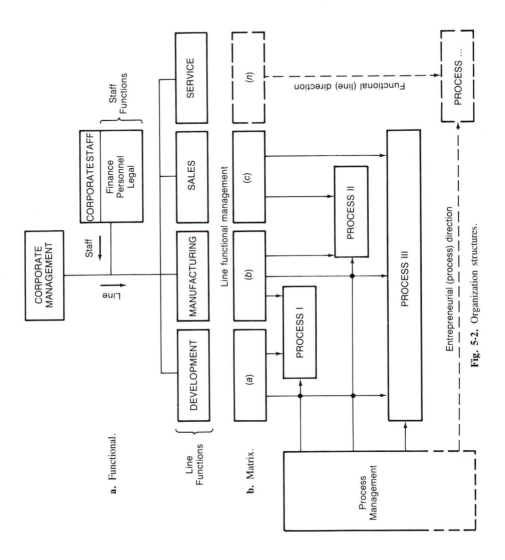

Fig. 5-2. Organization structures.

a. Functional.

b. Matrix.

Entrepreneurial organizations can have two levels of formality and permanency:

(1) Temporary, such as a project or task force, with a short life and to be replaced by other temporary or permanent structures.
(2) A permanent, alternate structure overlaid by other existing functional structures. This set-up allows critical skills and personnel to be regrouped to work toward stated common objectives, regardless of their position in the traditional structure (see Figure 4-6). *Matrix management* is a specialized form of permanent resource sharing relationships between alternate structures.

When implemented, the process management concept within an enterprise will result in some form of matrix management. Formal matrix management is implemented when the following three considerations are present:

(1) Need for multiple focus (functions–locations, functions–products, for example)
(2) Pressure for shared resources
(3) Requirement for multiple business objectives of equal priority, such as quality, cost, schedule, and so on

A matrix organization (Figure 5-2b) represents a balance between the advantages of functional and entrepreneurial organizations; it blends process management with the traditional functional hierarchy of the enterprise. The manager who does this balancing is usually a member of the senior management team within the enterprise. The two key paths of authority emanating from this senior manager are: (1) functional and (2) process management.

These paths may share a common infrastructure, such as budgets, personnel services, accounting methodology, and the like, or implement separate but related mechanisms. Obviously, this complex flow of information requires a clear definition of business processes, their interrelationships, and roles in the overall business environment. It is again common measurement parameters, such as the cost of quality, which help to balance and reconcile multiple paths and objectives within the matrix management system.

> It is beyond the scope of this text to explore further the justification and advantages, as well as the detailed characteristics, of matrix management; suffice it to say, that it is a feasible organizational approach and in fact has its greatest successes in high-technology industries and businesses.

Process management forces us to think through the basic decisions and activities independent of organizational structure. The management system provides a logical view and the appropriate relationships of how processes occur within the overall business environment. Given the policies and strategies of the business, with the right processes defined, the skills and staff can be built to meet the related business objectives and also select the right organizational structures. (In fact, processes can be built to monitor and study the management system itself.)

The Quality Function

All tasks required to ensure conformance—in both the management of intent (prevention) and management of outcome (control) areas—are performed in a process environment. Contrary to widespread opinion, these tasks are not performed primarily by quality professionals; instead, the majority of them are carried out as part of each of the numerous daily work activities within the process. Nevertheless, some quality-related tasks are sufficiently time-consuming to occupy the full time of specially trained employees such as inspectors, testers, cost accountants, instructors, and auditors, especially where the quality improvement approach is in transition between control and prevention. Other such tasks are performed on a part-time basis by people whose main job or profession is doing something else—design engineering, production control, or administration.

Three major activities in organizing for quality consist of (1) identifying the quality-related tasks and their interrelationships, (2) assigning clear responsibility for their performance, and (3) designing logical pieces of work to be assigned down to the worker (task) level.

Few resources in any company are scarcer than those related to quality management (statistical knowledge and experience, measurement training, process planning, and control skills), and no source of knowledge can contribute more to productivity and competitive position. It is therefore very important to give this skill and knowledge base the best possible chance for continued improvement. Good management ensures that everyone has a chance to (1) obtain the necessary education and training, (2) take direction from competent management and improve on an ongoing basis, and (3) perform in a measured, organized environment. Quality work carried out here and there in a company, fragmented and uncoordinated, will not show predictable improvements. Good management requires the systematic creation and organization of quality-related skills—within the organizational structures described in Figure 5-2.

The quality organization within the matrix management framework ensures that quality management has the benefit of overall competent direction, usually by the process owner. As quality-related training and guidance are under firm leadership, such a scheme also ensures continued skills development and improvement.

There will be in each major operation a quality manager or coordinator. In a matrix management environment, the *quality manager* in an operating unit (division) is responsible to two people—to the functional head of the division for day-by-day output of procedures and analysis, and to the process owners for continued quality support work, such as process education. The quality manager will coordinate the teaching and dissemination of quality-related materials, policies, procedures, techniques, and the like for management and for everyone else, including suppliers.

To influence managerial and organizational behavior, quality must be managed from a high level down into the organization. The enterprise *quality executive* is appointed with the responsibility for implementing the quality policy and related procedures and practices throughout the organization. This is a key position and should be filled from among the most capable executives available. People will judge the importance of the quality effort by the caliber of its top manager. Duties of this quality executive include:

- Developing an overall strategy and plan for implementing the quality policy, including the definition and selection of processes and their owners
- Working with the process owners to ensure that process management integrity is consistently implemented throughout the business
- Working with support and staff functions to ensure the proper functioning of the management system (accounting methods to include quality-related items in the measurements; personnel practices for implementing the appropriate personnel evaluation and compensation system to reward quality performance and to provide the necessary education and training; internal audits to monitor compliance with the quality policy)

The quality executive must make a special effort to ensure that everyone in the business recognizes the importance of quality improvement and the need to implement the quality policy in their respective areas—particularly where the understanding about quality and its rewards are traditionally not high (nonmanufacturing areas). In short, the quality executive is responsible for the successful functioning of the management system for quality.

To ensure its effectiveness the quality function must be exercised in an objective and independent manner, and organized such that its head in each unit (quality director or manager) shall report directly to the general manager of that unit and be on the same organizational level as the functions whose quality performance is being measured. The quality function shall be staffed with professionally qualified personnel whose responsibilities and deployment are determined by their specialized skills and training in:

- Product acceptance at all levels
- Supplier/vendor quality
- Quality and process engineering techniques (data analysis and reporting, planning, qualification approval of products, processes and procedures, quality education, corrective action and audits)
- Product safety
- Consumer relations
- Quality assurance

The most valuable actions the head of the quality function can take are the prevention of problems by heading them off and by recommending action or redirection at the proper time. This is very much a matter of management style and involves a human element that transcends responsibilities spelled out in procedure manuals and organization charts. Quality managers are good at selling, just as they are good practitioners of their craft. They know that the way to make top management quality-conscious is to make them comfortable with the concepts and rewards of quality in their own terms. Since managing quality has much to do with people management, quality managers must also be people oriented: They must be able to work with people and motivate them by demonstrating what they can receive from their commitment to the concept of quality.

Users (customers, consumers) deserve to receive exactly what has been committed to them based on their requirements. Therefore, the identification, investigation, resolution, and future prevention of user problems are actions that require the most professional experience and training. There are four basic action phases in *consumer relations*:

(1) Prevention, involving all activities aimed at helping users avoid developing problems through misinformation or lack of education/training. Prevention also includes establishing early warning systems to detect any potential user problems; it assumes the existence of a competent quality management system.
(2) "Problem contacts" (information centers) so users can reach the provider for remedy whenever they have a problem with the work product.
(3) Repair or exchange of defective items inadvertently passed on to users.
(4) Feedback for correction: the process that produced the problem must also be adjusted or upgraded.

Quality assurance comprises activities which determine how well the company's quality mission and policies are being carried out. Assurance, by definition, is procedure-driven and operates mainly on the basis of documents. One approach to quality assurance requires prior preparation of detailed quality plans plus subsequent reviews and audits to establish that the plans are adequate and that they are being followed. Placement of the assurance function within an organization has been debated intensively, mainly around the question of "checks and balances." In theory, the assurance function should report to the general manager because it is charged with reviewing the job of quality management itself. In practice, such an arrangement means that the assurance function receives little competent supervision, and therefore, the usual practice is to make the assurance function subordinate to the quality manager. This is done more so since only a very small staff is needed to provide quality assurance.

5.3 Communications

Communications deals with the flow of information within the business, including all the processes under consideration. As we examine processes based on their structural characteristics, we must also examine the flow of information through the organization in terms of these processes. Communication within the organization and, most importantly, within management will largely determine the success or failure of the process.

Information Flow

Within a process, the carrier of the information flow—that is, the communication network—is the organization. As organizational structures grow in size, significant changes take place in the flow of information within them. The larger the process (and therefore the component organizations), the more information will flow horizontally among the various subprocesses and activities which make up the total process. (In large processes more than two thirds of the information flows horizontally, crossing organizational and functional boundaries.)

In establishing effective communications, three important considerations apply:

- *Authority*: The decision on how the information should flow, from what sources and to what destinations. At the time a process is established, this authority is exercised by top management. It is also top management who decides on what information should emanate from the process upward to senior management and what communications channels should exist among the various processes. For information flow within the process, the process owner is responsible for both direction and volume.
- *Information sources*: It is always more important to establish what the source of information is than who should receive it and when. Authenticity, accuracy, and timeliness all critically depend on the information source.
- *Information distribution*: The direction of information flow and the destination of information distributed. In determining the recipients of the various information items, the "need to know" principle is applied by those in authority.

The authority and responsibility paths of organizations serve as parallel information paths for communications. Whatever the organizational structure, communication is tailored to the two major branches of quality management: control and prevention.

Information related to the current status or the outcome of the process is grouped in various control documents and reports. *Control information* has the following characteristics:

- It is organizationally aligned, generally reflecting management responsibilities.
- It comprises all important controllable elements of the process that effect its contribution to overall business objectives.
- It is assessment-oriented in the sense that it facilitates evaluation of actual performance against requirements.

- It spans relatively short periods of time and is generated on a timely basis to facilitate corrective action.

Information dealing with the future—that is, with intended outcome—is consolidated in the various types of planning documents and reports. *Planning information* has the following characteristics:

- It covers longer periods of time and focuses on long-term trends.
- It is directive in form and content.
- It serves as the basis for quality improvements, the assessment of performance against general business objectives, and the evaluation of overall process effectiveness, efficiency, and adaptability, as well as a benchmark for formulating new objectives or plans.

In quality management terms, the elimination of worker-controllable defects almost always generates only control communications; the elimination of management-controllable defects, on the other hand, will normally require both control and planning information.

Within the process organization, quality functions can act as specific channels of communication for quality-related information among all concerned—in effect serving as an information network. The problems of communication generated by the high degree of specialization in modern industry are well known. For example, workers may not understand the significance of newly introduced, close tolerances to which they are held for proper product performance; inspection may not be aware of the product characteristics considered critical by product engineering until production has already started and items have been shipped to customers. With proper communication channels established and the appropriate information furnished—in many cases through the quality professionals—most of these information barriers can be removed.

Another critical consideration in communications is the *accuracy* and *precision* of the information; in obtaining and maintaining a quality commitment, the *clarity* of the communications is most important. The imprecise use of quality terminology cannot be tolerated because it will lead to inconsistencies and errors in both communicating intent and in measurements of actual performance.

There has been considerable progress in establishing improved and consistent terminology in quality management to meet the purposes of precision and accuracy of communications. Establishing a systematic exchange of information among the various functions that make up the process is indispensable for meeting requirements. Specifically, such flow of information should include data about, for example, the cost of quality. Another important branch of information is communication about methodologies, tools, and techniques that prove invaluable in the management of quality and in process control.

Early warning is another valuable role of communications within the process and to the recipients of its output. Such data will be invaluable in the event of nonconformances, product failures, or anticipated product repair or recall actions.

5.4 Management Support Mechanisms

With information being a key component of the process, *information systems* must certainly be part of the overall management system as a special class of tools supporting process management.

Information systems are particularly helpful in the following key areas of quality management:

- *Managing intent*: Advanced techniques, such as simulation, modeling, project planning, and scheduling (PERT, critical path methods)
- *Managing outcome*: Data accumulation, reduction, analysis, and reporting; statistical analysis; information retrieval and query; automatic inspection and testing; real-time process control, where applicable to technological processes and other quality management-related techniques
- *Process description, analysis,* and *documentation*

Examples for specific information systems applications in quality management include process review (computer modeling or simulation of information flow through a business process) and field quality evaluation (the collection, reduction, and analysis of field service data for the purpose of management reporting and potential improvements to the process).

Within an enterprise, several business processes (for example, product lines or associated services) must be coordinated from a management standpoint to support a stated quality policy. Consequently, the effective use of information systems in support of these processes may also require some level of standardization within information systems, particularly in the areas of process analysis and programming, data collection, validation, and reduction.

> The modern organization of industrial or business work processes introduces the concept of *cooperative processing,* which is a hierarchical information flow concept from the highest level to the individual work station. In the context of an entire business or enterprise, the highest level of system is called the enterprise system, normally supported by information systems in a central host (mainframe) configuration. At the next lower level, work groups are defined on the basis that they share common information within themselves—organizationally termed as departments. Departments, in turn, include teams or individuals at a workstation level. Cooperative processing, then, comprises three distinct levels: (1) enterprise systems, (2) department systems, and (3) workstations.

> Managing quality within the information systems function is, by definition, another requirement for overall quality and process management. However, its details are beyond the scope of this discussion.

> One key area from the standpoint of information systems support, and rather exciting from a technological viewpoint, is automated measurement systems. In the control of more and more technological processes, instruments are directly connected either to a central host computer system, dedicated minicomputers, or even

personal computers. Rather than use the central host for generating quality control reports, analyses and the like, it is possible to use a minicomputer or personal computer for the collection of data from, say, a test laboratory on a periodic basis and provide both interim reports and analyses. The results of these reports and calculations can then be transferred to a central data bank for future retention, query, and use by process management or the top management of the enterprise. To date, minicomputers and personal computers have been interfaced with practically every conceivable type of instrument found in industrial research and testing laboratories. With the advent of low-cost personal computers with relatively large memories and backup storage capabilities, the use of desk calculators for the analysis of quality-related measurement data has given way to these new technologies. (However, some of the programmable calculators, which have function key access to many statistical functions, including standard deviation, variance, correlation coefficient, linear regression, F and t tests, are still very much in use for cost-effectiveness reasons.)

Advanced Techniques

The computer puts in the hands of the quality manager the capability of utilizing more advanced techniques than just the statistical analysis of data, using desk calculators or personal computers. The field of *operations research*[2] provides quality management with a number of advanced techniques, used mainly in managing intent; that is, in designing a process or in attempting to predict its performance.

Simulation techniques are aimed at answering questions which begin with "What would happen if. . .?" Essentially, simulation is a substitution of a computer model for an existing business process or system.[3] In a number of companies, quality managers and industrial engineers jointly study process flows for general feasibility, increased productivity, and cost reduction. Computer simulation of process flows using *discrete techniques* permits evaluation of the effect of changing such variables as the number of inspection stations, gradations in the flow of raw materials, and the like. In the field of automated process control, where engineers deal with ongoing physical or chemical processes and must take into account process perturbations, *continuous techniques* permit modeling and studying computer-collected data on an ongoing basis to determine the appropriate response function to avoid under- or overcontrol.[4]

---

[2]Operations research is the application of scientific methods to the operation of a system (or process) that has alternative possibilities for attaining its specific objectives, in order to provide those in control with the optimum solution(s) to the given problem(s).

[3]A detailed discussion of simulation methods is outside the scope of this text. The interested reader is directed to the numerous books available on the subject, in particular [19], [20], and [25] in the Bibliography.

[4]For a detailed description of the General Purpose Simulation System (GPSS), a typical discrete simulation package, see "General Purpose Simulation System/360—Application Description," Form H20-0186 (White Plains, NY: IBM Corporation), or refer to [25] in the Bibliography. One of the better known continuous simulation programs, the Continuous System Modeling Program (CSMP), is described in "System/360 Continuous System Modeling Program—Application Description," Form H20-0240 (White Plains, NY: IBM Corporation).

Model planning and building is a methodology used independently or in conjunction with simulation, in which case it is the first step in the overall simulation approach. Models are usually mathematical formulations of an industrial, technological, or financial process. After verifying that the model is pertinent and valid, a programmer generally converts it into computer language and makes it ready for the appropriate analytical procedures.

For certain quality management functions, deploying resources (human resources, materials, equipment, and so on) and scheduling the appropriate activities becomes a time-consuming part of the planning or project management function. Much time can be saved by using carefully constructed computer programs, scheduling techniques, and allocation methods, taking into account skills, capabilities, time required to complete individual tasks, and the like. These are particularly useful when a wide variety of quality control projects are under way or when critical products are being introduced. With the problems of project management, it is important to meet inspection planning and quality control schedules. The use of network control and critical path techniques (CPM, PERT) for identifying bottlenecks in both overall project planning and within the quality control portion of the project itself can avoid oversights and missed schedules while contributing to strict resource and cost controls. These techniques are useful both for enterprise-wide coordination of quality efforts and the management of individual processes.

> As an example, the Pareto principle can be automated to identify, say, the "ten most chronic quality problems." By doing this periodically and using automatic information retrieval and query techniques from the quality management information data bank, progress in overcoming these problems can be highlighted in a faster and more economical way. The interrelation between production losses, difficulties in manufacturing, preshipment inspection, and customer experience should produce a more responsive quality system. Under quality management information systems (quality data base) it will be possible for any executive to query the data bank and to examine quality performance historically in comparison with program forecasts.
>
> A log of the number of queries to the quality data bank and the types of questions asked could provide additional insight into senior management's concern and commitment.

DISCUSSION QUESTIONS

1. Define the term *management system*. What is the key concept of management systems planning? What are the key objectives of a management system? What are its components?
2. Relate the three basic stages of quality management to basic process management issues. What are the corresponding process assessment rating levels?
3. Discuss the control aspects of complex work processes. Explain the principles of process organization in terms of subdivision into manageable subprocesses and activi-

ties. Name at least one process example, in specific terms, from your own work experience.

4. Define the term *policy*. Explain how it differs from instructions, guidelines, or procedures. Explain why a policy statement on quality is critical for the success of quality management.

5. Give at least four examples for subject matter appropriate for quality guidelines and instructions.

6. Explain the role of secondary, or indirect users in formulating product requirements.

7. Explain the economic advantages of industrial standards over government regulations or legislation. Give at least two major advantages of standardization. Can you name any disadvantages?

8. Explain the basic characteristics of functional and entrepreneurial organizations. Discuss their relative advantages and disadvantages. What is a matrix organization?

9. Describe the role of a position that is called a function within the matrix management framework.

10. Describe the duties of the quality executive responsible for the enterprise quality function. Describe the skills and training of the quality professional staff.

11. Name the three important considerations in establishing effective process communications.

12. Define the terms *control information* and *planning information*. Explain the difference between the two.

13. Describe the role of information systems in support of process management. What key areas are they most helpful in?

14. Name at least three advanced management techniques that are used to support various phases of process management.

Part III EXCELLENCE THROUGH PROCESS MANAGEMENT

6

PROCESS MANAGEMENT IMPLEMENTATION

The purpose of this chapter is to help the practicing manager implement the concept "quality improvement through process management." It does so by guiding the reader in the selection and application of the actions, techniques, and tools discussed in earlier chapters through the three major stages of quality improvement: *commitment, consolidation*, and *maturity*.

In each stage, at least three steps are required for the continuing implementation of quality improvement:

(1) The necessary elements of the *management system* must be developed and put in place to allow the selection and management of the business processes, through which the management of quality will be implemented.

(2) The appropriate concepts and techniques of *prevention* must be applied, in combination with the complementary aspects of *control*. The two together form the "quality management template," representative of that particular stage of quality improvement.

(3) The appropriate *process management* measures must be taken to provide the management framework for implementing quality management and, subsequently, process optimization as well.

At the outset, many organizations will have some level of quality control in place—that is, certain elements of quality management or even process management. Others will have to start "from scratch," with the sole motivation, and a powerful one at that, being the continued viability of their business. To proceed in either case there are two prerequisites: *management's conviction* that quality is achievable and the *commitment* to implement an all-out, consistent quality improvement effort with the ultimate objective of "zero defects."

6.1 Stage One: Commit to Quality

The purpose of the *commitment stage* is to (1) establish a management commitment to quality improvement and (2) implement this commitment in terms of management infrastructure and process management measures in the shortest possible time.

In the following, we will address these actions in more detail, grouped into the three steps mentioned earlier, as they apply to this stage.

The commitment stage is made up of two phases: (1) *introduction* and (2) *initial implementation.*

Introduction, that is, getting the program off the ground by taking certain specific actions, may take anywhere from three to 12 months, depending on the size of organization, complexity of the processes to be set up, and the resources invested. The *initial implementation* phase, which is the second part of the commitment stage, comprises the bulk of activities: the first-time problem definition, defect identification, and defect removal; the first-time calculation of the cost of quality and the implementation of defect-cause analysis. At the end of this phase, which may require anywhere from six to 18 months, the basics of process management—ownership, controls, measurements, and corrective actions—are in place, and the overall organization is positioned to the concept of continued improvements to zero defects. The financial and process management infrastructure, and the cost of quality data base are also in place, the initial education is completed, and so are the initial efforts for dominant problem definition and defect-cause removal. From this point on, quality management becomes an ongoing effort repeating much of what was done at the outset with continued improvements to the process to achieve conformance to requirements in the work product, along with maximum efficiency and productivity in the process.

6.1.1 The Management System for Commitment

Once the top management of the enterprise has recognized the need for an organized and consistent quality improvement effort and has committed itself to its implementation, systematic measures can be taken in preparation for its introduction. These measures are among the responsibilities inherent in the *management system.*

INTRODUCTION PHASE

The first measure is to formulate and publish a clear *policy statement* on the subject of quality, covering the entire enterprise.

The main purpose of a quality policy is to establish, beyond a shadow of a doubt, top management's commitment to quality. It must be clear to all employees that defect-free work is not only possible but that it is expected and ranks in importance with objectives related to cost and schedule. Often people assume that pronouncements on quality apply only to manufacturing or to the technical community; therefore, the policy must make it clear that quality is everyone's responsibility, including office workers, administrators, service personnel, and, above all, line managers.

The chief executive officer or general manager of a company is responsible for formulating a quality policy and then reaching agreement with the corporate executive for quality on the proper level of quality operations to be established in each business function (marketing, development, manufacturing, service, and the like). It is again the general manager's responsibility to publish this policy and to take affirmative steps to ensure that all employees understand that *the quality policy of the enterprise is to conform to requirements exactly as stated, or to cause the requirements to be formally changed to meet user expectations.*

Consequently, statements of policy on quality should be clear, unambiguous, and brief.

Examples for policy statements on quality:

"We will perform defect-free work for our clients and our associates. We will fully understand the requirements for our jobs and the systems that support us. We will conform to those requirements at all times." (Philip Crosby Associates, Winter Park, Florida)

"In order to improve quality we shall provide clearly stated requirements expecting each person to do the job right the first time in accordance with those requirements, or cause the requirements to be officially changed." (Bechtel Power Division, Ann Arbor, Michigan)

"We will deliver defect-free competitive products and services on time to our customers." (IBM Communication Products Division, Research Triangle Park, Raleigh, North Carolina)

The public commitment of the company to quality is marked by the *publication* of the quality policy. It is also the *first of five key documents* in the quality management effort (see Figure 6-1).

To facilitate the administration and practical implementation of the quality policy, this document must be accompanied by specific *guidelines* and *instructions,* to both management and employees. Among others, these guidelines must address the following questions related to quality:

- *Objectives*: If the organization is serious about quality, specific quality objectives must be established, along with a system of recognition and rewards for their attainment. It must be clear to everyone that not only missed schedules or cost overruns will draw senior management attention

but defects in products and services, and variations against user requirements will be viewed with equal seriousness.

- *Measurements*: Once objectives have been established, people must be clear
  about their meaning. If they are to meet requirements then they must be
  given specific guidelines and instructions for each work activity and task,
  making it clear that measurements of performance against requirements
  must be established at all levels within the organization.
- *Attainment*: To meet requirements and to be productive, workers within the
  process must be given the wherewithal—such as education and training,
  techniques and procedures, and the knowledge and skill to use them—to
  achieve stated objectives.
- *Management*: This dynamic state is attained through common implementation of process management.

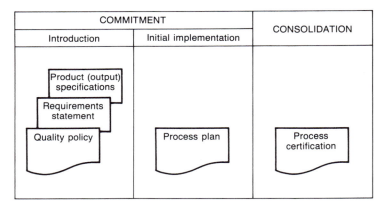

Fig. 6-1. The five key documents of quality management.

Common implementation is a key concept laid down in the guidelines. It
means that not only is the quality management effort based on a common policy
but that it will also be implemented on a common schedule throughout the
enterprise. There are no "pilot efforts" or "lead projects" to be established for
the purpose of experimentation or testing; whether they have to do with the
manufacturing or personnel function, engineering or marketing—or whether the
processes involve field activities, planning, administration, billing, or order
entry—they must proceed on a coordinated and compatible schedule, against at
least one common management measurement: the cost of quality. In other words,
the quality management effort is consistent "across the board," to be effective
and successful.

When prepared at the operating unit, division, or location level, quality
guidelines and procedures include the preparation of a formal *plan* for process

management, requirement statements, measurements, quality assurance, and the like. They incorporate such things as formal systems for education, design reviews, vendor qualification, inspection and test, process control, assessment and feedback, and so on. *Quality manuals* are published which outline the formal plans, procedures, and definitions of responsibility, authority and accountability, organization charts, and the like. At division or location level, the management system calls for *audits* which will determine the extent to which plans are adequate and implementable.

Aside from organizational instructions and guidelines, *practices* may be prepared for business processes and the functional units they cover. For example, they can be developed for reliability programs, service and maintenance, administrative processes, issue resolution, and the like.

The publication of the quality policy and its accompanying guidelines and instructions also represent the first major *communication* within the management system: management's commitment to quality. Beyond that, the form of communication continues to be the steady flow of instructions, especially of a financial or business controls nature, from company management and, to an even greater extent from the process owners, related primarily to the procedural component of their processes: requirements, specifications, process plans, reports, and so on.

The next important measure within the management system is to establish the *organization for quality*. It comprises several key elements:

- Establishment of *new processes* and the selection of *existing processes* for implementing the process management approach to quality improvement. (The assignment of process owners will be discussed in greater detail in Section 6.1.3.)
- A *quality improvement team* (QIT) is set up, representing the key functions of the enterprise, to serve as the "administrative arm" to top management through the entire quality improvement effort. The QIT is the highest body of issue resolution as related to quality and is, for all practical purposes, the "steering committee" for quality.
- If they did not previously exist, the need for *professional quality organizations* and staffs is assessed and the appropriate functions are established, including quality engineering, quality assurance, and so on.

Since process management is the preferred approach to quality improvement, the process owners and their organizations represent the "line management" of quality. Within each process the activities primarily related to process design and planning, and certain aspects of control (e.g., detection) will require the deployment of quality professionals, such as quality engineers, testers, product acceptance personnel, and so on.

Once in place, process owners are responsible for establishing their appropriate process organizations, which will invariably be implemented as some form of matrix management (see Section 5.2). The latter, in turn, results in multiple paths of communications, command and control, authority and responsibility. In many instances parallel reporting relationships will emerge: line and functional. However, this multiplicity of lines of communications and reporting relationships is manageable by means of common measurement parameters, such as the cost of quality and the strict and clear definition of business processes, their relationships, and their role in the overall business environment.

> Parallel line relationships exist in practically every modern corporation. A chief financial officer, reporting to the chief executive officer, is responsible for the financial condition and health of the corporation. At each manufacturing facility or development laboratory, for example, there is a local controller who is responsible for the financial performance of that specific operation. He reports *in line* to the manager of the facility and on a *functional* basis to the chief financial officer. Because of the complex nature of today's business, accounting procedures, and tax environment, the financial direction of the plant or laboratory is ultimately provided by the chief financial officer. No one questions the feasibility of this organization or its value and no problem arises from the fact that the local controller reports to two people. Other dual reporting structures are found in the environmental, personnel, legal, security—and quality functions.

In addition, and especially in larger enterprises, it is desirable to establish a *quality staff* along with its management structure, following the traditional functional (manufacturing, engineering, marketing, service) or divisional structure of the company. This quality staff structure is not part of process management; rather it belongs to the permanent management system which supports the quality management efforts across the various organizational or functional entities. In larger companies, this permanent quality staff may also be location-oriented in terms of plants, development laboratories, or field offices. The term *quality function*, on the other hand, always refers to the collection of quality professionals deployed in the various process activities and engaged directly in the management of intent or outcome within a given process.

One chief responsibility of the quality function is *product acceptance,* comprising:

- *Inspection*: Visual, mechanical, or electronic inspection results in a collection of data which, after proper study and analysis, permit evaluation of product or service status. Each measurement is planned and conducted by trained professionals who are organizationally independent from those they are inspecting.
- *Testing*: Part of the acceptance activity is accomplished through the use of mechanical or electronic test equipment to determine the material, structural, or functional integrity of a given work product. This activity ranges from components testing in purchasing and receiving to functional and systems testing at the end of the assembly line. The only purpose of testing

is to determine whether or not the work product will perform to the basic *specifications.*[1]

Supplier and vendor quality requires special attention in terms of product acceptance and defect elimination because, especially in high-technology businesses, components, supplies, raw materials, or services enter the enterprise on a continued basis in ever-increasing volumes. Although supplier quality operations traditionally focus mostly on product or materials controls, it should be remembered that in many cases the largest single supplier to an enterprise can be the vendor of administrative or financial services, such as insurance companies, banks, and the like.

> *Supplier quality engineering,* in most cases, complements purchasing in that it assesses the quality management capabilities of vendors and suppliers.
>
> Acceptance of supplier items, through acceptance inspection and testing—which should properly take place on the supplier's premises—is carried out consistent with the concepts of supplier quality engineering and is a consequence of it. (In the maturity stage, this is all preplanned and carried out in conjunction with supplier quality engineering activities.)

Quality engineering began as an application of statistical knowledge to the design of sampling plans for inspection and control charts for production control. With widening experience, quality engineers redirect their efforts to the broader aspects of process design, quality planning, and defect prevention.

Quality engineering is responsible for determining and planning the quality-related work of the rest of the organization (or the process). Among other things, quality engineers determine how, in the management of outcome (control) phase, the work product should be inspected, tested, and then monitored during its life in the user's hands. Establishing these requirements and measuring results are what quality engineering is all about:

- *Planning:* Most quality departments pay their way, but at the outset they may be expensive, especially as resources and time are expended on process planning, design, and related activities. For this reason, it is only reasonable that planning should become a key part of quality engineering. Everything that happens in the process, then, will be a predictable event and not a reaction to surprise.
- *Data analysis and reporting:* Each inspection or test brings about two results. First, the product is either accepted or rejected—the acceptance

---

[1]One of the most critical error prediction and test problems in high-technology industry, particularly in computer systems and communications, is that of software. For a comprehensive treatment of the subject, refer to H. Remus and F. L. Bauer, "Program Transformations and Programming Environments," *NATO ASI Series*, P. Pepper, ed. (New York, NY: Springer Verlag, 1984).

decision. Second, the measurement must be recorded; by accumulating such recorded measurements and analyzing them, the quality engineer can determine exact current and projected future quality status.

- *Corrective actions:* All the work related to planning, inspection, testing, measuring, data analysis, and reporting could be a waste of time unless it leads to the removal of defects and the prevention of their recurrence. Therefore, the real strength and value of quality engineering lies in prevention. Today, most nonconformance problems, with the exception of accidents and other unforeseeable events, are preventable. All that is required is some organizational discipline and professional direction.
- *Audit:* A planned examination, after the fact, of an activity or process carried out either (1) by determining conformance to design and procedures in the process or (2) by critical analysis of the work product resulting from the process. Conducted properly, there is no method more fruitful in exposing shoddy process planning, insufficient training, or inadequate controls—in brief, poor process management.

Product safety can always be handled with minimum expense when faced maturely and in a businesslike fashion. In most product safety problems, the basic cause is usually a lack of sound judgment on the part of management—usually some individual manager. Often it is the result of trying to achieve a short-range goal by cutting corners and sacrificing long-range advantages. Product safety need not be a legal problem—it is primarily an ethical one.

> The safety aspects of the 63rd Street subway tunnel in New York City represent a case in point. The structural concrete elements were poured in a deficient way and, as a result, did not meet basic materials and safety standards. The inspectors of the City and Metropolitan Transit Authority apparently missed this negligence on the contractor's part and accepted the work product. Since the project was already significantly behind schedule, it is very likely that they had little motivation to cause any further delay by reporting shoddy performance and thereby causing additional and time-consuming repair actions. The subsequent investigation by an independent consultant led to no better resolution and ended up in litigation, the suspension of further Federal funding of the project, and an indefinite delay in its completion—all at the taxpayers' expense.[2]

The logic of determining the balance between line activities and those of the various quality groups is based on such considerations as the extent to which line departments have been trained to perform their work activities, prior record of performance, the volume of work, the general operating practices of the company in work assignment (for example, use of staff versus line), and the overall quality

---

[2]*The New York Times*, August 18, 1985, pp. 1–34.

improvement strategy—that is, the mix of prevention versus control. The variable nature of these considerations means that the job of organizing is never finished; changes in any of these factors require corresponding changes in organizational structure as well.

Responsibility may be assigned to several categories of organizational units: "nonquality" functions, such as design, manufacturing, service, marketing, and the like, to carry out routine tasks within their responsibility; "line" quality departments such as inspection and test; "staff" quality groups, with tasks mainly of a planning, reporting, analytical, or coordinating nature; outside agencies, such as vendors, service organizations, and so on.

Organizational reporting of *information systems* within the overall management system is a key factor in establishing optimum support capabilities for quality management. Ideally, priorities for computing services should be established on the basis of team decisions. When the priorities for computer access, systems analysis, and programming are favorable, both the process owner and the quality functions are content to receive information services from some other organizational entity, as the information systems department. Such an arrangement enables process management and the quality functions within it to give attention to their primary mission without becoming deeply involved with a support specialty. However, when total information service needs exceed available capacity, alternate arrangements may have to be made and, short of turning to outside sources (purchased services), increasing reliance on stand-alone personal computer work stations could be the best alternative.

The management system for the commitment stage also specifies the reporting relationships with respect to other processes and process owners, as well as the general management of the business.

Of the management support mechanisms, *education* represents a major investment in the introductory phase. Quality education takes three basic forms:

(1) Conceptual and procedural orientation (awareness and fundamentals)
(2) Direct skill development and improvement, including the use of management techniques, tools and aids, as well as statistical process control
(3) Continuing communication of quality-related ideas, achievements, and case-study material that serve as needed information and motivators to make quality improvement an ongoing objective in everybody's mind

All three are aimed at both managers and nonmanagerial employees; during the introductory phase the focus is on the first two, and the objective is that every single worker has a completed version of both, as appropriate for the individual's responsibilities within the work process.

In the education program, both quality fundamentals and achievements are illustrated by case studies; the management material is heavily oriented toward illustrative examples using the cost of quality and other efficiency and productivity indicators to show the economic underpinnings of "doing the job right the first time."

The dual focus of the motivational and education efforts established during the introductory phase is maintained through the entire quality improvement effort: management's responsibility is resource and cost-driven, whereas other professionals and nonmanagerial employees are focusing on the various procedures, practices, and activities related to worker-controllable defect prevention.

Another key aspect of the introductory phase is *employee motivation* for maximum participation and contribution to the quality improvement effort. This has both communications and people management aspects. The former may include the entire spectrum from posters and newspaper articles through presentations and meetings to the electronic media; the latter ranges from individual objective setting, group activities, through team competition, to various forms of recognition.

In the management systems support area, *personnel management* maintains a dual focus on the motivation of managerial and nonmanagerial people. Managers at all levels are motivated primarily by the prospect of new and enhanced management tools (among them, process management and cost of quality) to help them attain their business objectives. Beyond this all employees, managerial and nonmanagerial, are motivated through professionalism, the need for quality to assure business survival in a highly competitive world, and the role of quality in reducing costs and its consequent direct contribution to the profitability of the business.

One of the most important management activities during the introductory phase is the *commitment of resources*, both human and financial, to the quality improvement effort. One area requiring significant investment is education—both company-wide and at the process level. Another significant area of investment is the establishment of processes and, within them, the deployment of the various quality functions, with associated facilities and equipment. The third area of increased initial levels of investment is administration, as related to the measurement system and especially to the cost of quality. Work aimed at establishing a cost of quality database (for example, data gathering) must start right at the beginning of the introductory phase. This work is driven by financial management, usually from the accounting side. To make this possible, in turn, requires the deployment of financial skills and resources within each process as part of the process owner's organization so that cost data can be gathered and managed at the process level, but also consolidated at the enterprise level for overall financial control and business measurement purposes.

The introductory phase is completed when (1) processes are selected, (2) process owners and their organizations are in place, (3) both conceptual and skills-oriented quality education is complete, and (4) the cost of quality database is established, ready to receive actual cost measurement data.

INITIAL IMPLEMENTATION PHASE

The start of this second phase of the commitment stage is marked by the readiness of the entire enterprise to start the quality improvement effort on a common schedule and against consistent, common measurements.[3]

Although some defect removal and quality improvement may have already taken place in various parts of the organization, the key to the start of initial implementation is the *commonality* of the effort.

In the practices and procedures area, the various measurement and reporting schemes are extended to all the subprocesses and, where appropriate, down to the individual task (worker) level.

As one aspect of the measurement system, the *process performance rating* scheme is now in place and by the time the initial implementation phase is completed, *all* processes are expected to be assessed to operate at a rating level of "4."

From an organizational standpoint, *quality circles* are established where appropriate or necessary. They represent an *organizational alternative* which management has at the point of initial implementation for the introduction of *participative management* by concentrating *like skills* (quality professionals, production supervisors, design engineers, and so on) or *related* human resources (members of a department, first-line managers in a given function, and so on) for problem analysis, defect identification, or the resolution of a particularly complex problem. When they are established, attention should be given to the fact that they are usually aimed at lower levels of the organization or the process and, therefore, unless they receive continuing management attention, they will have difficulty in maintaining momentum once they accomplish their initial purpose.

> Quality circles are not a mandatory ingredient of the quality improvement program. Rather, they represent another optional tool aiding process management, specifically in the area of control (detection and correction) where multiple functional or organizational entities must interact in the process of eliminating worker-controllable defects. Thus, quality circles are primarily facilitators of communications and decision making among interacting functions or organizations. The lowest level of quality circle, obviously, is the single department where the interacting parties are individual employees or workers.

The initial implementation phase is also characterized by the early completion of basic *process-related education*; that is, education in process theory, process analysis tools and techniques, and process management. Quality educa-

---

[3]If we adopt Philip Crosby's terminology and 14-step approach to quality improvement, the initial implementation phase starts with Zero Defect Day, which represents a public commitment to continuing quality improvement with "zero defects" as the ultimate goal.

tion now shifts from these fundamentals to the more advanced topics of process control, process capability (related to effectiveness), process efficiency, productivity, adaptability, and their measurements.

From a people management standpoint, initial implementation offers an excellent opportunity for the recognition of innovation and leadership during the introductory phase where examples of outstanding performance provide a high level of motivation to other employees (peer effect).

In summary, the four key measures taken to launch the quality improvement effort emanate from top management:

- Management commitment (policy statement, guidelines and procedures, communications, and the selection of processes)
- Quality organization (establishment of process ownerships and organizations, quality improvement teams and staffs)
- Management support mechanisms (education, cost of quality database and supporting administrative/accounting infrastructure)
- Commitment of resources

6.1.2 Quality Management for Commitment

INTRODUCTION PHASE

The cost of quality gets its first evaluation and is used as a *reporting tool* and as an indicator of process effectiveness. (Nothing is quite so effective as having cost data show competing areas that one department has more effective methods of reducing defects than others.) Quality improvement is coordinated by a *quality improvement team*—a direct representation of line management. Their purpose is to begin to establish a process as well as the attitudes that will last for a long time, in other words, the beginnings of a continued quality improvement effort.

The introduction of a new quality improvement effort, by definition, must start with two basic activities: (1) a review of already existing *experience* related to quality management and (2) *problem analysis,* ranging from the overall process level down to individual activities and tasks, to establish the nature and magnitude of the quality problem. As a consequence, the management of quality in the initial phases of commitment will be focusing more on *outcome* than on intent, as effective prevention can be based only on a comprehensive understanding of the problem and established experience in defect identification and removal.

At the process or subprocess level, problem analysis focuses on the process itself, in the form of *process analysis.* This is a disciplined exercise using established tools and techniques, such as *department activity analysis* (DAA), *structured analysis* (SA), and *process analysis technique* (PAT).

Quality circles can also be used as an effective vehicle of communication and group analysis of quality-related problems.

Management of Intent. During the introduction phase the *requirements subprocess* is the key activity of prevention-oriented management. More than likely, problem analysis will show that a significant proportion of quality-related problems emanate from a flawed or incomplete requirements statement. If a formal requirements process does not exist, it must be established at this point; if it does, it requires a total review and analysis to ensure timeliness, completeness, and responsiveness to user needs and expectations. In either case, a new *requirement statement* must be produced which is the *second of the five key documents* of the quality improvement effort (Figure 6-1). This work will probably last through the better part of the introduction phase; it will have to be followed during initial implementation by measures to ensure the disciplined review, acceptance, and assurance of requirements as an integral part of the process. Specifically, the creation of requirements is followed by their review by both user representatives and by those of the provider. Preferably, the provider, through design or requirements acceptance personnel, has already participated in requirements creation; in any case, the requirements review is the *latest* point at which the provider should get involved in the requirements process and contribute meaningfully toward the completion of manageable requirements. Any delay beyond this point will likely result in divergence between requirements and specifications, or a loss of time in the requirements acceptance and assurance process which follows.

Based on and closely linked to the requirements process is the *design of the work product*—be it durable goods, information services, or administrative output—which, as will be seen later, is closely followed by the *design of the process* (or its updating). The product design effort leads to the work product *specifications* which represent the *third of five key documents* in the quality management effort (Figure 6-1).

In business and industry the traditional relationship between the requirements and design efforts was *serial*: first, the requirements statement was produced and submitted to the product designers. The work product design effort then followed as a repetitive process through the various design reviews, redesigns, and final approval for implementation. In today's world of sophisticated requirements and complex work product solutions, but more importantly because of quality considerations, a more effective approach to producing specifications is a *parallel*, joint effort with the requirements creation and review process. The coupling of the requirements and design efforts is made possible by the appropriate guidelines, procedures, and communication mechanisms in a total quality management environment where requirements are considered to be an integral part of managing intent and, as such, a subprocess in the overall process under consideration.

The introduction phase also sees the establishment of the *measurement system,* specifically: the units of measure and the related process variables are defined; measuring devices, sensors, and instruments are selected, purchased, installed; and the various parameters of the management system, such as accuracy, precision, and the like, are determined. Gauge analysis helps identify the magnitude of the measurement error which is inherent in the measurement system installed for the process.

The predictive aspects of the appraisal/test activities include the *product design test plan*, which is the formal framework for reviewing the work product specifications and predicting key parameters which may affect quality in the finished product, such as reliability and serviceability. At this point, the selection of statistical design aids also takes place, along with some universal planning tools for both process analysis and design. The design of the work product is aided by Pareto analysis, project management, and control tools such as Gantt charts and PERT diagrams. Among the statistical aids for prevention are those related to the analysis and prediction of failures and failure rates for manufactured products (reliability prediction): frequency distributions, probability paper, control charts, and, if needed, certain advanced statistical techniques.

> In the analysis of both common and special causes of variations, the Pareto principle is equally applicable: A few factors will usually account for most of the total problem, while the remaining contributors, however many, account for only a small part. This principle is especially important in the initial sizing of a problem because it defines priorities for the improvement projects and highlights that the improvement effort should be deployed disproportionately over the various functions, departments, products, and other components of the process.

Process capability prediction is an important aid during process design: the parameter known as *process tolerance* is specified in advance and then, upon completion of the design effort, attempts are made at predicting the process capability which is an anticipated characteristic of the *process in operation*. Such predictions can be based on the completed process design, process simulation, laboratory experiments, or observation data derived from a preproduction testing of the process itself. In any case, process capability prediction is part of *prevention;* the determination of actual process capability is part of *control* whereas actions upon the process, resulting in process capability improvements, again belong to the management of *intent*.

Thus, process capability, as an inherent process characteristic, can be viewed as the bridge between prediction and correction, intent and outcome. As a parameter of actual process performance, it can be measured during the detection phase; as an inherent operating characteristic of the process, it can first be established during the process design phase and then improved through changes to the process during the process adjustment phase.

Once statistical design aids have been selected, the methodology for calculating process capability is put in place.

Management of Outcome. As key concepts related to the term *control* are discussed in terms of their implementation, the reader should be reminded that this term is used in two specific contexts:

(1) *Quality control* is synonymous with the management of outcome and comprises the specific sets of activities which make up detection and correction.
(2) *Process control* is a subset of quality control and comprises the activities aimed at the detection and elimination of special causes of variations in the process, which in turn leads to *statistical control*: a stable and predictable state of the process.

The *process plan*, discussed below includes: (1) measurement system, (2) process control methodology, (3) process capability methodology, (4) procedures for requirements acceptance and assurance, and (5) criteria for requirements adaptability.

Within quality control it is *detection* that is being actively pursued during the introductory phase—specifically, defect identification and defect-cause analysis. Both of these, in turn, require the use of statistical control tools, mainly in the form of data analysis (frequency distributions, tally diagrams, statistical calculations), control charts, and statistical inference (estimation and, occasionally, test of hypothesis).

The analysis of data, obtained from process observations and measurements, leads to defect discovery and identification. Control charts establish the presence of special causes and the extent of common causes, and defect-cause analysis is used to establish the true linkage between causes and variations. A supporting *controllability study* separates special (worker controllable) causes from common causes of variation.

The first criterion for worker self-control: the workers' knowledge of what they are expected to do commonly derives from the following key sources:

• Work product specifications: Usually a written document, such as standards, a sample work product, or other tangible definition of the end result to be achieved.
• Process plan or specification: Again, a written document comprised of specific instructions (verbal or written) or other definition of the means by which the end result is to be attained.
• The definition of responsibilities: Decisions to be made, actions to be taken and by whom.

It is management's responsibility to ensure that these sources exist and jointly contribute to the knowledge required. In many cases, checklists are developed to ensure that they exist and have been clearly communicated.

For self-control, the second criterion is that workers have the means of knowing whether their performance conforms to specifications or not. Although in some situations the normal human senses are sufficient to establish this knowledge, in most contemporary, complex product and service situations, human senses must be supplemented by a well-designed and implemented measurement system, including appropriate instrumentation.

Where workers are expected to use instruments to carry out measurements on the work product, it is of course necessary to provide them with the appropriate training. The more complex the measurement system and associated instrumentation, the more important it is to motivate workers to obtain the necessary education and follow instructions so that measurements are carried out in a consistent and reliable manner. Where workers do not have access to the instruments themselves, arrangements must be made for feedback of the essential performance data from someone who has the responsibility for the actual measuring. To meet the criteria for good feedback, modern technology is used, most notably computers for analyzing and summarizing data and work stations for presenting the results on an individualized basis.

The third criterion for self-control is the ability of workers to adjust their performance to meet specifications. This is achieved either through action on the work product (output) or through action on the process.

Adjusting the *process* requires the presence of a number of management-controllable factors, the most important of which are:

- The process must respond to adjustment in a predictable, cause-and-effect manner.
- The process must be capable of operating within given tolerances.
- Workers must know (that is, must be trained in) the use of procedures and mechanisms for process adjustments, the reasons behind them, and the results to be expected. (If the process requires close interaction between humans and other inanimate components such as equipment or materials, the definition of process capability must include certain capabilities attributed to the human element, among them, strength, attention span, responsiveness, and the like.)

Additionally, a study of management-controllable defects is carried out to determine their distribution within the process, or among the various organizational or functional units associated with the process. In most cases Pareto analysis is used to support this study.

Concurrent with the defect identification work deriving from data analysis, a *problem analysis* effort is undertaken using other sources of information such as end-user complaints, and other problem-solving techniques (group brainstorming or quality circles, for example) to provide further defect identification. One basic technique here is the *listing* of basic user data in order of importance. Typically, such listings appear in forms such as complaint rate by customer, unit or total repair cost by product type, unit repair cost by defect type, and so on. Obviously, the principal purpose of these listings is to permit further analysis by Pareto methods. Since detection in this phase focuses on identifying the causes of defects, problem analysis takes the form of cause/effect studies, supported by suitable analytical tools, such as *Ishikawa-diagrams*.[4]

---

[4]For a more detailed description of Ishikawa-diagrams, see [18] in the Bibliography. See also E. Kindlarski, "Ishikawa Diagrams for Problem Solving," *Quality Progress*, December 1984, pp. 26–30.

Another defect identification technique is the analysis of *external failure costs*, a standard category within the cost of quality. This category is made up of such cost elements as labor, parts, supplies, travel, and so on. These cost analyses are useful primarily to justify prevention programs as a matter of cost trade-off against repair expenditures in the field.

In the measurement and prediction of future failure rates and field performance, another useful technique is the *cumulative defect analysis*. This requires the dating of products to show when they were produced, sold, and installed, and when defects were detected. The concept of using the cumulative approach to data analysis has an even wider application: a related technique for predicting future performance is the concept of *growth curves*. This is based on the assumption that product performance will improve ("grow") with time, as a result of continuing quality improvement.[5]

The concluding activity of detection during the introductory phase is the *correctability analysis* to assess the feasibility of removing the causes of variation from the process components identified earlier during defect-cause analysis. The approach of correctability analysis is different for special causes and common causes of variation: the former may be removed through action on the output or the process, or both; the latter are always removed as a result of action upon the process.

> Special causes may be indicated by the sudden appearance of observations (data points) outside the control limits of a control chart. These may be caused by a minimum number of individual factors, resulting in sudden change but usually easily eliminated—by either workers or management. On the other hand, common (root) causes may manifest themselves by certain patterns (runs) within the control limits of a control chart. These may be the result of many individual causes, resulting in a chronic process condition; such causes are more difficult to eliminate and always require management action upon the process. Similarly, the causes of divergence can be eliminated only on the basis of management trade-offs and decisions which may result in changes to the inputs of the process.

Within *process control*, measures are taken to put process management in the position of not only removing defects during initial implementation but also removing special causes of variation, thereby bringing the process under statistical control as the overall objective of the commitment stage. Accordingly, procedures and tools are put in place, skills and resources are committed and schedules established for *remedial actions* during initial implementation. Of the statistical control tools, control charts are the prime support devices for the detection of special causes of variation. Supported by the results of the correctability study, quality management is positioned for corrective action during the next phase: initial implementation.

---

[5]For further detail and reading, see J. M. Juran and F. M. Gryna, Jr., *Quality Planning and Analysis* (New York, NY: McGraw-Hill Book Co., 1980), p. 485.

One of the key objectives of quality management during the introductory phase is to establish the *cost of quality database* for the process. Accordingly, data gathering for all cost of quality elements (failure cost, appraisal, and prevention costs) starts at an early point in time. Activities related to the cost of quality are concluded during the introductory phase by establishing cost measurements and reporting on the *cost of failure* in the process, to support the other concurrent activities of problem analysis, defect identification, and defect-cause analysis.

The cost of quality is the one key measurement that ties not only the various process components together but also bridges quality management and process optimization within the same process. It further links one process to the others, as well as to the overall management of the business; however, basic definitions and accounting instructions related to the definition and capturing of the cost of quality must emanate from the *management system* (which we understand as the general management of the business) so that consistent terminology and measurements are used throughout the company. This is particularly important with regard to the definition of and the distinction among the major cost of quality categories, including the cost of failure, appraisal, and prevention. The accounting systems of most business enterprises or organizations are not initially structured to accommodate these cost categories, which need to be developed and defined for the particular business and work product. Once this is done, the continuing task for accounting and financial management will remain the keeping and reporting of consistent cost of quality data within processes and across the business enterprise as new developments and technological and process changes necessitate further refinement, modification, and enhancement of the cost of quality structure and database.

INITIAL IMPLEMENTATION PHASE

Management of Intent. As the title suggests, all that was established and put in place during the introductory phase is put into *operation* the first time in the initial implementation phase. In other words, the introductory phase represents *deployment*; the initial implementation phase is the *startup* of all the activities required for total quality management and the preparatory phase for process optimization.

Within the *requirements process*, procedures for requirements acceptance are established and criteria are approved for requirements adaptability, that is, the management of future changes to the original end user requirements.

Based on the requirements acceptance procedures contained in the process plan, implementation of the measurement system includes establishing the *quality of requirements*. Along with this, the *quality of design* is also determined, which is in turn based on the *product design review* held as part of the appraisal/test activities earlier during this phase.

Based on the process capability measurement and calculation methodologies established during the previous phase, and using the process observations and measurement data gathered so far, *process capability calculations* are carried out to establish the actual value of this parameter for further analysis, assessment, and potential management action for improvement. Of the statistical design aids selected during the introductory phase, prime use is given to those supporting process capability measurements, for example, control charts and data analysis methods aimed at establishing the extent of common causes of variation in the process.

Process improvement using control charts is essentially an *iterative* procedure, repeating the three fundamental phases of the cycle:

(1) Observation and measurements: The process is run and data are gathered from observations and measurements made on the process output. (These data might represent measured dimensions, percentage of assemblies failing electrical test, the number of typographical errors in a document, the number of defects on a printed circuit board, and the like.) Data are converted to a form which can be plotted on a control chart.

(2) Control: Parameters known as *control limits* are calculated from the process output data; they represent the amount of variation that could be expected if only variation from common causes were present in the output. The control limits are drawn on the control chart as a guide to further analysis. (Control limits reflect the inherent variability of the process; they are not objectives.) Data are then compared with the control limits to determine whether special causes of variation are present, or whether the variation is stable and appears to come only from common causes. (Defect-cause analysis is used to further identify the special causes present in the process.) After appropriate, mostly local, corrective actions have been taken, further observations and measurements are made, data are collected, control limits recalculated if necessary, and any additional special causes studied and removed. At this point all uncontrolled variation has been eliminated and the process is considered to be operating in a state of *statistical control*.

(3) Process capability: Once the process is in statistical control, the capability of the process can be assessed; namely, the extent of variation from common causes. If this is excessive, the process itself must be investigated and corrective management action must be taken to improve it.

For continuing process improvement, these three phases are repeated on an on-going basis.

If applicable, performance objectives for work product reliability, availability, and serviceability are established during the initial implementation phase, based on the analysis of process observations and measurements gathered throughout the introductory phase. The statistical control tools selected for the support of quality management earlier are brought to bear on this problem, particularly data analysis and statistical inference.

The initial implementation phase sees the planned startup of activities related to correction: *defect removal* and *defect-cause removal*, as related to special causes of variation in the process. Just as problem analysis, defect identification, and defect-cause analysis were in the introductory phase, defect removal and special defect-cause removal in the implementation phase are "bottoms-up" activities: They start at the lowest levels of the organization. The basic vehicle of implementation is the individual worker; the team assigned to a single, defined task; or members of a department managed by a first-line manager. In this fashion a one-to-one linkage is established between individually identifiable defects and those responsible for their detection and elimination. Also, the commitment to quality assumes a real-life, definable, and measurable meaning with targets established both in terms of numbers and schedules. The ultimate objective of defect-cause removal in the initial implementation phase is to *remove all worker-controllable defects and their causes*. This "modus operandi" will continue throughout the entire quality improvement effort as far as individual employees are concerned; the aggregate effect, however, is the stabilization of the entire process, which thus will be under statistical control and therefore capable of continuing improvement at the completion of the commitment stage.

At this point those special causes of defects are removed which are worker-controllable and can be accessed through local action—in other words, which do not require management action on the process itself. The removal of the special causes of defects represents the *second half of the defect elimination cycle* (DEC). There are several possible approaches to this; the *four-step scheme* to be described here has been tried in several industrial and business processes.[6]

Since action on the output and action on the process are not necessarily sequential events but may proceed in parallel, it is convenient to define correction in those terms which are common to both output- and process-related actions of defect-cause removal. In this representation, then, correction is divided into four steps.

The purpose of *Step A* is to take the defect cause defined in defect-cause analysis and describe the conditions that will exist when that cause has been removed. That final condition of the process is defined as the "objective." The intermediate levels on the way toward meeting the objective are known as targets. Step A output is expressed in terms of objectives, targets, and time schedules. These should contain both quantitative and qualitative parameters, which are compatible with the desired future state. The output should reflect the following improvements:

• A *reduction in defects*, primarily as a result of reductions in rework, errors, and delinquencies. The term *craftsmanship* is sometimes used to impart the added notion that trying to do things better is necessary to meet competition and also to provide individual fulfillment—a matter of professionalism. "Better" can mean more func-

---

[6]For each step in the DEC there exists a set of tools and techniques—which fall into three categories:
  • Process analysis tools (CSF, DAA, SA, PAT)
  • Data analysis and presentation tools (tally sheets, scatter diagrams, cause/effect diagrams, frequency distributions, control charts, Pareto)
  • Process control/process improvement tools (simulation, pilot programs, control charts, trend charts, statistical control techniques)

tion, higher reliability, improved aesthetics, and the like. It also means anticipating a change in requirements, the inevitable result of progress.

- *Improved user satisfaction*, which is based on the assumption that user requirements are clear to all concerned parties, including the method by which process output will be measured against those requirements. This does not imply that requirements are static; rather that the targets are agreed upon with the user for both content and schedule.
- *Improved efficiency* (reduced cost for each unit of output), meaning the reduction of resources that are consumed in adding value to an input.
- *Improved productivity* (increased quality output for each dollar invested), meaning added value with less than a proportional increase in cost. (For instance, a 150 percent increase in revenue with a 30 percent increase in expenses; or a 30 percent improvement in product shipments without adding direct product costs.)

Definition of a measurement plan is the last action taken in Step A. Its main purpose is to confirm the feasibility of achieving the targets that have been established.

The purpose of *Step B* (selection) is to take the defect cause identified by DCA and select the most effective solution for its removal. The list of ideas for corrective action can be narrowed using data analysis techniques. Because this step usually develops a large number of alternatives, it is useful to classify the ideas *before selection* into such categories as incentives, procedural, information, and the like. Alternatives can then be quickly consolidated or eliminated through the application of decision matrices or other methods. The last action in Step B is to check to see that the proposed alternative solutions are directly supportive of the future state defined in Step A.

The purpose of *Step C* (solution) is to use the solution selected in Step B to produce an implementation plan, a detailed measurement plan, and a management commitment of resources and schedules to proceed. The last step in Step C is the actual execution of the implementation plan.

The purpose of *Step D* (process feedback) is to observe and track the results of the implementation, communicate the results to all interested parties and provide feedback into the process for the purposes of resetting it at an improved level, with defect causes removed and thus, their recurrence prevented. If all the targets have been reached, the new state of the process will become the new process itself, with problem solutions integrated into the normal business flow. The choice now exists either to set higher quality targets (restate requirements and, consequently, specifications) or maintain the new state of the process but introduce changes in productivity and efficiency objectives. In either case, a new quality management situation arises, where both intent and outcome have been redefined and must be managed accordingly.

During the initial implementation phase the *cost of quality* becomes a reporting tool over the *full range* of its cost categories. In regular intervals (monthly or quarterly) during this phase the major categories of the cost of quality are tracked and reported along with trends and incremental changes. This information will serve as useful input to cost of quality *analysis* and trade-off decisions later. The accurate capturing and tracking of the cost of quality data in the commitment stage is extremely important, both in absolute and relative terms. As suggested earlier, the introduction of a quality improvement effort requires nontrivial investment of resources at the outset which should be included in the total cost of quality as the quality management effort matures. Most of the activities emanating from the management system as well as those discussed under the management of intent will, obviously, be accounted for under the cost of prevention. Similarly, activities related to the gathering of data for the cost of quality database qualify under the cost of prevention. Almost without exception all the other activities under the management of outcome, carried out during the initial implementation phase, fall into the cost of appraisal category. The only exceptions are activities related to defect removal (remedy): they represent cost of failure.

6.1.3 Process Management for Commitment

Although technically speaking, process management encompasses both major ingredients of quality management—prevention and control—and all aspects of the defect elimination cycle, only those aspects will be discussed in this section which command the direct attention of the process owner and which are also visible to the general management of the business:

- Process design
- Work process implementation
- Process ownership
- Process management tools
- Process measurements (effectiveness, efficiency, and productivity)
- Process optimization

INTRODUCTION PHASE

The commitment stage from a process management standpoint will be different depending on whether (1) already existing and reasonably well-defined processes will have to be selected or (2) new processes defined, designed, and assembled for quality improvement. Most probably, however, most enterprises will find themselves in a position where a combination of the two cases will occur, namely, some existing processes can be selected for the more disciplined process management approach, while new ones will have to be established to help the enterprise focus on heretofore neglected or "untapped" areas.

The two approaches will eventually converge in the consolidation stage where a redesign effort may be needed to improve an already existing process. On occasion, a newly designed process will, due to unforeseen operational conditions, also have to be adjusted or even redesigned to meet new requirements.

The design of a *new work process* begins with an analysis of the user requirements in terms of business objectives and the definition of process activities which already exist or would have to be newly created, along with the needed process components—material and human. This analysis will also attempt to answer such basic questions as compatibility with basic policies and business goals of the enterprise, technical feasibility, financial viability, availability of trained skills and other resources, and so on.

The process analysis activities described above are usually supported by suitable analytical tools, such as DAA,[7] SA, and PAT. These tools are designed to help develop a structured description of the process, usually in terms of its inputs and outputs, information flow, activities with their component tasks, sometimes including volume and time-dependent factors and variables.

A satisfactory process analysis is followed by the *process design* effort, which describes in detail the basic components needed for implementing the process: people, procedures, materials, equipment, information, and energy. The process design also describes the various activities, their sequences and interrelationships, into which the various components have to be organized within the process. The tangible result of process design is the *process plan*, which is the *fourth of five key documents* in the process management effort (Figure 6-1).[8]

In general terms, the process plan describes *how* the process is supposed to operate, its basic form (departmental, tree, or serial), and its key measurements. The process plan also includes the measurement system for the process, as well as for the work product, methodologies for determining process control and process capability parameters, the procedures for requirements acceptance, the parallel development of requirements and specifications, and the criteria for requirements adaptation and change. In short, *the process plan is the process owner's blueprint for process management.*

The selection of *existing work processes* for total quality management is preceded by a less comprehensive analysis of the user requirements and a review of already existing, related business processes. This analysis is followed by a *selection procedure* in which business processes, the key to attaining identified business goals and quality objectives, are selected for the disciplined implementation of the process management approach. Although these processes may have been in existence and operation for some time, the new process management discipline may require a redefinition or a more formal, accurate, and complete documentation in the form of an *updated process plan* if one already did exist. In any case, the end result of work process selection for quality management is a *deployed work process*, described by a newly created or updated process plan.

In the case of newly designed processes, the rest of the initial implementation phase is taken up with their deployment. For processes which have already been in existence and which have been selected for continuing quality improvement, their full deployment is assumed at the *beginning* of the initial implementa-

---

[7]For a more detailed description of DAA, refer to "DAA, Everyone Can Use It," *Directions*, December 1984, pp. 19–20.

[8]Process design normally takes up a considerable portion of the introduction phase and the process plan may only be completed well into the initial implementation phase.

tion phase. With that, the entire commitment phase is shorter in time for enterprises which require little or no new process design effort.

One of the key events of process management during the introduction phase is the designation of a *process owner* for each selected or newly designed process. The owner, in turn, devotes most of his/her time during the introduction phase to the planning and deployment of the management mechanisms (such as the process office) for implementing total process management.

INITIAL IMPLEMENTATION PHASE

The process management system is primarily concerned with establishing the infrastructure for managing the process—specifically, process management council, the process office and their supporting functions (communications, information systems, finance, professional quality staff, and so on). By definition, these support functions should not represent an internal resource addition, as they are provided through the *directed* assignment of already existing capabilities from the traditional organization. While during the introductory phase management tools were used primarily in support of process *description*, during initial implementation tools of an *analytical* nature are required which can also capture and describe time-dependent changes within the process for the purpose of improvement. The PAT is one such tool which is finding increased acceptance and use as process improvements get under way as an organized, systematic activity.[9]

The definition and quantification of process attributes is another important task undertaken in this phase:

- *Effectiveness* relates to process status and the capability of improvement to produce defect-free output. The essence of effectiveness is (1) a stable process—that is, one which is in statistical control and (2) a process for which there exist adequate data and methodologies for determining process capability. The quantification of effectiveness is based on the assumption that there are no special causes of variation present and common causes are at the minimum level achievable without further major change to the process.[10]

- *Efficiency* and *productivity* are defined as *conformance at minimum cost,* and *increased conforming output at constant cost,* respectively. "Cost" in either case includes the cost of quality; the key task in quantifying these measurements is to establish the precise relationships between total cost (or unit cost) and the various elements within the cost of quality for analytical, cost trade-off and investment decision purposes. Depending on process

---

[9]For a more detailed description of PAT, refer to E. H. Melan, "Process Management in Service and Administrative Operations," *Quality Progress,* June 1985, pp. 52–59.

[10]"Major change" in this context means management-controllable change upon the process; it is assumed that all worker-controllable process changes have already been carried out.

makeup and the nature of its output, cost structures will vary greatly, as do the relationship and proportion of the various elements within the cost of quality. Relationships and linkages can be demonstrated through financial models and trend observations over time by the systematic variation of one cost element at a time, while observing and recording changes in the others.

- *Adaptability* is the inherent ability of the process to undergo change (as, for instance, in the deployment and relative role of such process components as people, equipment, and materials) without adverse impact on effectiveness and efficiency.[11]

6.2 Stage Two: Manage Quality

The second stage in the evolution toward maturity is also known as *consolidation*. It derives its name from the fact that the major components of quality management (prevention and control) and the organizational, design, and measurement aspects along with supporting activities of process management are consolidated, fully developed, and operational under the umbrella of process management. The only further outstanding objective is to improve the return on the investment in prevention on the *quality side*, as efficiency and productivity are improved on the *process side*, as a result of process optimization.

Requirements for *reaching* the consolidation stage are:

- The process is fully deployed, in operation, and in statistical control.
- The completed defect elimination cycle—the full "quality template"—is in place.
- Data and methodology are in place for the calculation of process capability and the measurement of process effectiveness.
- The process is assessed to be operating at rating level "4."

Some of the expected *results* of the consolidation stage are:

- All common causes of variation are removed from the process.
- Process output is in conformance to requirements.
- Vendors are part of process control; they are included in defect-cause analysis and removal.
- The cost of quality is used as a reporting and analytical tool so that quality management is achieved by cost trade-off (including vendors).
- Process efficiency and productivity are measured, tracked, and reported.
- Process certification is complete, and the owner is part of the overall business management system.

---

[11]Although this definition does not relate adaptability directly to process productivity, it can be shown that if efficiency can be held constant during change, productivity can always be improved from this base.

• Quality-related factors and measurements are routinely included in the performance evaluation of all managers.

6.2.1 The Management System for Consolidation

Procedures and guidelines are established for the *measurement* of process performance by the process owner for purposes of *process certification*. This becomes the *last of the five key documents* of quality management and its completion fully integrates the process owner and with it, process management, into the overall business management system. Process certification is subject to subsequent audit by company auditors who now follow a systematic *process audit* approach, as opposed to the traditional compliance-oriented audits of individual organizations, locations, or functions (for example, cash position, security and safety, inventory level, and so on).

During the consolidation stage, process performance assessment is expected to improve from rating level "4" to "3."

From an *organizational* standpoint, consolidation sees vendors and suppliers become part of the process organization and of quality management, particularly its control aspects (that is, the defect elimination cycle).

In the *personnel management* area, quality objectives, measurements, and indicators are made part of all managers' performance plans and evaluations. This means that quality management has entered the "management fabric" and has begun to be integrated into the traditional set of business and performance measurements.

6.2.2 Quality Management for Consolidation

Management of Intent. The prerequisite for starting consolidation is that the process is in statistical control, with all special causes of variation removed from it through combined action by management and workers on the output. Improvements to process capability can now be made by action on the process itself. At this point, only common causes of variation are present in the process. Their removal requires action on the process by either workers (where they have the ability and wherewithal to do so) or, more likely, by management. (A schematic representation of this concept is shown in Table 1-2.)

Management of Outcome. Throughout the consolidation stage, process control is maintained such that the process is continuing in a state of stability. Having removed all special causes of variation during the commitment stage, mechanisms and tools are in place (e.g., control charts) to routinely detect and eliminate any special causes of variation owing to unexpected and environmental changes, accidents, people problems, and the like. Problem handling is routinely handed down to the lower levels of the organization—more precisely, to the subprocess and task level. Process capabilities are well established and understood, and changes are routinely introduced without the risk of causing instability. When problems occur, the process is routinely returned to its state of minimum variability, that is, statistical control. Also, vendors are now routinely part of the process throughout the entire defect elimination cycle. As defect elimination focuses on common causes of variation, the relative weights of the causes in this category are again analyzed and determined by such tools as Pareto analysis. Detection and, especially the use of defect cause analysis (DCA) become routine both with respect to special and common causes of defects: they are part of the "management fabric."

During the consolidation stage, correction is aimed at full conformance, primarily by eliminating as many of the common causes of defects as possible, both in terms of process capability improvement and process change (adaptation), without impacting process efficiency or effectiveness. In terms of corrective action, the end objective of the consolidation stage is attained when any further changes to the process will begin to cause erosion of process efficiency or effectiveness. This objective is reached when variability of output, cost of quality, and process efficiency and effectiveness have been brought to a combined state of optimality, and when further improvement in process capability can only be achieved through major process redesign with no further impact on any of the other parameters. *This is the point when defect-free status (state of conformance) is reached.* The process is assessed to be operating at rating level "3."

The cost of quality is routinely used both as a reporting and an analytical tool for resource trade-off decisions in managing the optimal combination of prevention and control. All along during the consolidation stage the objective of quality management is to *reduce failure and appraisal cost to an absolute minimum*—consistent with the elimination of the majority of common causes of defects, and leading to the logical conclusion that if all causes (both special and common) of variation are removed then only prevention will continue actively using process resources. Consequently, the absolute magnitude of the cost of quality—which, by the way, now includes vendor cost of quality as well—*tends to approach its minimum level during the consolidation stage.*

6.2.3 Process Management for Consolidation

The consolidation stage means full focus on process management: its complete implementation along with full measurements and the *basics of process optimization* in place. This means that measurements on both efficiency and productivity are routinely produced, summarized, reported, and entered into a process optimization database. Reports are regularly generated for process management and general business review purposes; trends and changes in both efficiency and productivity are observed, tracked and analyzed, and compared with corresponding changes in the cost of quality (see Figures 5-1 and 6-2).

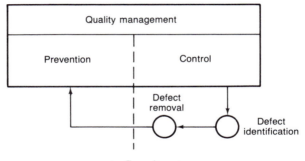

a. Commitment.

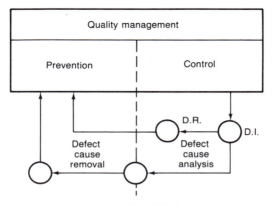

b. Consolidation.

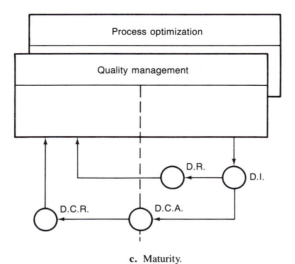

c. Maturity.

Fig. 6-2. Process management implementation model.

In the area of *process design*, the tools of simulation and experimentation are routinely used to determine the effects of proposed and approved actions on the process and changes to its design.

Because process controls are fully implemented, the result is a stable process which is under continuing improvement as a result of actions taken on the basis of continuing process capability measurements and analyses.

At the outset of the consolidation stage, the process management system requirement was the full implementation of process ownership, with the corresponding organization (process management council, process office) also in place. Toward the end of the consolidation stage, process ownership as a management function and control mechanism becomes fully integrated into the overall business management system, partially by means of process certification and partially through the reported results of process optimization, that is, efficiency and productivity. At this point process optimization is implemented for purposes of reporting and analysis, and is ready for improvement and incorporation into the overall business plan—objectives and measurements—in the next stage of maturity.

During the consolidation stage, process measurements are in fact used to enhance process readiness for full integration into the management system:

- Ability to produce fully conforming output.
- Efficiency and productivity measured and also linked to the cost of quality and total process cost.
- Adjustments and changes to the process routinely made in the course of eliminating management-controllable defects, while maintaining its effectiveness and efficiency.

It should be noted that consolidation is the one stage in which some of the *leading* American enterprises and business organizations find themselves today. Depending on the size of the organization and the nature of its business, it may take years, if not a decade or more, through the consolidation stage before full and pervasive quality management *maturity* can set in.

6.3 Stage Three: Quality—A Way of Life

Maturity is attained when both major components of process management—quality and process optimization—are fully operational, in balance, and tied together by common measurements, such as the cost of quality.

The key requirements for *reaching* the maturity stage are:

- Completed process certification
- Routine quality management by cost trade-off
- A state of conformance in the process output that can further be improved only through major process redesign

The expected *results* of the maturity stage are:

* Balanced and combined management of quality by return on investment in prevention
* Process optimization with established links between the cost of quality, total process cost, efficiency, and productivity
* "Best of breed" processes

6.3.1 The Management System for Maturity

The procedures and practices in force ensure that quality objectives and measurements form an integral part of the overall company *business plan*. The cost of quality is included—both as an objective and a business measurement. Continuing quality improvements are built in as matter of business planning. The process is assessed to be operating at rating levels "2" to "1" throughout the maturity stage.

During this stage, *personnel management* moves to include quantitative and specific quality measurements in the performance evaluations of *all* employees assigned to the various business processes. Quality education is continuing on a routine basis, conveying new results to all concerned and maintaining the high level of general quality education and skill training to keep up with turnover and the assignment of new employees and managers to the processes.

The cost of quality is used primarily as a leverage on productivity and profitability and, accordingly, as an *investment tool* for continuing improvement in both process productivity and efficiency. The linkage between the cost of quality and productivity improvements is quantified in terms of financial and resource indicators. The contribution of quality to productivity and profitability, therefore, is also part of the business management process, as they directly contribute to the "bottom line" through established linkages to traditional business measurements, such as revenue, volumes, product cost, inventory, asset turn, profit, and so on.

6.3.2 Quality Management for Maturity

Management of Intent. In the maturity stage the quality management effort is dominated by, and with the the the passage of time approaches, *pure prevention.*

Process capability is consistently improved to new process tolerance limits. (These had earlier been enhanced and improved through major redesign to meet changing user requirements.) During this stage all common causes of variation are absent through consistent and continued action on the process and as a result, the process is producing defect-free output on a *consistently predictable* basis. Vendors, by definition, are part of process capability improvement and, hence, of continued quality improvement.

The cost of quality is used primarily as an investment tool, and quality management is essentially *management by return on investment in prevention.* In absolute terms, the cost of quality is the amount which represents the cost of conformance. (Again, the total cost of quality includes vendor cost as a matter of course.)

Management of Outcome. Investment in process control is greatly reduced, since process redesign has resulted in a situation where all special causes of variation have not only been removed but the emergence of any new ones is prevented through appropriate mechanisms in the process itself.

Beyond prevention, the cost of nonconformance approaches zero in the maturity stage. The process itself is enhanced to include increased emphasis and reliance on end user feedback, and the use of service data to measure conformance to requirements, in addition to reliance on defect prevention at earlier points within the process. *The process is a true, user-driven preventive system.*

6.3.3 Process Management for Maturity

With a major investment having been made in process redesign at the conclusion of the consolidation stage, a new and improved *process plan* signals the onset of maturity. In terms of resource deployment and the arrangement of process components, the new process mirrors the enhanced orientation of quality management toward full prevention. As a result, the work process now being implemented also shows improvements not only in terms of producing defect-free output but also in terms of maximum efficiency and productivity. Consequently, it can be rated as "best of breed" with respect to all similar (competing) processes.

The process management system is now known as *total process management*, a concept which combines quality management and process optimization as a single management task, functioning on the basis of established common measurements and totally integrated resources, communications, and organization. It is a pervasive way of life within the total business enterprise.

During the maturity stage, process management has the clearly stated objective that any redesigned version of the process, while producing defect-free output, should also operate at a higher level of effectiveness and efficiency than its predecessor version. This, in fact, is one of the fundamental differences between consolidation and maturity. In consolidation, adaptability objectives were limited to *maintaining* efficiency and effectiveness; in maturity, process changes resulting in defect-free output must go hand-in-hand with *improvements* in process optimization as well.

It should be pointed out that the maturity stage of quality management represents a "never-ending," continuing improvement effort, both in the theoretical and practical sense. Very few, if any, enterprises in American business have attained this level of performance so far. Nevertheless, by virtue of its quantifiable objectives and measurability of results, the maturity stage is worth striving for because *it is the assured state of maximum profits and competitive position, as determined by quality and optimal levels of productivity.*[12]

---

[12]The recognized linkage between quality and productivity has recently resulted in proposed approaches to their *integrated management*. See [12] in the Bibliography.

DISCUSSION QUESTIONS

1. Name the three basic steps required for continuing quality improvement in each of its major stages. Give at least two examples for each step—preferably each in a different stage.

2. Name the two phases of the commitment stage. Describe key activities in each.

3. Describe the three key publication activities during the introduction phase. Explain the purpose and rationale for each.

4. Name and describe the key elements of the organization for quality during the introduction phase.

5. Describe the three basic forms of quality education. Explain their purpose and role and discuss implementation aspects.

6. Describe, in your own words, the basic aspect of the initial implementation phase.

7. Explain the concept of common implementation. Why is this the preferred approach to quality management?

8. Describe the process performance rating scheme used for process assessment. Explain the conceptual meaning of each rating level "5" to "1."

9. Discuss quality circles. Are they a mandatory or a necessary ingredient of the quality improvement program—or are they just an organizational alternative?

10. Name and briefly describe the five key documents of quality improvement.

11. Define the terms *quality control* and *process control*. Explain the difference between them.

12. Discuss how the cost of quality, as one key measurement, ties together the various process components.

13. Name the key "bottom up" correction activities in the introductory and implementation phases of quality improvement. What is the ultimate objective of defect removal and elimination?

14. What corrective action takes place in the second half of the defect elimination cycle? Discuss the four-step scheme used, in terms of the purpose of the activities and the output of each of these steps.

15. Discuss the various process management-related activities in the introduction and initial implementation phases. In your discussion examine the situation with already existing and defined processes, as well as the one where new processes must first be identified and defined.

16. What are the key items in a process plan? Describe, in your own words, what the process plan is and its role in process management.

17. Define the process attributes *effectiveness*, *efficiency*, and *adaptability*. What is the difference between efficiency and productivity? Give at least one specific example of a measurement applicable to each.

18. What are the requirements for entering the consolidation stage? What are some of the key results expected in this stage?

19. Discuss the procedural, organizational, and personnel management aspects of the management system for consolidation.

20. What is the purpose of prevention (management of intent) during the consolidation stage?

21. Discuss quality control (management of outcome) during the consolidation stage, in terms of special causes, problem handling, process capability, and corrective actions. What is the prime objective of quality management during the consolidation stage?

22. What does the consolidation stage mean in terms of process management? What are the basics of process optimization?

23. What are process measurements used for during the consolidation stage?

24. Discuss, in your own words, the conditions under which maturity in quality management can be attained. What are the key requirements for reaching this stage?

25. What are the expected results of the maturity stage?

26. Discuss, in your own words, the major aspects of quality management (prevention and control) during the maturity stage. How is the cost of quality used? How would you characterize quality management from a business viewpoint during this stage? Why is financial investment in process control greatly reduced?

27. What is total process management? Describe it in your own words. What is the fundamental difference between consolidation and maturity in terms of the effectiveness and efficiency of the process?

28. What is the difference between consolidation and maturity in terms of process adaptability objectives?

29. What is the meaning of the maturity stage in terms of such business goals as low cost, productivity, profitability, and competitiveness? Discuss, in your own words, how total process management contributes to the attainment of these.

7

CASE STUDY IN QUALITY MANAGEMENT

7.1 Introduction

The purpose of the case study in this chapter is to illustrate, through a real-life business experience, the actual implementation of a quality improvement effort over time—from inception through the consolidation stage—where the process management approach is well established and functioning and where the establishment is well positioned for continued movement toward maturity. (In essence, this case study represents the actual implementation of the staged general progression described in Chapter 6.)

The case study is based on the quality improvement effort—and, primarily its management aspects—which was initiated at IBM Sterling Forest in 1980, moved into the consolidation stage in 1983, and has been continuing in the process management mode to the present time. Everything in the case study is based on events and activities that actually happened; a few results and their interpretations have been extrapolated in the interest of consistency with today's management philosophy and the terminology of this book, without compromising the integrity of business results or financial facts.

Sterling Forest is the home of several organizations within the IBM company. The one which is subject of this case study is the Information Systems Center, one of the largest and most concentrated collection of information systems professionals, data systems, and telecommunications equipment and supporting management infrastructure within IBM. The mission of the Center is that of an information servicer, primarily to users internal to IBM. This mission comprises such data services as software development, batch and on-line information processing services, and telecommunication services including network management and operation. Organizationally, the Center is part of one of IBM's product groups; however, in carrying out its mission it provides its products and services to a corporate and worldwide set of end users. Over the years the quality improvement effort at Sterling Forest involved between 500 and 800 employees at any given time.

For purposes of this case study, the Center will be treated as a "business establishment" because, for purposes of quality management, it has essentially behaved as an independent business unit, with self-contained measurements, dedicated resources, and a very low dependence on external inputs for achieving its objectives. Also, while the functional and organizational entities described in this study are real, some of the designations and the related job titles have been altered in order to achieve a "generic consistency" that also coincides with the terminology and definitions used elsewhere in the text. Note, however, that the term *initial implementation*, used in earlier chapters, has been replaced by *common implementation* to stay consistent with the original usage at the Center.

Present tense will be used throughout the case study, even though it covers events that have occurred over a number of years. What was learned over these years is described in detail in the material that follows.

One of the fundamental lessons learned at Sterling Forest—and this is also true for most organizations which have been through some form of quality improvement—is that *quality is a business process problem*, not merely a problem of quality control in engineering or production.

The second point learned is that quality is primarily a *people problem*—not a yield or productivity problem, although yield and productivity are part of it, especially in manufacturing. Neither is it a cost problem, although the cost of quality is a key management parameter in managing the overall process, or a problem of quality professionals, or the so-called "quality department." It is a *line management problem*, dealing primarily with the human element of the overall business process.

What we also know now is that while the objective of traditional quality improvement efforts has been to manage the outcome—for example, the finished products coming out of a manufacturing process or documents produced by a design or administrative organization—*modern quality management must focus on both the intent and the outcome*. This means that by managing the intent, management must also plan and invest and then begin again by managing changes to the process depending on the outcome. Modern quality management has become a full-circle, feedback-driven process management effort, as opposed to an after-the-fact approach of traditional quality control and product improvement.

Within the process management concept, the Sterling Forest experience showed that *the requirements process is part of managing the intent*; in fact, delineating the requirements is a vital ingredient of the overall quality management approach. If we accept the definition of quality as conformance to requirements, then quality can only be managed if the requirements process measures up to the standards of the rest of the management effort—that is, if it is treated and measured as part of the overall process.

Also, it is my belief that *the cost of quality is the key measurement and management tool* in the management of the overall process. This may seem somewhat controversial, especially in certain manufacturing circles, where there are people who will say that the cost of quality is one of many indicators, but certainly not the key management tool. My view is that the cost of quality allows managers, for the first time, to make meaningful and consistent trade-offs—because that is what management of resources is all about. The only way trade-offs and priority decisions can be made in managing quality is on the basis of cost, which is the common denominator to the many process ingredients management has to deal with. It is my contention that if the cost of quality is not used in this fashion, the entire quality management effort will be less than successful. One can have slogans, posters, education, and partial process management—such as defect tracking, reporting, and the like—but as a management effort, without the ability to manage resources through cost, it will be always out of control.

The organization for which the quality improvement effort was implemented is a straightforward functional organization, as shown in Figure 7-1. Top management of the establishment comprises the director, for whose position the term *general manager* will be used in the case study. Reporting to him were, at the outset of the quality improvement effort, eight functional managers, representing four line and four support functions:

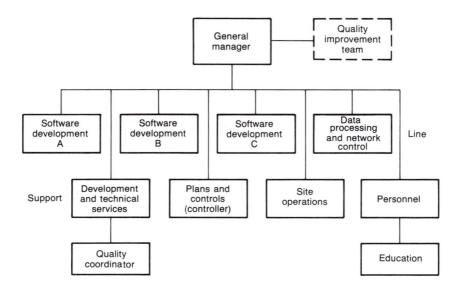

Fig. 7-1. Organizational structure of case study establishment (Sterling Forest).

- Software development A
- Software development B
- Software development C
- Data processing and network control center
- Development and technical services
- Plans and controls (controller)
- Personnel
- Site operations (engineering, maintenance, and security)

This functional organization endured through the years, with one exception: As the management focus on application development—especially in terms of quality and productivity measurements—increased and the first elements of a process management approach to applications development were introduced, the three application development functions were consolidated under a single, functional "super manager," responsible for the overall application development process throughout the establishment.

7.2 Commitment Stage

7.2.1 Management System

INTRODUCTION PHASE

In the wake of the food and energy shocks of the 1970s American business finds itself in an environment marked by increasingly fierce domestic and international cost-competitive pressures, rising inflation, and accelerating capital and labor costs. Alarmed by a declining productivity growth, growing unemployment, a deteriorating balance of payments, and an increasing percentage of foreign competitors in American markets, government officials, bankers, and business executives are looking for solutions to save our collective economic future.

While financial and technological measures aimed at improved productivity have been under way since the early to mid-1970s, it is recognized more and more that to stay competitive, as well as to fuel further productivity, the *quality* of American work products, whether destined for domestic markets or foreign, must also be improved by a significant margin.

Top management of the parent Corporation, as well as the general manager of the establishment have been focusing on the problems and challenges of quality for some time. The corporate-wide policy decision is now made to give quality top priority: "first among equals" when it comes to trade-offs against cost, schedule, or return on investment.

The quality improvement effort at the establishment starts with an *all-day meeting*, attended by the general manager, the heads of the eight functions that make up the establishment, and a representative of top Corporate management who introduces the subject, enunciates the Corporate quality policy, and outlines the general objectives and measurements related to quality management. The following additional subjects are on the agenda of this "quality improvement kickoff" meeting:

- *Motivational themes*: It is decided that for the entire employee population quality is to be presented as (1) a clearly stated business objective, to be pursued as a matter of "business survival" in the face of quality-oriented, cost-effective competition and as a direct contributor to improved profitability; and (2) a matter of attitude, not a staff assignment or temporary program; that is, the continuing pursuit of quality is never to end. In addition, managers are to be motivated by the new tools related to quality management, such as the cost of quality, which should further their ability to achieve their business objectives to the satisfaction of their users. To make this point, real-life case studies and examples are included in the management briefing material to show that it is always less costly to do "the job right the first time," and that there is clear evidence for the increasing cost leverage of prevention over appraisal, let alone over the correction of failures which have already occurred. Last but not least, an appeal is made to managers' intuitive recognition that there is a real quality leverage on productivity: One person's quality output contributes to the increase of the recipients' productivity.
- *Education plans*: These are drawn up for (1) the immediate education of all managers in "quality fundamentals"; (2) a corresponding education of all nonmanagerial employees, tailored to their individual functions and departmental activities and to be given by their first- and second-line managers over a period of two months; and (3) extended and more specialized training of selected individuals (such as the yet-to-be-named establishment quality coordinator and members of the quality improvement team, to be established as a result of the meeting) in quality management-related techniques, such as problem analysis, defect elimination, cost of quality accounting and reporting, and the like.
- *Action plan*: Agreement is reached on the initial steps to be taken for the introduction of the quality improvement program. These are to be: (1) the appointment of an establishment quality coordinator; (2) the naming of a quality improvement team; and (3) data gathering for the cost of quality data base and evaluation.
- *Implementation approach*: It is decided that the establishment will follow a "common" approach of implementation; that is, every function and every department within the organization will start its share of the quality improvement effort at the same time, using essentially the same methodologies and management objectives. The key common measurement for the establishment will be the *cost of quality*.

The common implementation approach is very important. Its "across the board" philosophy means that a pilot project is not initiated in one department "on speculation" and, depending on results, implemented elsewhere as well. In fact, if the cost of quality is accepted as one key common measurement for the entire organization, starting the quality improvement effort at the same time in every function and organization is the right decision and the only alternative, because without a common and consistently developed database for the cost of quality, the quality approach will not become the pervasive and effective management tool that it should be. Common implementation helps create the management system and supporting infrastructure to be really successful. It means everybody, from secretaries and administrative employees all the way to high-level technical professionals and top management, will be doing the same thing at the same time. Surely, as the quality management effort continues over the years, there will be inconsistencies and discontinuities; there will be some leaders and some stragglers; some inequities and some stagnation. But the intent is to *start* together across the board and continue in a coordinated, consistent, and measurable way as much as it is possible.

- *Process identification and ownership*: Through its common implementation phase, quality improvement will be based on departmental processes. That is, in terms of process management *each departmental organization will be considered a self-contained process.*[1] Accordingly, the process owner will be the respective department manager. (As will be seen later, the subsequent decision to define applications development as a pervasive business process will lead to reorganization and the reassignment of process ownership as well.)
- *Quality circles*: The departmental process management approach obviates the creation of separate quality circles. Each department is expected to act in a "bottoms-up" mode, that is, as a collection of professionals in their own right (including their manager), jointly addressing and resolving quality-related problems and thereby acting as a "quasi-quality circle."

Following the quality management kickoff meeting, the following two months are devoted to the implementation of the initial steps approved at the meeting.

The general manager and the eight functional managers participate in a three-day seminar on quality fundamentals provided by an outside consultant.[2] Based on the information obtained at the seminar, the general manager, together with the functional managers, the newly appointed quality coordinator, and a few financial and technical specialists, form an "education task force." This task force, over a four-week period, develops the quality education material to be given to all managerial and nonmanagerial employees within the establishment.

---

[1]A department comprises a first line manager and the employees—usually five to ten in number—reporting to him or her.

[2]Philip Crosby Associates, Winter Park, Florida.

While the task force is at work, the rest of the managers within the establishment (approximately 60 to 70 people) also attend, in groups of ten to 15, the quality seminar provided by the outside consultant. Upon their return, the quality education material is ready to be given out to the employees, which again constitutes another four-week period of training.

A *quality coordinator* for the establishment is appointed. While this position is not a managerial position and does not carry direct responsibility for the attainment of quality objectives, it is intended to be a formal staff function to carry out such administrative and coordinating activities as measurements and schedule tracking, assistance in issue identification and resolution, contact with outside quality activities, and so on. The quality coordinator reports to the functional manager of development and technical services, but functions informally as the "quality assistant" to the general manager. This person is also the "keeper" of the establishment's *quality control book*, which contains the establishment quality management plan and the schedule of all events related to quality management. (These include, for example, the quarterly cost of quality review meetings in the general manager's office, recognition events, meetings of the quality improvement team, and so on.)

The establishment *quality improvement team* (QIT) comprises one manager, preferably second-line, from each of the functions reporting to the general manager. Membership on the quality improvement team is based on a one-year assignment for each member. As mentioned earlier, the QIT is the highest level management body for issue resolution within the establishment. This is the reason for membership by second-line managers—the team is expected to make on-the-spot decisions as it works its way through the various interdepartmental and interfunctional issues that emerge in the course of managing problem identification, defect removal and elimination, the allocation of resulting costs, and so forth. The team also acts as the advisory body to the general manager in both setting direction and resolving issues at the highest level in the establishment. Team members carry out their normal management responsibilities without any significant change, and membership on the team is an additional responsibility to their normal managerial duties. (Experience over the years shows that QIT members spend approximately 15 to 20 percent of their total work time on matters related to quality improvement.)

Last but not least among the initial steps of introducing the quality improvement effort, *data gathering* for the common establishment of the *cost-of-quality database* commences within a few weeks after the quality management kickoff meeting. This work is carried out by financial analysts from the controller's department. The key task here is to augment the conventional accounting system by the various cost-of-quality categories: prevention, appraisal, and external and internal failure. At the same time, a financial planner establishes and publishes the related *definitions* so that each department manager, working with assigned financial analysts, can begin identifying cost elements related to any of the above cost of quality categories. By and large, the work related to the cost of quality is methodological at this point, and its purpose is to provide guidance and general direction to the various line organizations as they develop their cost-of-quality data in a "bottoms-up" mode.

With the initial steps implemented or under way and the education of the entire employee population on the fundamentals of quality completed, there are two management actions still required during the introductory phase: (1) the commitment of resources and (2) communications and recognition.

The quality improvement effort requires a preplanned commitment of resources in the following areas:

- Incremental workload resulting from management and staff assignments related to the introduction of the quality effort. This pertains to the quality coordinator and quality improvement team, data gathering for the cost-of-quality database, education (instruction and attendance), and the preparation of procedures, guidelines, measurement plans, and other employee communications.
- Workload (incremental or displaced) at the departmental process level, related to problem analysis, defect identification, cost-of-quality studies, and so on.
- Incremental workload in support functions, such as data processing, personnel, and site operations. From the outset, the cost-of-quality database is designed for an automated approach: The database is built and installed as part of the site administrative support system; it is accessible for updating by the controller's department and for on-line query by all managers with a "need to know" authorization. From a site operations standpoint, planning for Zero Defect Day requires the commitment of both people and financial resources to cover planning, logistics, audiovisuals, fees for outside speakers, and entertainment, just to mention a few key items.

These resource commitments become part of the establishment *quality plan* which is maintained and tracked by the quality coordinator. This individual is also responsible for either the direct safeguarding or the tracking and updating of the *five key documents* of quality management:

- Quality policy statement
- Requirements statements
- Work product specifications
- Establishment quality plan (later to become the process plan)
- Process certifications

A visible, sustained, and well-communicated *management commitment* to quality is critical for the success of the improvement effort. Such a commitment must be "top down" and credible by virtue of management's active presence and participation in all aspects of the effort, but especially where direction and decision making are required. This is a prerequisite for the motivation of all workers in the organization to commit their time, energy, and creativity to quality improvement. Of equal importance, especially during the introduction and initial implementation phases, is the *recognition* of leadership, creativity, and unusual achievements displayed by groups or individual employees. Thus the two important themes of communications are (1) what is expected and why, and (2) acknowledgment and recognition of accomplishments.

From the beginning, *communications channels* are utilized to get across these basic messages to the entire employee population; to communicate rules, guidelines, and procedures; and to report progress or the establishment of new objectives:

- *Site newspaper*: In addition to frequently published editorials on the subject of quality, a permanent column is set aside for quality-related reporting.
- *Defect tracking and removal charts*: Reflecting departmental progress in the identification, tracking, and elimination of key defects, these charts are on public display and are updated regularly by designated individuals from the respective departments.
- *"Quality Corner"*: A tableau installed in the main lobby of the establishment displaying the pictures of recent quality achievers. Every two to three months the pictures are replaced by those of new achievers.

Beyond these formal and permanent channels of communication, other means of recognition are also used on an ongoing basis: financial awards, recognition breakfasts and luncheons for individuals or groups, and so on.

COMMON IMPLEMENTATION PHASE[3]

From a management viewpoint, the common implementation phase has the following two key objectives:

(1) To establish the management system prerequisites for a systematic implementation of continuing quality improvement through the process management approach.
(2) To secure the commitment and participation of the entire employee population.

Toward the attainment of the first objective, a *process education plan* is drawn up to provide selected managers and workers with instruction in the basics of business process management, and the use of process analysis tools such as structured analysis (SA), departmental activity analysis (DAA), and process analysis tool (PAT). General guidelines are established for the selection of processes, the assignment of process owners, and process measurements (effectiveness, efficiency, and adaptability).

The commitment and participation of all employees is reaffirmed at a formal event known as Zero Defects Day (Commitment Day, or Defect-free Day). The format for this is a half-day "all hands" meeting, attended by top executives

---

[3]Referred to also as "initial implementation phase" in Chapter 6, and elsewhere in the book.

of the parent Corporation and invited guest speakers from the outside quality community. The prerequisites for this event are:

- Completion of all education in quality fundamentals
- Cost-of-quality database available for tracking and reporting purposes
- Completed problem analysis and defect identification work at the departmental process level
- Completed quality improvement plan in terms of defect removal/elimination objectives and schedules at the departmental level
- Communication channels established and functioning for measurements and reporting purposes
- Departmental processes identified and ownership assigned

7.2.2 Quality Management

INTRODUCTION PHASE

Since quality management is the sum total of managing intent and outcome—prevention and control—the key decision to be made relates to the *balance* of these two components of quality management.

During the introduction phase, the foundations are laid for preventive activities to be implemented as soon as information becomes available, from continuing cost-of-quality measurements and analysis to the type and magnitude of investments needed in prevention.

The first quality management activity to be undertaken is a review of the existing *quality-related experience base* within the establishment. Virtually every business organization or company has developed some, if limited, experience with inspection, sampling, accuracy checking, and other techniques of quality control—be it related to administration, production, or service.

In the case under study, the existence of a considerable body of quality-related experience is confirmed in two areas: applications development and data processing services.

Quality-related experience in software development comprises:

- Several years' experience in the "phased" development of software products, where the product in question moves through a number of well-identified and controlled *phases*, from inception through release and installation. The reviews, checks, and balances associated with this process (also known at the "phase review process") provide a ready-made framework to incorporate reviews and checkpoints related to defect elimination and cost-of-quality objectives.
- For several years the software development organizations have operated under a *design and code inspection* process. This includes recommended inspection of software design and the resulting code, by specially trained and selected review personnel. This is recognized as an important form of prevention to be built into the overall quality management scheme.

- Improved *technology*: programming techniques and development practices already in use will contribute further to the preventive aspect of overall quality management.

For several years prior to the introduction of quality improvement, the data processing center has been operating on the basis of "service-level agreements," which represent measurable performance targets committed to groups of users. Since service-level agreements are based on user requirements, meeting these targets should represent "quality service." In addition, the data processing center has, for some time, used several measurements to track workload buildup and equipment utilization—to provide feedback for future capacity planning. Again, using quality management terminology, the tracking of service-level agreements is part of control; prudent capacity planning to anticipate future user requirements is a key component of prevention. Measurement data related to equipment utilization and operating costs can contribute to future process efficiency measurements.

Two further factors are recognized as key contributors to successful quality improvement:

(1) The highly self-contained cost structure of the establishment allows easy capturing of most elements of the cost of quality.
(2) The attitude and commitment of both managers and nonmanagerial employees is fundamental to the success of quality improvement. A young, technically vital and professional population is particularly helpful and easy to motivate; accordingly, measures are taken for the continued enhancement of technical vitality and professionalism. (As an example, management makes a public commitment to the technical and financial support of professional publications, originating within the establishment, on subjects related to quality improvement.)

Beyond the review of the existing quality-related experience base, three further activities related to prevention are established in all software development departments:

(1) A streamlined requirements/specifications process, implemented jointly and *in parallel* between the software developers and the users' representatives. This process is to take the place of the traditional, serial approach where the user representatives first develop the requirement statement which is then submitted to development for review and acceptance, in turn followed by the subsequent development of product specifications. This serial approach is not only time-consuming but also leaves room for misunderstandings and errors in the process, sometimes to be discovered only after the completion of specifications and well into product development.[4]

---

[4]One of the major software development successes was the release and installation of a software package related to engineering design automation. The specifications for this product were developed using the new parallel methodology; the approach contributed significantly to the easy installation and virtually defect-free performance of the product years later.

(2) Having experienced several cases where the original requirement statement was found to be incomplete and had to be redone after the completion of specifications, a formal procedure for *requirements acceptance* is established, with the responsibility for its administration and implementation assigned to the development and technical services function.

(3) Mandatory product design reviews, also known as "design inspection." Although software development has been using mandatory code inspection for some time, a similar process aimed at error-free design only becomes mandatory with the introduction of quality improvement.

Having decided that the initial implementation of quality improvement will be done through the management of departmental processes, by definition "across-the-board" quality management must start with outcome-related activities, because in most areas there is no clear understanding or definition of the quality problem, let alone the defects causing it.

Problem analysis marks the first quality management activity, undertaken simultaneously by all departments of the establishment and leading to the identification of defects that may exist within individual departments. Defect removal will then become the fundamental quality improvement target of all members of the department. At the departmental level, problem analysis is conducted in a "roundtable" format, with the department manager and all members participating. In line with the quality work plan and schedule agreed upon at a departmental level, a series of problem analysis sessions is held over a period of several weeks, usually comprising one or two half-day sessions every week, until all quality-related problems are defined and the defects causing them identified. The general scheme of problem analysis is as follows:

- The department is identified as a single process comprised of several major activities (subprocesses) carried out by one or more members of the department.
- Key inputs to the departmental process are identified and documented; normally they originate in other departments or, in exceptional cases, outside the establishment.
- The prime output (work product) of the department (or, alternatively the prime output of each major departmental activity) is identified and documented.
- "Quality problems" are identified as (1) the results of receiving input not meeting departmental needs or requirements, or (2) conditions resulting from the department turning out defective work products. (At the individual worker level, problems can be identified by answering the question, "What is the result of not doing my job right the first time?")

It is important to differentiate between problems and defects: problems are conditions resulting from defects "upstream," or leading to further defects "downstream." However, defects can always be related to an existing requirement or specification, while problems usually cannot. Here are two examples of problems detected at the departmental level:

- Toward the end of every week, 10 to 15 percent of employee time cards, collected and submitted for processing on Monday, are returned to the personnel department for the correction of errors. The problem manifests itself primarily in added workload for the personnel staff as well as those who submitted or authorized the time cards in the first place. An analysis of the problem reveals three types of possible defects that can cause the return of time cards: (a) manager's signature missing, (b) incomplete attendance/absence information, and (c) coding or arithmetic errors. The solution would be the assignment of a part-time employee to detect and correct these three types of defects; this action will be more than justified by potential savings in overall processing costs and time delays.
- The facilities maintenance department has been receiving a number of complaints from employees about the time it takes to complete various repair and adjustment jobs (replacement of cracked windows, repair of malfunctioning thermostats, installation of power outlets, and so on). The obvious solution would be to allocate more personnel and thereby expedite the work. However, a detailed analysis shows that while most repair actions do not take excessive amounts of time, the real problem is the perceived lack of responsiveness. Introduction of an automatic and timely feedback procedure dramatically improves satisfaction.

In practice, problem analysis, which comprises these conceptual steps, is facilitated by such tools as the "Five-stage Problem-solving Process" (see IBM Form No. Z320-0755) or the *department activity analysis* (DAA)—both widely used during this phase of the effort. (See also Section 6.2.1.)

COMMON IMPLEMENTATION PHASE[5]

Depending on the number, severity, and complexity of quality-related problems, the problem analysis activity at the departmental level may cover a period of four to eight weeks. The resulting defect identification marks the end of the introduction phase and, at the same time, the beginning of *common implementation*.

At this point every department has entered the *defect elimination cycle* (DEC) by having identified one or more defects which, together with their causes, must be removed as part of the continuing quality improvement effort. (The key to defect identification is to first focus on those defects whose elimination is within the department's control; that is, address problems with departmental solutions.)

Once defects are identified, the defect elimination cycle continues with three control activities: (1) completion of defect identification in terms of quantifiable,

---

[5]Referred to also as "initial implementation phase" in Chapter 6, and elsewhere in the book.

objective measurements of nonconformance and specified relationship to one or more departmental activities; (2) defect-cause analysis; and (3) defect removal (with or without cause).

Just as the problem analysis leading to defect identification takes place in a departmental work-session setting, so does the validation of defects as specific quantifiable nonconformances. If the defect occurs within the department, it is related to one or more specific departmental activities. With quantifiable measurements established and agreed upon, a schedule for defect removal is created, with measurable targets identified on a periodic basis to ensure a continuous downward trend in defects remaining. This applies to those defects for which a cause is not known, but whose correction is within the department's control.

Finally, an attempt is made to identify possible causes for the defects, both within and outside the department. *Defect-cause analysis* (DCA) is a fairly straightforward, logical process, but, again, in practical implementation it is aided by such prioritization tools as Pareto analysis or tools for establishing cause-and-effect relationships, as Ishikawa-diagrams (see Section 6.2.2).

Information related to defect identification, measurements, and quantification, as well as elimination responsibilities, is summarized in the *defect elimination document* shown in Table 7-1. The document both tabulates an action plan to cause a downward defect trend and it also shows the relationship between the identifiable nonconformances and the original quality problem.

Here are some examples of defects established at the departmental level:

- In the finance department, erroneous entries in such documents as budget submission, expense accounts, or expense reports are all considered individual defects. Their measurement is the variation from the correct amount, in dollars and cents. The defect cause in most cases is human error; occasionally, it is an error in the source document or other input. If human error is prevalent, the removal of defect cause may require (1) the retraining or replacement of personnel involved in the particular activity or (2) correction or clarification of existing instructions and guidelines pertaining to that activity.

- In facilities maintenance, a defect resulting in customer dissatisfaction with responsiveness is the lack of a timely acknowledgment and status report back to the requester. The cause for this defect is the lack of a procedure calling for the feedback. Once a procedure is established and meticulously followed, user satisfaction is dramatically improved.

- Symptomatic of another facilities maintenance quality problem is the general level of discomfort in a number of offices on account of high temperatures and humidity during the summer. The problems underlying this symptom are: (1) temperature in excess of the maximum allowable 78 degrees Fahrenheit, given relative outside humidity of 92 percent; and (2) restricted airflow. Causing these problems, respectively, can be:

    malfunctioning thermostats

    reduced cooling capacity due to the loss of one of the cooling towers

Table 7-1. Defect Elimination Document

Control Dept.	Problem		Defect				Defect Removal		Defect Cause			Defect-Cause Removal	
							Responsibility					Responsibility	
	Symptom(s)	Description	Related Requirement	Description of Nonconformance	Measurement	Occurrence (Dept.)	Dept.	Name	Description	Origin (Dept.)	Controllability	Dept.	Name

partially open air vents

an obstruction in the air supply ducts

Although the symptom itself (discomfort) cannot easily be quantified and measured, the underlying problem (temperature gradient) is precisely measurable in terms of degrees of Fahrenheit.

• The problem of time cards returned to the personnel department is the result of three defects: (1) manager's signature missing, (2) incomplete attendance/absence data, and (3) errors in coding or arithmetic. The cause of the first defect could be unavailability of the manager due to business travel; for the second and third, it could be human error or the lack of explicit and easily accessible instructions for filling out time cards. Once identified, the first two causes can be removed by local action, while the latter requires personnel management action affecting the entire establishment.

The identification and quantification of defects is followed by *defect removal*, when this is possible and within the control of the department, and *defect-cause analysis*, as a matter of course. The latter in turn may lead to causes that are beyond departmental, or even functional, control. The identification of defect causes and associated costs is the one area that requires most of the interdepartmental and interfunctional resolution of issues, as well as a cooperative effort in working through costs. The management mechanism used for this purpose is the quality improvement team, which represents all functions and meets regularly to address such issues.

Defect-cause analysis utilizes essentially the same prioritization and cause-and-effect tools as problem analysis (Pareto, Ishikawa). The causes of nonconformances thus identified have to be further separated into those controllable by individual workers and those controllable only by management. This is determined through the controllability analysis, conducted as part of the overall defect-cause analysis; a new element is the added qualification (controllable by local or management action), shown in Table 7-1.

The last corrective step carried out at the departmental level during the implementation phase is the removal of worker-controllable defect causes. The elimination of these is targeted and scheduled according to the format shown in Table 7-1. Similarly, the results of these actions are displayed on the department's defect tracking and removal charts described earlier.

The *availability* and *reliability* of planned and existing on-line services, data processing equipment, and power supply and heating-ventilating-air conditioning (HVAC) equipment is recognized as a critical issue of performance prediction and, consequently, prevention.

Beyond actions related to the management of intent and outcome, the third major quality management thrust is the *cost of quality evaluation*. Just as most of the work related to the defect elimination cycle was initiated and carried out at the departmental level, so is this. With accounting guidelines and a definition of major cost-of-quality categories already prepared and distributed by the controller's organization, each department proceeds through the steps of this evaluation:

- Outputs of the departmental process are identified and documented.
- Individual departmental activities (subprocesses) producing these outputs are also identified and defined in terms of three distinct categories of tasks: (1) prevention, (2) appraisal or test, and (3) failure correction.

This particular step within the cost-of-quality evaluation proves quite time-consuming, as care must be taken that these definitions are consistently used and applied across the entire establishment. Issues and disputes, especially related to "borderline cases" are often resolved through management decision rather than consensus. Examples of such cases include:

- Does the unit testing of software code belong to prevention or test (appraisal)?
- Does functional test of software fall into the category of appraisal or failure correction? How about system test or environmental testing?
- Does the cost of all calls made on the "Help" line automatically add to the cost of failure?

Once subprocesses have been broken down into these three categories of tasks, financial analysts are assigned by the controller's department and applicable cost elements are apportioned to the various categories, creating an accurate *cost of quality database*.[6]

Figure 7-2 shows cost-of-quality trends and the relative size of cost-of-quality categories at the establishment level for the first three years of the quality improvement effort. The total cost of quality, as well as the categories of prevention, appraisal, and failure cost, are shown in Figure 7-2a as percentages of the annual expense budget. While both appraisal and failure costs show a definite downward trend as percentage of the total expense, the cost of prevention increases slightly during the second and third fiscal year—a result of consciously planned investments in that category. The linkage between these investments and the coincidental decline in appraisal and failure costs is not obvious from the charts; indeed, further analysis is needed to establish the cause-and-effect relationship.[7]

Figure 7-2b shows the relationship of the cost of quality to total annual expense in dollar terms for the same three fiscal years. Here we can see that in absolute dollar terms the cost of quality stayed "flat" over the three-year period,

---

[6]Although all initial cost of quality data are gathered from the departmental level in a "bottoms-up" fashion, routine tracking and reporting of the cost of quality continues generally only at the functional level. The analysis is extended down to the departmental level only where unusual trends or variations warrant it. Normal reporting frequency to functional and general management is on a quarterly basis; unusual situations or out-of-line conditions will be tracked and reported monthly. By the end of the common implementation phase, cost-of-quality reporting becomes part of the regular establishment measurement system.

[7]Seasonal effects—time-dependent fluctuations in work content and mix—may account for some of the cost changes. These have to be discounted before establishing the true leverage of preventive investments on appraisal and failure cost avoidance or reduction.

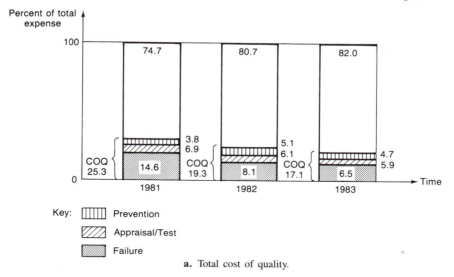

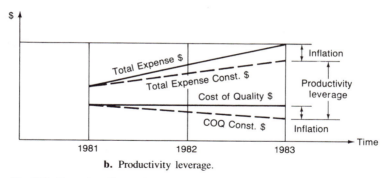

Fig. 7-2. Cost of quality performance of case study establishment.

but in constant dollars (adjusted for inflation and pegged to the value of the dollar at the beginning of the first fiscal year) it shows a marked decline of approximately 4 percent year to year. Meanwhile, overall expenses rose by approximately 5 percent year to year on the average, adjusted for inflation over the period. In this context, then, the productivity leverage of quality improvement can be clearly established.

7.2.3 Process Management

INTRODUCTION PHASE

From a process management viewpoint, the management decision to utilize the departmental process as the basic vehicle for quality improvement essentially means that:

- All defects (but not their causes), which are addressable through local (departmental) action, will be removed at least for some time. All worker-controllable defect causes will also be removed and, consequently, the related defects permanently prevented from recurring.
- The work process of the entire establishment will be stabilized (brought under statistical control), ready for continual and permanent quality improvement through management actions upon the process itself.

Achievement of these two results is the objective of the *commitment stage*, from introduction through common implementation.[8]

COMMON IMPLEMENTATION PHASE

Sometime after completion of the introduction phase and with considerable experience gained in the resolution of interdepartmental and interfunctional issues, management comes to the realization that of all the activities and processes within the establishment, *software development* proves to be the ready candidate for a more sophisticated process management approach, by virtue of its complexity and interdepartmental nature:

- The development and delivery of a single software module usually requires the cooperative, joint effort of several departments.
- From the beginning on, software development has been well structured in terms of separable and definable actions related to prevention, test, and failure correction.
- Project management techniques and accounting practices to track development costs provide the needed basis for the consistent use of the cost of quality as a management tool across the entire software development effort.

Consequently, toward the end of the implementation phase, software development is redefined as a *single technical process* and organizationally consolidated under a newly appointed software development "super manager" who is also given process ownership responsibility. Within the establishment this then becomes the first *functional process*, made up of over a dozen departmental subprocesses. Each of these essentially continues to follow the traditional phase process for software development, with on-demand support functions and services (such as requirements acceptance and assurance, data administration, database design, data processing, and telecommunications services) shared by all the subprocesses on a preplanned basis.

Within the software development process, the focus continues to be on *control*; that is, the detection and correction of errors as early in the process as

---

[8]Although initially no interdepartmental or interfunctional processes are identified for purposes of direct process management, the selection of the departmental process as the basic vehicle of quality improvement will turn out to be a good choice because it can be shown that both approaches eventually accomplish the same process management results, even though the initial, departmental approach will take more time.

possible. But software development is also among those few processes within the establishment in which, based on the analysis of the cost-of-quality trends of the first two to three years, consciously planned trade-off decisions can be made:

- Cutback of exhaustive functional and systems testing, especially in the real-time, network-based application environments where it is simply impossible to capture all the possible test cases and combinations of operational conditions.
- Establishment of new, direct, on-line, and real-time end-user services (information center) to assist in the resolution of user problems arising from system complexity, network interaction, and performance problems. Such types of problems are more prevalent in today's network-based environment than functional or coding errors.
- Increased investment in preventive measures such as design inspection, code inspection, and test plan inspection. The selection and redefinition of software development activities for process management purposes is aided by the process analysis technique (PAT).

At just about the same time when software development is redefined as a functional process and, as a consequence of the availability of reliable cost-of-quality data and continued management attention to productivity, the need for a more comprehensive business measurement system arises. In a series of management meetings chaired by the general manager, a new *business measurement process* is defined and process ownership is assigned to the manager of plans and controls (controller). After much discussion, *business system planning* (BSP) is chosen as the documentation and planning vehicle for the new process. (See also Section 6.2.1.)

> This technique is particularly useful in cases where the process did not previously exist and where it can primarily be defined as a complex system of information flow with definable and quantifiable needs in terms of type, amount, and frequency of information, along with its intended use. The model also includes the available and expected information sources and specific destinations. Although BSP provides thorough and detailed results and will yield a complete process model, its one major drawback becomes evident early in the game: Since it is an interview-driven tool, its success is highly dependent on the availability of key management and professional personnel for exhaustive tutorials, interviews, and feedback sessions.

7.3 Consolidation Stage

From the day of the quality management kickoff meeting to Zero Defect Day at the end of the introduction phase, about ten months have elapsed at Sterling Forest. From there, it takes another 2 1/2 years to the point in time when software development is redefined as the first functional process. At this point also, work begins on the newly established business measurements process, and the cost of quality is firmly established as the pervasive reporting tool to track progress in the quality improvement effort.

The establishment enters the consolidation stage with another *milestone meeting*: the "business process management kickoff" meeting, chaired again by the general manager and attended by all functional managers and the then incumbent members of the quality improvement team. This meeting establishes the following priority of objectives for the consolidation stage:

- Substantial increase in the number of processes (either new or existing) selected for the process management approach.
- Increased attention and resource commitments to prevention and process improvement.
- Expanded use of the cost of quality for reporting and analysis to achieve "management by cost trade-off" as the norm rather than the exception.
- Quantification of the linkage between quality and productivity improvement, especially as it relates to the interdependence of processes within the establishment.

7.3.1 Management System

The guidelines for process selection and the assignment of process ownership, along with the process owner's responsibilities, were published toward the end of the commitment stage. At the beginning of the consolidation stage, the rules for process assessment, the rating criteria, and the certification procedure are communicated to all managers, but in particular to the newly assigned process owners. (For the rating criteria, see Table 4-4; the process owners' responsibilities are discussed in more detail in Section 4.3.)

At this point, two of the *process owners' responsibilities* are given special attention: (1) process organization and team selection, and (2) process rating and certification. In line with parent Corporation and establishment guidelines, both must be accomplished on a predetermined schedule to ensure general and positive progress toward total process management.

Another dimension is added to the measurement of this progress by the introduction of specific quality responsibilities into all *managers' performance evaluations*. These responsibilities are stated as measurable objectives in their performance plans:

- Evidence of continued quality improvement: All meaningful defects identified and documented, and progress toward their elimination tracked within each department or major departmental activity.
- Scheduled quality measurement and progress review meetings held and reported.
- Maintenance of visible public displays documenting progress toward defect elimination, by defect type.
- Regular cost-of-quality reporting and analysis prepared at least on a quarterly basis.

- Responsiveness in the prompt handling of interdepartmental and interfunctional quality issues.
- Recognition of quality achievements (leadership, innovation and creativity, meeting or "beating" targets).
- Managers' display of leadership and imagination in the use of quality-related methodologies and aids (education, quality circles, problem and process analysis tools, and so on).

In addition to these quality responsibilities, which appear in virtually every manager's performance plan, some managers are given additional, quantified, or time-dependent objectives (for example, cost of quality reduction targets and schedules).

The "general health" and overall progress of the quality improvement effort is also tracked by the general manager through specific quarterly measurements, normally prepared by the quality coordinator in these areas:

- Progress in defect elimination: actual versus objectives; defect elimination trends.
- Departmental and individual employee participation in the various measurable quality activities, for example, the defect elimination cycle. (The definition of minimal employee participation in quality improvement is the commitment to the elimination of at least one identified defect.)
- Use of the cost of quality as a management reporting and analysis tool.
- Demonstrably declining overall cost of quality, with special focus on cost of failure reduction.
- Demonstrable cause-and-effect relationship between increased cost of prevention and failure cost reduction.
- Evidence of cause-and-effect relationship between quality and increased productivity.

Throughout the commitment stage and well into the consolidation stage, a "dual focus" is maintained on objectives and related measurements, in the interest of better manageability:

(1) Managers' focus and responsibilities are directed to the cost of quality and, later on, to specific aspects of process management, such as measurements of process improvement and process certification.
(2) The nonmanagerial employees' focus is on continuing (worker-controllable) defect elimination.

7.3.2 Quality Management

From the standpoint of managing *intent*, the two major preventive activities continuing into the consolidation stage are (1) process improvements in software development, and (2) continued, aggressive implementation of the streamlined, parallel requirements/specification process.

Process improvements include:

- Introduction of *function points* as the consistent measurement of software functional content.
- Enhanced and improved design and code inspection procedures.
- Increased investment in capital equipment and indirect support of the development process through use of personal computers, office systems, and information center services within the software development functions—leading to improvements in quality and process productivity.

By the time the consolidation stage is reached, the new streamlined requirements/specification process is considered an important source of payoff and a major contributor to the reduction of both appraisal and failure costs. Patterned after the outstanding example of the recently completed design automation application package, this approach is now made mandatory for all new software development efforts.

On the *outcome* side, the defect elimination cycle, including the mechanism for the removal of defect causes, is in place in every department and every identified, standalone process—across the board. Targets are set for the complete elimination of all identified worker-controllable defects and their causes in order to achieve overall process stability.[9]

A particularly important step in the area of defect elimination is the inclusion of all software *vendors* in the process. This requires comprehensive quality education for vendor personnel, similar to that received by all other employees of the establishment. In fact, vendors are considered an extension of the software development process for quality management purposes.

A major breakthrough in the measurement of quality improvement is the expanded use of the cost of quality as both a reporting and analytical tool, leading to the capability of "managing by cost-tradeoff." Two examples of resource trade-offs and shifting from appraisal and failure correction toward prevention-type activities are:

- Replacement of a failure-prone electrical substation even though it was purchased only a few years before. Projected cost avoidance and outage reductions helped offset the high rate of capital asset write-offs resulting from this action.
- In the software development process, increased investments are made in data administration, database design, and support activities, as well as code inspection, against the alternative of increased functional and performance testing. Actual defect elimination rates experienced in the inspection process over the past two years indicate significantly better payoff as against the number of defects actually eliminated through testing.

---

[9]An example of the far-reaching defect-cause removal effort is site operations' way of addressing traffic safety problems in the parking lot. Actual accidents and violations of traffic rules (whether or not resulting in an accident) are treated as defects and attacked through their causes.

The consistency of the cost of quality as a reporting and analytical tool is significantly enhanced by the continued tuning and updating of the cost-of-quality database as an increasingly homogeneous and consistent source of information. This is further helped by discarding the data gathered during the first fiscal year (essentially the introduction phase of the quality improvement effort) and the reconciliation of the cost-of-quality databases from fiscal year to fiscal year after that.

In line with one of the stated business objectives of the establishment (that is, to be the low-cost provider), the cost of quality reduction targets are chosen such as to ensure an overall "minimum cost" functioning of the entire establishment. This essentially is the first step toward developing a planning and measurement methodology to ensure the continued, and measurably improved efficiency and productivity of selected processes.

It is during the first year of the consolidation stage that initial attempts are made to establish quantified links between the cost of quality (more precisely, the cost of prevention) and the resulting productivity improvements experienced by recipients (end users) of the establishment's work products. Specifically, a series of measurements are carried out on the perceived and real improvements in the productivity of design engineers at one of the large development laboratories which uses on-line design automation and engineering records management services. Work habits, throughput improvements, and various other factors are measured at several levels of subsecond response time to arrive at net productivity measurements. These show conclusively that meeting successively shorter response time requirements (and thereby providing improving, quality service) lead to direct increase in work output per time unit by all professional users surveyed.

7.3.3 Process Management

Within a year into the consolidation stage, the following new processes are selected, with owners assigned, and the basics of process management introduced:

- Software release and control
- Equipment installation
- Emergency change in the data processing center
- Data processing operations
- Network control

In each of these cases, process improvement is established as the basic and ultimate vehicle for quality improvement. In each case it is the process owner's responsibility to carry out a detailed process analysis, establish process improvement objectives, and extend them down to each individual employee's performance plan as specific and measurable targets. (Within another year, process ownership is assigned to over a hundred identified processes and sub-processes.)

7.4 The Road to Maturity

To this day, the quality improvement effort is continuing, with the establishment well into the consolidation stage. Although it may take several more years before it reaches the point of maturity and pervasive process management operating at an assessment rating level of 1, management is confident that it is well positioned for achieving that result. And certain conclusions can already be drawn about results and accomplishments that are definite and measurable, and cannot be debated. Also, during the years of the quality improvement effort, challenges have surfaced that can teach lessons to those who currently find themselves in a similar stage of evolution in their journey toward quality. The following discussion of these will conclude the case study.

7.4.1 Conclusions

Experience clearly shows that the successful *introduction* of the quality improvement effort depends on the following key factors:

- Visible, "top-down" initial management commitment
- Initial commitment of resources and management time
- Participation by all managerial and nonmanagerial workers, in their assigned responsibilities, throughout the effort
- The "quality attitude," in which responsibility lies with line management and their employees, not the quality staff or quality professionals
- Quality improvement is a continuing effort, not a short-range program

Full participation is one obvious objective at all levels of the establishment. This is tracked and reported regularly to departmental and functional management and made visible at the general manager's level. Line management commitment to and ownership of the solution of quality problems is further ensured by keeping the size of the professional quality staff to an absolute minimum.[10]

The continued, successful *implementation* of quality improvement requires:

- Continued and unrelenting "top-down" management direction and participation.[11]
- Continuing investment of both financial resources and management time—

---

[10]In the case under study the organization chart of the establishment lists only one full-time employee whose title includes the word *quality*—that of the quality coordinator. Quality-related activity is carried out by line organizations, particularly line managers, in some cases on temporary assignment to a specific quality responsibility, such as the quality improvement team.

[11]The Quality Improvement Team (QIT) is replaced by the Quality Management Council (QMC) which includes the general manager and the functional managers reporting to him or her. The responsibilities of the council are: quality policy, monitoring progress, and recognition of quality accomplishments. In this fashion, top management is directly and continuously involved in the management of the overall quality effort.

especially when it comes to preventive, "upfront" expenditure of resources, usually not easily justifiable when the payoff may be years away.
* A well-documented, detailed plan for the quality improvement effort maintained as a "live" document by the quality coordinator (process plan).
* Ongoing education and training.
* Visible display and recognition of quality accomplishment, both at the process and individual employee level.[12]

It can also be concluded that a significant number of *difficulties* have to be overcome, beginning with the introduction phase. Some of these are:

* Difficulty in articulating and differentiating between quality problems and the defects which cause them; between defect and defect causes, especially when these are not measurable or not within the control of one department or a single process.
* The resolution of interprocess, interdepartmental, or interfunctional conflicts—which is typical of matrix management environments—is one of the most challenging management tasks throughout the quality improvement effort. In many cases, however, the problem is eventually resolved through consistent and systematic cost accounting that may lead to the cause of defect itself. Also, stubborn interfunctional or interdepartmental quality problems can be overcome by the process management approach, using appropriate process definition to include both the potential sources and recipients of defects through successive linkage of subprocesses.[13]
* Cause-and-effect relationship between problems and defects is more difficult to establish in a managerial, decision-making environment. Here again, the process management approach, namely, the definition of decision making or administration as a business process, establishes a helpful attitude in eliminating defects and their causes, primarily through process improvement.
* Personnel and employee relations concerns, unique to quality improvement, including:

    (1) Rewarding quality penalizes professionalism: The notion here is that a professional, by definition, does "the job right the first time." According to this type of thinking, professionals automatically do quality work, and therefore rewarding quality achievements degrades professionalism and promotes unprofessional behavior.
    (2) Difficulty of establishing mutually acceptable and measurable quality objectives as part of an individual's performance plan, in light of the fact that many of these measurements and objectives derive from par-

---

[12]Recognition programs, in the consolidation stage, place special emphasis on recognizing those who have improved key business processes.

[13]A good example of this in the case under study was the redefinition and consolidation of departmental software development processes to a single, albeit more complex, software development process.

tial experience or incomplete data. (The timing of the introduction of quality responsibilities and objectives into performance plans, accordingly, is a critical consideration.)

(3) Especially in a product environment, it is difficult to get away from the traditional view that, when "the chips are down," schedules take precedence over other cost or quality considerations. It takes consistent management direction and equally consistent action to maintain the "quality first among equals" view as management trade-offs are continuously made against other business objectives.

The *schedule* portion of the quality improvement plan and the timing of certain key events can be of great help in managing the overall quality improvement effort and in the evolution through the various stages toward maturity.

Yearly events may include:

• Preparation or updating the quality improvement plan (process plan)
• Changing membership of the quality improvement team
• Review and updating of process assessment and certification

Events planned on a *quarterly* basis comprise:

• Cost of quality status and trends
• Process efficiency and productivity measurements
• Recognition events for quality achievers
• Review of "health indicators" of overall quality improvement effort

The following activities may be scheduled in *monthly* cycles:

• Quality improvement team meetings
• Review of departmental and individual employee participation in defect elimination activities in key "problem areas" or processes
• Updating visible displays of defect elimination status and defect trends

7.4.2 Challenges

When we look at those issues and challenges an establishment is still facing well into the consolidation stage, it is easy to see why quality improvement should be an ongoing and never-ending process. Major challenges which require significantly more work and the investment of nontrivial resources include:

• The pervasive use of the *cost of quality as an investment tool* to demonstrate, on the basis of actual cost data, the benefits of a given investment in prevention. This is done in terms of real reductions in the cost of appraisal and failure as a projected result. This relationship should be extendable over a wide range of recipients of the work product, remote both organizationally and physically from the provider (among them, interdepartmental, interfunctional, and interestablishment linkage, showing that increased prevention will assuredly lead to decreased appraisal and failure costs).

- Quantified linkage between *quality improvement* and *increased productivity*, on an interdepartmental, interfunctional, or interestablishment basis. This requires a significant amount of process effectiveness and efficiency measurement and data gathering activity, extended sometimes over several years.
- Quantified linkage between *process measurements* and *traditional business indicators* (revenue, profit, volumes, inventory, asset turn, and the like).
- Methodologies and management guidelines for the routine resolution of interfunctional, interestablishment conflicts that may arise from the process management approach.
- Vendor and supplier quality: The leverage of increased prevention and the linkage between quality and productivity should be extendable to those vendors whose work products and services are essential inputs to the provider's various business processes. Again, process management offers a logical and straightforward solution in that the definition of the affected processes is extended to include the related vendor activities and work products. Under this concept, the vendors simply become part of the extended process, under the management and responsibility of the process owner. The various elements of the management system, such as procedures and guidelines, education, and the various communication channels are simply extended to cover the vendor; the same applies to process management disciplines, tools and aids, and process measurements as well.

As these challenges are faced and overcome, quality improvement becomes more and more embedded in the fabric of everyday business management, assuming its true contribution to business success through the "triangle of excellence." Here, the continuing fostering and enhancement of people's *professionalism* leads to consistently conforming *quality* output as a matter of course resulting, in turn,

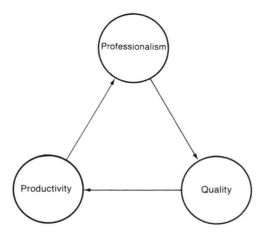

Fig. 7-3. The triangle of excellence.

in the improved *productivity* of other professional recepients. They then combine that with their ongoing professional development to maintain technological and management leadership and to contribute to competitiveness and the "bottom-line" profitability of the enterprise (see Figure 7-3).

GLOSSARY

ACCURACY—The closeness of the average of a series of repeat measurements to the accepted true value. The smaller the difference between measurements and the true value, the more accurate the measuring device. If the difference is due to a systematic error in the measurement process, the measuring instrument is said to be "out of calibration."

ACTIVITY—The collection of tasks performed to change inputs into outputs. (*See also* Subprocess.)

ADAPTABILITY—A process characteristic needed to maintain process effectiveness and efficiency, as requirements and the operating environment change over time. Capability for improvement to meet changing requirements.

AIM—*See* Goal.

APPRAISAL—The act of judging as to quality, status, or value.

AVAILABILITY—The probability that a product, when used under specified conditions, will perform satisfactorily every time it is called upon.

BEST OF BREED—A process is "best of breed" when its overall performance, in terms of effectiveness, efficiency, and adaptability, is superior to all comparable processes.

BIAS—A systematic error, resulting in change to the inherent accuracy or precision of an instrument.

CAUSE—An established reason for the existence of a defect.

CAUSE-AND-EFFECT DIAGRAM—A problem-solving tool based on the graphic representation of the causal relationships among process components used to analyze the potential causes of variation. Referred to also as *fishbone-diagram* or *Ishikawa-diagram*.

COMMON CAUSE—A source of variation in the process output that is inherent to the process and will affect all the individual results or values of process output. (Also called *root* cause.)

CONTROL—The set of activities employed to detect and correct deviation in order to maintain or restore a desired state. A past-oriented approach to quality management.

CONTROL CHART—A graphic representation of measured actual process performance relative to computed control limits shown as limiting lines on the chart. The prime purpose of the control chart is to detect *special causes* of variation in the process.

CORRECTION—The totality of actions to minimize or remove variations and their causes.

COST OF APPRAISAL—Money spent to measure and assess completed work products against stated requirements. Costs incurred to determine nonconformance.

COST OF FAILURE—Money spent on correcting defects or using defective work products; cost associated with things that have been found not to conform to requirements, as well as the evaluation, disposition, and public relations aspects of such failures. Costs resulting from the occurrence of nonconformances (defects).

COST OF PREVENTION—Money required to prevent defects and to "do the job right the first time." Costs incurred to reduce the total cost of quality.

COST OF QUALITY—The sum of the costs of prevention, appraisal, and failure. The key financial measurement tool which ties process control and process optimization into a total process management effort. It can be used both as an indicator and a signal for variation (more often, patterns of variation), as well as a measure of productivity and efficiency.

CUSTOMER—The recipient that must be satisfied with the output (work product) of the process. (In the commercial sense, a customer acquires products through a form of compensation.)

DATA—Information or a set of facts presented in descriptive form. There are two basic kinds of data: *measured* (also known as *variables* data) and *counted* (also known as *attribute* data).

DEFECT—Any state of nonconformance to *requirements*.

DETECTION—An outcome-oriented approach to quality management based on the identification of nonconformances after the fact; its result is the identification of defects and their causes.

DEVIATION—Any nonconformance to a *standard*.

EFFECTIVENESS—A process characteristic indicating that the process output (work product) conforms to requirements.

EFFICIENCY—A process characteristic indicating that the process produces the required output at minimum cost.

FISHBONE-DIAGRAM—See Cause-and-Effect Diagram.

FREQUENCY DISTRIBUTION (of a *discrete* variable)—The count of the number of occurrences of individual values over a given range.

FREQUENCY DISTRIBUTION (of a *continuous* variable)—The count of cases which lie between certain predetermined limits over the range of values the variable may assume.

GAUGE CAPABILITY—The accuracy, repeatability, reproducibility, and stability of measurements combined into a single parameter. Considering the measurement system as a subprocess of the overall process in question, "gauge capability" can be defined as the process capability of that subprocess.

GOAL—That which one proposes to accomplish or attain, with an implication of sustained effort and energy directed to it over a longer range.

GOODS—Items related primarily to personal use, such as food, clothing, furniture, books, and the like.

HISTOGRAM—A frequency distribution represented in the form of a vertical bar chart.

HYPOTHESIS—An assertion made about the value of some parameter of a population.

INPUT—Materials, energy, or information required for the process to complete the activities necessary to produce a specified output (work product).

MAXIM—A statement of a general truth with the purpose of providing a base for general direction or conduct in an area of endeavor.

MEAN TIME BETWEEN FAILURES (MTBF)—The average time between successive failures of a given product.

MEASUREMENT—Method(s) employed to determine, in a quantified form, the actual status of a process variable or product attribute.

NEED—A lack of something requisite, desired, or useful; a condition requiring provision or relief. Usually expressed by users or customers.

OBJECTIVE—A statement of the desired result to be achieved within a specified time. By definition, an objective always has an associated schedule.

OFFERING—Specific combination of products and services provided in a "packaged" form to satisfy certain specialized needs. (The products in this context are sometimes also known as *deliverables*.)

OUTPUT—The specified end result (work product) of the process, required by the recipient (customer).

PARETO DIAGRAM—A problem-solving tool based on the ranking of all problems or sources of variation according to their relative contribution to some specified parameter, such as cost or total variation.

PLAN—A specific course of action designed to attain a stated objective.

POLICY—A statement of principles and beliefs, or a settled course, adopted to guide the overall management of affairs in support of a stated aim or goal. It is mostly related to fundamental conduct and usually defines a general framework within which other business and management actions are carried out.

POPULATION—A large collection of items (product observations, data) about certain characteristics of which conclusions and decisions are to be made for purposes of process assessment and quality improvement.

PRECISION—The closeness of a group of repeat measurements, to a mean value. The smaller the difference between the group of repeat measurements and the mean value, the more precise the instrument. Precision is an indicator of the repeatability, or consistency, of the measurement.

PREVENTION—A future-oriented approach to quality management that achieves quality improvement through corrective action on the process.

PROBLEM—A question or situation proposed for solution. The result of not conforming to requirements or, in other words, a potential task resulting from the existence of defects.

PROCESS—A system *in operation* to produce an output of higher value than that of the sum of its inputs. A process is also defined as the *logical organization of people, materials, energy, equipment, and procedures into work activities designed to produce a specified end result* (work product).

PROCESS CAPABILITY—A measure of the inherent uniformity of the process.

PROCESS CONTROL—The set of activities employed to detect and remove *special causes* of variation in order to maintain or restore stability (statistical control).

PROCESS IMPROVEMENT—The set of activities employed to detect and remove *common causes* of variation in order to improve process capability. Process improvement leads to *quality improvement.*

PROCESS MANAGEMENT—Management approach comprising *quality management* and *process optimization.*

PROCESS OPTIMIZATION—The major aspect of process management which concerns itself with the *efficiency* and *productivity* of the process; that is, with economic factors.

PROCESS OWNER—A designated manager, within the process, who has authority to manage the process and responsibility for its overall performance.

PRODUCTIVITY—The value added by the process divided by the value of the labor and capital consumed.

PRODUCT—Item of both personal and general use, related more to convenience, comfort, and productivity—such as appliances, vehicles, cameras, office and data processing equipment, and so on.

PROVIDER—Individuals or organizations from whom work products originate—including agricultural producers, manufacturers, public utilities, educational institutions, vendors, and the like.

QUALITY—Conformance to requirements.

QUALITY CONTROL—The totality of activities comprising *detection* and *correction*.

QUALITY OF DESIGN—Conformance of *specifications* to *requirements*.

QUALITY IMPROVEMENT—Quality management over time, in the face of changing requirements.

QUALITY MANAGEMENT—The totality of management actions aimed at achieving conformance of the work product to requirements. (Known also as *Quality improvement*.) It includes both the management of intent (prevention) and the management of outcome (control).

QUALITY OF PROCESS—Conformance of the *work product* to *specifications*.

QUALITY OF REQUIREMENTS—Conformance of *requirements* to known user *needs* and the *expected manner* in which they are to be met.

RANGE—The difference between the maximum and the minimum value of data in a *sample*.

RECIPIENT—The most general and consistent definition of all those individuals or organizations for whom work products are provided. When a work product is acquired with some form of compensation in return, the recipient is known as a *customer.* If the acquisition is for the direct use of the work product, the recipient is known as the *user.* The *end user* is one who receives the intended benefit of the work product. (End users of consumable products—food, fuel, clothing, and the like—are known as *consumers.*)

RELIABILITY—The probability of a product entity's performing its specified function under specified conditions, without failure, for a specified period of time.

REMEDY—A change that can successfully remove or neutralize a defect.

REPEATABILITY—The variation of repeat measurements, carried out by one inspector on the same work product, using the same measuring device.

REPRODUCIBILITY—The variation in measurement averages, when multiple inspectors carry out repeat measurements, each on the same work product, using the same measuring device.

REQUIREMENT—A formal statement of a *need* and the *expected manner* in which it is to be met. (The recipient's view of the work product.)

SAMPLE—A finite number of items taken from a population.

SCATTER DIAGRAM—A graphic method of data representation for analytical purposes. It is used to determine if a cause-and-effect relationship exists.

SERVICE—Activities related to goods and products (delivery, maintenance, and the like) to ensure conformance or offered by themselves, such as transportation, education, electricity, and so on, to meet user requirements.

SIMULATION—The technique of observing and manipulating an artificial mechanism (model) that represents a real-world process which, for technical or economical reasons, is not suitable or available for direct experimentation.

SPECIAL CAUSE—A source of variation in the process output that is unpredictable, unstable, or intermittent. Also called *assignable* cause.

SPECIFICATION—A document containing a detailed description or enumeration of particulars. Formal description of a work product and the intended manner of providing it. (The *provider's* view of the work product.)

STABILITY (of measurements)—The variation in measurement averages when repeat measurements are carried out over a specified time period.

STABILITY (of process)—A state of statistical control.

STANDARD DEVIATION—A parameter describing the spread of the process output, denoted by the Greek letter sigma, σ. The positive square root of the *variance*.

STATISTIC—Any parameter which can be determined on the basis of the quantitative characteristics of a *sample*.

- A *descriptive statistic* is a computed measure of some property of a set of values, making possible a definitive statement about the *meaning* of the collected data.
- An *inferential statistic* indicates the confidence which can be placed in any statement regarding its expected accuracy, the range of applicability of the statement, and the probability of its being true. Consequently, decisions can be based on inferential statistics.

STATISTICAL CONTROL—The status of a process from which all special causes of variation have been removed and only common causes remain. Such a process is also said to be *stable*.

STATISTICAL ESTIMATION—The analysis of a sample parameter in order to predict the values of the corresponding population parameter.

STATISTICAL METHODS—The application of the theory of probability to problems of variation. There are two groups of statistical methods:

- *Basic statistical methods*: Relatively simple problem-solving tools and techniques, such as control charts, capability analysis, data summarization and analysis, and statistical inference.
- *Advanced statistical methods*: More sophisticated and specialized techniques of statistical analysis, such as the design of experiments, regression and correlation analysis, and the analysis of variance.

STATISTICAL PROCESS CONTROL—The use of statistical techniques to analyze a process through its various outputs so as to take appropriate actions to establish statistical control and improve process capability.

STATISTICS—The branch of applied mathematics that describes and analyzes empirical observations for the purpose of predicting certain events in order to make decisions in the face of uncertainty. Statistics, in turn, is based on the *theory of probability*. The two together provide the abstraction for the mathematical model underlying the study of problems involving uncertainties.

STRATEGY—A broad course of action, chosen from a number of alternatives, to accomplish a stated goal in the face of uncertainty.

SUBPROCESS—A large collection of activities and tasks performed to change inputs into outputs.

VARIABLE—A data item which takes on values within some range with a certain frequency or pattern. Variables may be *discrete,* that is, limited in value to integer quantities (for example, the number of bolts produced in a manufacturing process); discrete variables relate to *attribute data.* Variables may also be *continuous,* that is, measured to any desired degree of accuracy (for example, the diameter of a shaft); continuous variables relate to *variables data.*

VARIANCE—In quality management terminology, any nonconformance to *specifications*. In statistics, it is the square of the *standard deviation.*

VARIATION—Any nonconformance or deviation; differences among individual results or outputs of a process. The generic term for defects, nonconformances, deviations, and so on.

ZERO DEFECTS—The term used to describe a state free of measurable variation; the state of full conformance to requirements.

STATISTICAL SUMMARY

Numerical Methods: Descriptive Statistics[1]

Consider the random variable X, of which a finite set of values $x_1, x_2, \ldots x_n$ are observed. For this finite sample, a number of *descriptive statistics* can be defined which, with proper interpretation, are equally applicable to both discrete and continuous random variables.

1. Central Tendency Statistics

A finite set of values of a random variable (a sample) can be analyzed to describe the central tendency of that variable. Geometrically, the central tendency is the *shape* of the frequency distribution curve associated with that variable.

Definition: The *sample mean* $\bar{x}$ of a finite set of n values $x_1, x_2, \ldots, x_n$ is

$$\bar{x} = \frac{x_1 + x_2 + \ldots + x_n}{n} \tag{A.1}$$

The mean is also called the "average" in everyday language. In the continuous case, the mean can geometrically be interpreted as the location of the center of gravity of the area under the frequency distribution curve (Figure 3-4a).

---

[1]Adapted, with permission of the publisher, from *Introduction to Scientific Computing* by G. A. Pall (New York: Appleton-Century-Crofts/Plenum Publishing, 1971).

Definition: The *median M* of a finite set of values $x_1, x_2, \ldots, x_n$ is that value of the numerically ordered elements of the sample which gives an equal number of values above and below it. In the continuous case, the median can geometrically be interpreted as the location of the average ordinate associated with the frequency distribution curve (Figure 3-4a).

Definition: The *mode m* is the value of the random variable X which occurs most frequently. In the continuous case, the mode can geometrically be interpreted as the location of the maximum ordinate associated with the frequency distribution curve (Figure 3-4a).

2. Dispersion Statistics

A finite set of values of a random variable X may be analyzed to compute statistics that measure the dispersion (or variability) of X about its mean. Geometrically, dispersion is the *spread* of the frequency distribution curve associated with that variable.

Definition: The *range R* of a finite set of ordered values $x_1, x_2, \ldots, x_n$ is defined as

$$R = x_n - x_1 \tag{A.2}$$

Definition: The *sample variance*, s^2, of a finite set of values $x_1, x_2, \ldots, x_n$ is defined as

$$s^2 = \sum_{i=1}^{n} \frac{|x_i - \bar{x}|^2}{n-1} \tag{A.3}$$

Definition: The *standard deviation s* of a finite set of values is defined as the positive square root of the sample variance.

Kurtosis describes the *peakedness* of the frequency distribution curve: The curve can be *leptokurtic* (peaked), *mesokurtic* (medium), or *platykurtic* (flat) (see Figure 3-4b).

Another descriptive statistic that can be computed for a finite set of values is the measure of *skewness*. In the continuous case, it can geometrically be interpreted as the *symmetry* of the frequency distribution curve. Positive skewness means that the tail of the distribution curve is stretched to the right; negative skewness to the left (Figure 3-4c).

Note that n, $\bar{x}$, and s refer to statistics calculated for a finite sample; the corresponding population parameters are denoted by N, μ, and σ, respectively. The formula for the *population variance* is

$$\sigma^2 = \sum \frac{x - \mu}{N} \tag{A.4}$$

Numerical Methods: Probability Distributions[2]

The limitations of graphical methods, such as histograms and tally diagrams, in describing and analyzing observation data can be overcome by using numerical descriptors, namely *parameters* (computed from populations) and *statistics* (computed from samples). In many industrial and business applications, the occurrences of nondeterministic (that is, probabilistic) events form patterns that can conveniently be described by *probability distributions*.

1. Discrete Probability Distributions

Definition: If a random variable X can assume a finite, or countably infinite, set of values, X is referred to as a *discrete random variable*.

Definition: Given a real number x within the range of a discrete random variable X, the probability that the random variable X will assume the value x is specified by the *probability function* or *probability distribution $f(x)$* (Figure A-1a).

Definition: Given a real number x within the range of a discrete random variable X, the probability that the random variable X will assume values ξ less than or equal to x, is described by the *cumulative distribution function $F(x)$* (Figure A-1b).

In the following, two discrete probability distributions will be discussed that are of special interest in quality control.

A. BINOMIAL DISTRIBUTION (Figure A-2a)

The binomial distribution giving the probability for x successes in n independent trials with θ, probability for success in any given trial (constant from trial to trial) can be written in the form

$$f(x) = b_n(x; \theta) = \binom{n}{x} \theta^x (1 - \theta)^{(n-x)}$$
$$(x = 0, 1, 2, \ldots, n) \qquad (A.5)$$

The binomial probability distribution depends on the two parameters n and θ. It applies to situations commonly referred to as repeated trials with binary outcomes, or sampling with replacement.

The mean and variance of the binomial distribution are, respectively,

$$\mu = n \theta$$
$$\sigma^2 = n \theta (1 - \theta) \qquad (A.6)$$

Application: Determining the probability of x occurrences of an event E in n independent trials, where E has a constant probability of occurrence on each trial.

B. POISSON DISTRIBUTION (Figure A-2b)

This important probability distribution can be derived as the limiting form of the binomial distribution, when $\theta \twoheadrightarrow 0$ and $n \twoheadrightarrow \infty$, such that $n\theta$ remains constant.

---

[2]Reprinted, with permission of the publisher, from *Introduction to Scientific Computing* by G. A. Pall (New York: Appleton-Century-Crofts/Plenum Publishing, 1971).

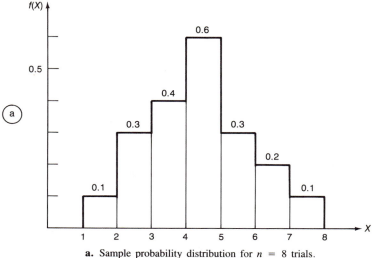

a. Sample probability distribution for $n = 8$ trials.

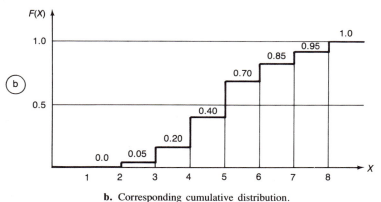

b. Corresponding cumulative distribution.

Fig. A-1. Graphical representation of discrete probability distributions.

Source: Reprinted, with permission of the publisher, from *Introduction to Scientific Computing* by G. A. Pall (New York: Appleton-Century-Crofts/Plenum Publishing, 1971).

The Poisson distribution is defined by

$$f(x) = p(x; \lambda) = \frac{\lambda^x e^{-\lambda}}{x!}$$

$$(x = 0, 1, 2, \ldots, n) \qquad \text{(A.7)}$$

where $e = 2.7182 \ldots$. The probability distribution depends on the single parameter λ. It has many applications in its own right: It can be used to approximate the binomial distribution for very large samples (n is very large) and to describe occurrences of certain events within given intervals of time.

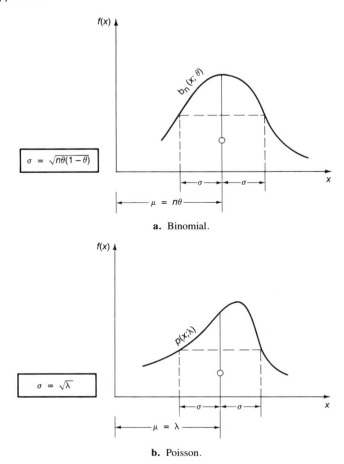

a. Binomial.

b. Poisson.

Fig. A-2. Discrete probability distributions.

Source: Reprinted, with permission of the publisher, from *Introduction to Scientific Computing* by G. A. Pall (New York: Appleton-Century-Crofts/Plenum Publishing, 1971).

The mean and variance of the Poisson distribution are, respectively,

$$\mu = \lambda$$
$$\sigma^2 = \lambda \tag{A.8}$$

Application: Same as for the binomial distribution, but particularly for very large samples, or when there are many opportunities for the occurrence of an event E, but a low and varying probability on each trial. Of special interest are occurrences of events within given time intervals.

As one of the most important discrete probability distributions, the Poisson distribution has been tabulated for practical reference (see Appendix B).

2. Continuous Probability Distributions

Definition: If a random variable X can assume more than a finite or countably infinite set of values, X is referred to as a *continuous random variable*.

Definition: The probability that the continuous random variable X assumes a specific value is described by the *probability density function* $f(x)$ associated with it.

The probability density corresponds to the probability distribution function of the discrete case. Since the density function represents the distribution of a continuous random variable, the probability of any given values can be predicted based on the associated areas under the density curve.

Definition: Given the random variable X, its probability distribution or density is said to be in *standard form* if $\mu = 0$ and $\sigma = 1$.

The need for using standardized random variables arises when tabulating values of probability distributions, cumulative distributions, or density functions. We now discuss three continuous density functions that are of importance in quality control.

A. EXPONENTIAL PROBABILITY DENSITY (Figure A-3a)

The exponential density function for $\theta > 0$ is defined by:

$$f(x) = \begin{cases} \dfrac{1}{\theta}\, e^{-(x/\theta)} & (x > 0) \\[2mm] 0 & (x \leqq 0) \end{cases} \qquad \text{(A.9)}$$

The probability that the variable X assumes a value less than or equal to x is

$$P(X \leq x) = \begin{cases} \dfrac{1}{\theta}\, \int_0^x e^{-\xi/\theta}\, d\theta & (x > 0) \\[2mm] 0 & (x \leq 0) \end{cases} \qquad \text{(A.10)}$$

The mean and variance of the exponential density are, respectively,

$$\mu = \theta$$
$$\sigma^2 = \theta^2 \qquad \text{(A.11)}$$

Application: The exponential density is used in the calculation of probabilities related to the failure of products or systems. It is also used in those situations when it is likely that more observations will occur below the average than above.

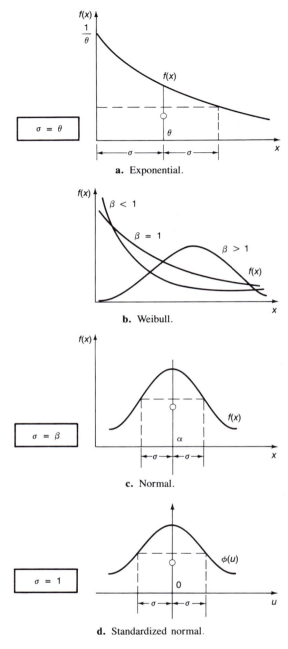

a. Exponential.

b. Weibull.

c. Normal.

d. Standardized normal.

Fig. A-3. Continuous probability distributions.

Source: Reprinted, with permission of the publisher, from *Introduction to Scientific Computing* by G. A. Pall (New York: Appleton-Century-Crofts/Plenum Publishing, 1971). Portion **b** is reprinted, with permission of the publisher, from *Quality Planning and Analysis* by J. M. Juran and F. M. Gryna, Jr. (New York: McGraw-Hill Book Co., 1980).

B. WEIBULL PROBABILITY DENSITY (Figure A-3b)

The Weibull density function is described by the general form

$$f(x) = \alpha\beta (x - \gamma)^{(\beta-1)} e^{-\alpha(x - \gamma)\beta} \tag{A.12}$$

where α = scale parameter, β = shape parameter and γ = location parameter. In practice, the shape parameter β varies from 0.25 to 5.0; note that for $\beta = 1$, the Weibull density function reduces to the exponential probability density.

Application: The Weibull probability density is used to describe a wide variety of variation, including departures from the exponential and normal distributions. As it can approximate many shapes of distributions, in practice it helps reduce the problem of fitting one of the more common distributions to the data.

C. NORMAL PROBABILITY DENSITY (Figure A-3c)

The normal density function is described by

$$f(x) = \frac{1}{\beta\sqrt{2\pi}} e^{\frac{1}{2}\left(\frac{x - \alpha}{\beta}\right)^2} \tag{A.13}$$

The probability that the variable X assumes a value less than or equal to x, is

$$P(X \leq x) = \frac{1}{\beta\sqrt{2\pi}} \int_{-\infty}^{x} e^{\frac{1}{2}\left(\frac{\xi - \alpha}{\beta}\right)^2} d\xi \tag{A.14}$$

Application: The normal probability density is used to describe the patterns of measurement errors, physical properties, or other natural or economic phenomena which are symmetrically distributed about some average value (for example, the mean), and where there is a concentration of observations about the average.

The curve representing the normal density function is commonly referred to as the "bell-shaped" curve. The mean and variance of the normal probability density are, respectively

$$\mu = \alpha$$
$$\sigma^2 = \beta^2 \tag{A.15}$$

The normal probability density function with mean μ and variance σ^2 is given by

$$N(x; \mu, \sigma^2) = \frac{1}{\sigma\sqrt{2\pi}} e^{\frac{1}{2}\left(\frac{x - \mu}{\sigma}\right)^2} \tag{A.16}$$

The standardized normal density function (Figure A-3d), for $\mu = 0$ and $\sigma^2 = 1$, takes the form

$$N(x; 0, 1) = \frac{1}{\sqrt{2\pi}} e^{-\frac{x^2}{2}}$$

(A.17)

As the normal probability density function is a key tool in statistical analysis, areas under the standardized normal density curve—which represent corresponding probabilities—have been tabulated for convenient reference (see Appendix B). Specifically, this tabulation contains the values of

$$\Phi(u) = \frac{1}{\sqrt{2\pi}} \int_{-\infty}^{u} e^{-\frac{x^2}{2}} dx$$

(A.18)

for $u = 0.00, 0.01, 0.02, \ldots$ where

$$u = \frac{x - \mu}{\sigma}$$

(A.19)

Examples of calculating probabilities Φ from the standardized normal density function are shown in Figure A-4.

Other probability density functions (for example, χ^2, t, and F) are important in certain types of data analysis and statistical inference, but less used in finding the probabilities associated with occurrences of the *specific values* of a random variable.

Operating Characteristic (OC) Curve[3]

The OC curve for an attributes plan (sample containing a finite number of countable items) is a graph of the percent defective in the lot p versus the probability P_a that the sampling plan will accept a lot. As p is unknown, a probability must be stated for all of its possible values.

Figure A-5a shows an "ideal" OC curve where it is desired to accept all lots p_c defective or less, and reject all lots having a defect level greater than p_c. All lots less than p_c defective have a probability of acceptance of 1 (certainty); all lots greater than p_c defective have a probability of acceptance 0 (impossibility). In fact, however, some sampling risk always exists as no sampling plan can discriminate perfectly; therefore, the objective is to make the acceptance of good lots much more likely than the acceptance of bad lots.

An acceptance sampling plan basically consists of a sample size n and an acceptance criterion c, which represents the maximum percent defectives allowed

---

[3]Adapted, with permission of the publisher, from *Quality Planning and Analysis* by J. M. Juran and F. M. Gryna, Jr. (New York: McGraw-Hill Book Co., 1980).

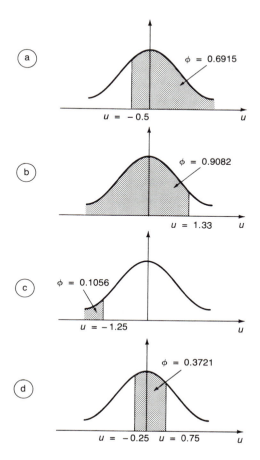

Fig. A-4. Examples of calculating probabilities Φ from the standardized normal probability distribution function.

Source: Reprinted, with permission of the publisher, from *Introduction to Scientific Computing* by G. A. Pall (New York: Appleton-Century-Crofts/Plenum Publishing, 1971).

in the *sample* before the *lot* is rejected. For example, a sample of n is to be randomly selected from a lot. If c defectives or less are found, the lot is accepted; if more than c defectives are found, the lot is rejected. The sample could, since it was drawn from a much larger population, by the laws of chance, contain 0, 1, 2, . . ., n defectives. It is this inherent sampling variation that causes some good lots to be rejected and some bad ones to be accepted.

The generalized OC curve is shown Figure A-5b. Its shape is uniquely determined by n and c. The shaded area at the peak of the curve shows conformance readily accepted by the sampling plan (the probability of rejecting a conforming lot is α); the shaded area under the tail of the curve shows conformance

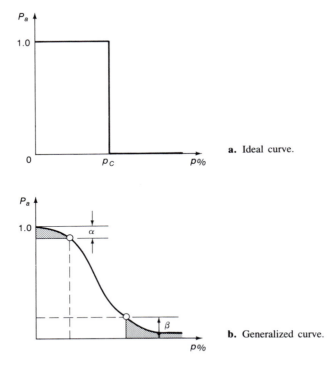

Fig. A-5. Operating characteristic (OC) curve.

readily rejected by the sampling plan (the probability of accepting a nonconforming lot is β).

With the risks thus stated in quantitative form, a judgment can be made on the adequacy of the sampling plan. The OC curve for a specific plan states *only the chance* that a lot having p percent defectives will be accepted by the sampling plan. The OC curve does not (1) predict the conformance of lots; (2) state a confidence level with respect to a specific value of p; or (3) predict the final conformance of lots after all inspections have been completed. (It should be noted that the OC curve is often represented by the Poisson probability distribution.)

APPENDIX B

STATISTICAL TABLES

Table B-1. POISSON PROBABILITIES

x	values of λ								x
	0.1	0.2	0.3	0.4	0.5	0.6	0.7	0.8	
0	0.90484	0.81873	0.74082	0.67032	0.60653	0.54881	0.49659	0.44933	0
1	0.09048	0.16375	0.22225	0.26813	0.30327	0.32929	0.34761	0.35946	1
2	0.00452	0.01637	0.03333	0.05362	0.07581	0.09878	0.12166	0.14379	2
3	0.00015	0.00109	0.00333	0.00115	0.01263	0.01975	0.02838	0.03834	3
4		0.00005	0.00025	0.00071	0.00157	0.00296	0.00496	0.00766	4
5			0.00001	0.00005	0.00015	0.00035	0.00069	0.00122	5
6					0.00001	0.00003	0.00008	0.00020	6
7								0.00001	7
8									8
9									9
10									10

x	values of λ								x
	0.9	1	2	3	4	5	6	7	
0	0.40657	0.36788	0.13534	0.04978	0.01831	0.00673	0.00247	0.00091	0
1	0.36591	0.36788	0.27067	0.14936	0.07326	0.03369	0.01487	0.00638	1
2	0.16466	0.18394	0.27067	0.22404	0.14653	0.08422	0.04461	0.02234	2
3	0.04939	0.06131	0.18045	0.22404	0.19537	0.14037	0.08923	0.05212	3
4	0.01111	0.01532	0.09022	0.16803	0.19537	0.17547	0.13385	0.09122	4
5	0.00200	0.00306	0.03608	0.10082	0.15629	0.17547	0.16062	0.12772	5
6	0.00030	0.00051	0.01203	0.05040	0.10420	0.14622	0.16062	0.14900	6
7	0.00003	0.00007	0.00343	0.02160	0.05954	0.10444	0.13768	0.14900	7
8			0.00085	0.00810	0.02977	0.06527	0.10326	0.13038	8
9			0.00019	0.00270	0.01323	0.03626	0.06883	0.10140	9
10			0.00003	0.00081	0.00529	0.01813	0.04130	0.07098	10
11				0.00022	0.00192	0.00824	0.02252	0.04517	11
12				0.00005	0.00064	0.00343	0.01126	0.02635	12
13				0.00001	0.00019	0.00132	0.00519	0.01418	13
14					0.00005	0.00047	0.00222	0.00709	14
15					0.00001	0.00015	0.00089	0.00331	15
16						0.00004	0.00033	0.00144	16
17						0.00001	0.00011	0.00059	17
18							0.00003	0.00023	18
19							0.00001	0.00008	19
20								0.00002	20

x	values of λ								x
	7	8	9	10	11	12	13	14	
0	0.00091	0.00033	0.00012	0.00004	0.00001				0
1	0.00638	0.00268	0.00111	0.00045	0.00018	0.00007	0.00002	0.00001	1
2	0.02234	0.01073	0.00499	0.00227	0.00101	0.00044	0.00019	0.00008	2
3	0.05212	0.02862	0.01499	0.00756	0.00370	0.00176	0.00082	0.00038	3
4	0.09122	0.05725	0.03373	0.01891	0.01018	0.00530	0.00268	0.00133	4
5	0.12772	0.09160	0.06072	0.03783	0.02241	0.01274	0.00699	0.00372	5
6	0.14900	0.12214	0.09109	0.06305	0.04109	0.02548	0.01515	0.00869	6
7	0.14900	0.13959	0.11712	0.09007	0.06457	0.04368	0.02814	0.01739	7
8	0.13038	0.13959	0.13176	0.11260	0.08879	0.06552	0.04573	0.03043	8
9	0.10140	0.12408	0.13176	0.12511	0.10853	0.08736	0.06605	0.04734	9
10	0.07098	0.09926	0.11858	0.12511	0.11938	0.10484	0.08587	0.06628	10
11	0.04517	0.07219	0.09702	0.11374	0.11938	0.11437	0.10148	0.08435	11
12	0.02635	0.04812	0.07276	0.09478	0.10943	0.11437	0.10994	0.09841	12
13	0.01418	0.02961	0.05037	0.07290	0.09259	0.10557	0.10994	0.10599	13
14	0.00709	0.01692	0.03238	0.05207	0.07275	0.09048	0.10209	0.10599	14
15	0.00331	0.00902	0.01943	0.03471	0.05335	0.07239	0.08847	0.09892	15
16	0.00144	0.00451	0.01093	0.02169	0.03668	0.05429	0.07188	0.08655	16
17	0.00059	0.00212	0.00578	0.01276	0.02373	0.03832	0.05497	0.07128	17
18	0.00023	0.00094	0.00289	0.00709	0.01450	0.02555	0.03970	0.05544	18
19	0.00008	0.00039	0.00137	0.00375	0.00839	0.01613	0.02716	0.04085	19
20	0.00002	0.00015	0.00061	0.00186	0.00461	0.00968	0.01765	0.02859	20
21		0.00006	0.00026	0.00088	0.00241	0.00553	0.01093	0.01906	21
22		0.00002	0.00010	0.00040	0.00120	0.00301	0.00645	0.01213	22
23			0.00004	0.00017	0.00057	0.00157	0.00365	0.00738	23
24			0.00001	0.00007	0.00026	0.00078	0.00197	0.00430	24
25				0.00002	0.00011	0.00037	0.00102	0.00241	25
26				0.00001	0.00004	0.00017	0.00051	0.00129	26
27					0.00002	0.00007	0.00024	0.00067	27
28						0.00003	0.00011	0.00033	28
29						0.00001	0.00005	0.00016	29
30							0.00002	0.00007	30
31								0.00003	31
32								0.00001	32
33									33
34									34
35									35
36									36
37									37
38									38
39									39
40									40

Table B-1 (*continued*)

x	values of λ						x
	15	16	17	18	19	20	
0							0
1							1
2	0.00003	0.00001					2
3	0.00017	0.00007	0.00003				3
4	0.00064	0.00030	0.00014	0.00006	0.00003	0.00001	4
5	0.00193	0.00098	0.00048	0.00023	0.00011	0.00005	5
6	0.00483	0.00262	0.00138	0.00071	0.00036	0.00018	6
7	0.01037	0.00599	0.00337	0.00185	0.00099	0.00052	7
8	0.01944	0.01198	0.00716	0.00416	0.00236	0.00130	8
9	0.03240	0.02131	0.01352	0.00832	0.00498	0.00290	9
10	0.04861	0.03409	0.02300	0.01498	0.00946	0.00581	10
11	0.06628	0.04959	0.03554	0.02452	0.01635	0.01057	11
12	0.08285	0.06612	0.05035	0.03678	0.02588	0.01762	12
13	0.09560	0.08138	0.06584	0.05092	0.03783	0.02711	13
14	0.10244	0.09301	0.07996	0.06548	0.05135	0.03875	14
15	0.10244	0.09921	0.09062	0.07857	0.06504	0.05164	15
16	0.09603	0.09921	0.09628	0.08839	0.07724	0.06456	16
17	0.08473	0.09338	0.09628	0.09359	0.08632	0.07595	17
18	0.07061	0.08300	0.09093	0.09359	0.09112	0.08439	18
19	0.05574	0.06989	0.08136	0.08867	0.09112	0.08883	19
20	0.04181	0.05592	0.06915	0.07980	0.08656	0.08883	20
21	0.02986	0.04260	0.05598	0.06840	0.07832	0.08460	21
22	0.02036	0.03098	0.04326	0.05596	0.06764	0.07691	22
23	0.01328	0.02155	0.03197	0.04380	0.05587	0.06688	23
24	0.00829	0.01437	0.02265	0.03285	0.04423	0.05573	24
25	0.00497	0.00919	0.01540	0.02365	0.03362	0.04458	25
26	0.00287	0.00566	0.01007	0.01637	0.02456	0.03429	26
27	0.00159	0.00335	0.00634	0.01091	0.01728	0.02540	27
28	0.00085	0.00191	0.00384	0.00701	0.01173	0.01814	28
29	0.00044	0.00105	0.00225	0.00435	0.00768	0.01251	29
30	0.00022	0.00056	0.00127	0.00261	0.00486	0.00834	30
31	0.00010	0.00029	0.00070	0.00151	0.00298	0.00538	31
32	0.00005	0.00014	0.00039	0.00085	0.00177	0.00336	32
33	0.00002	0.00007	0.00019	0.00046	0.00102	0.00203	33
34	0.00001	0.00003	0.00009	0.00024	0.00056	0.00119	34
35		0.00001	0.00004	0.00012	0.00030	0.00068	35
36			0.00002	0.00006	0.00016	0.00038	36
37			0.00001	0.00003	0.00008	0.00020	37
38				0.00001	0.00004	0.00010	38
39					0.00002	0.00005	39
40						0.00002	40

Reprinted, with permission of the publisher, from *Introduction to Scientific Computing* by G. A. Pall (New York: Appleton-Century-Crofts/Plenum Publishing, 1971), pp. 194-197.

Table B-2. AREAS UNDER THE STANDARDIZED NORMAL PROBABILITY DENSITY FUNCTION

u	$\Phi(u)$	u	$\Phi(u)$	u	$\Phi(u)$	u	$\Phi(u)$	u	$\Phi(u)$	u	$\Phi(u)$
0.00	0.5000	0.51	0.6950	1.01	0.8438	1.51	0.9345	2.02	0.9783	3.20	0.9993
0.01	0.5040	0.52	0.6985	1.02	0.8461	1.52	0.9357	2.04	0.9793	3.40	0.9996
0.02	0.5080	0.53	0.7019	1.03	0.8485	1.53	0.9370	2.06	0.9803	3.60	0.9998
0.03	0.5120	0.54	0.7054	1.04	0.8508	1.54	0.9382	2.08	0.9812	3.80	0.9999
0.04	0.5160	0.55	0.7088	1.05	0.8531	1.55	0.9394	2.10	0.9821		
0.05	0.5199	0.56	0.7123	1.06	0.8554	1.56	0.9406	2.12	0.9830		
0.06	0.5239	0.57	0.7157	1.07	0.8577	1.57	0.9418	2.14	0.9838		
0.07	0.5279	0.58	0.7190	1.08	0.8599	1.58	0.9429	2.16	0.9846		
0.08	0.5319	0.59	0.7224	1.09	0.8621	1.59	0.9441	2.18	0.9854		
0.09	0.5359	0.60	0.7257	1.10	0.8643	1.60	0.9452	2.20	0.9861		
0.10	0.5398	0.61	0.7291	1.11	0.8665	1.61	0.9463	2.22	0.9868		
0.11	0.5438	0.62	0.7324	1.12	0.8686	1.62	0.9474	2.24	0.9875		
0.12	0.5478	0.63	0.7357	1.13	0.8708	1.63	0.9484	2.26	0.9881		
0.13	0.5517	0.64	0.7389	1.14	0.8729	1.64	0.9495	2.28	0.9887		
0.14	0.5557	0.65	0.7422	1.15	0.8749	1.65	0.9505	2.30	0.9893		
0.15	0.5596	0.66	0.7454	1.16	0.8770	1.66	0.9515	2.32	0.9898		
0.16	0.5636	0.67	0.7486	1.17	0.8790	1.67	0.9525	2.34	0.9904		
0.17	0.5675	0.68	0.7517	1.18	0.8810	1.68	0.9535	2.36	0.9909		
0.18	0.5714	0.69	0.7549	1.19	0.8830	1.69	0.9545	2.38	0.9913		
0.19	0.5753	0.70	0.7580	1.20	0.8849	1.70	0.9554	2.40	0.9918		
0.20	0.5793	0.71	0.7611	1.21	0.8869	1.71	0.9564	2.42	0.9922		
0.21	0.5832	0.72	0.7642	1.22	0.8888	1.72	0.9572	2.44	0.9927		
0.22	0.5871	0.73	0.7673	1.23	0.8907	1.73	0.9582	2.46	0.9931		
0.23	0.5910	0.74	0.7703	1.24	0.8925	1.74	0.9591	2.48	0.9934		
0.24	0.5948	0.75	0.7734	1.25	0.8944	1.75	0.9599	2.50	0.9938		
0.25	0.5967	0.76	0.7764	1.26	0.8962	1.76	0.9608	2.52	0.9941		
0.26	0.6026	0.77	0.7794	1.27	0.8980	1.77	0.9616	2.54	0.9945		
0.27	0.6064	0.78	0.7823	1.28	0.8997	1.78	0.9625	2.56	0.9948		
0.28	0.6103	0.79	0.7853	1.29	0.9015	1.79	0.9633	2.58	0.9951		
0.29	0.6141	0.80	0.7881	1.30	0.9032	1.80	0.9641	2.60	0.9953		
0.30	0.6179	0.81	0.7910	1.31	0.9049	1.81	0.9649	2.62	0.9956		
0.31	0.6217	0.82	0.7939	1.32	0.9066	1.82	0.9656	2.64	0.9959		
0.32	0.6255	0.83	0.7967	1.33	0.9082	1.83	0.9664	2.66	0.9961		
0.33	0.6293	0.84	0.7995	1.34	0.9099	1.84	0.9671	2.68	0.9963		
0.34	0.6331	0.85	0.8023	1.35	0.9115	1.85	0.9678	2.70	0.9965		
0.35	0.6368	0.86	0.8051	1.36	0.9131	1.86	0.9686	2.72	0.9967		
0.36	0.6406	0.87	0.8078	1.37	0.9147	1.87	0.9693	2.74	0.9969		
0.37	0.6443	0.88	0.8106	1.38	0.9162	1.88	0.9699	2.76	0.9971		
0.38	0.6480	0.89	0.8133	1.39	0.9177	1.89	0.9706	2.78	0.9973		
0.39	0.6517	0.90	0.8159	1.40	0.9192	1.90	0.9713	2.80	0.9974		
0.40	0.6554	0.91	0.8186	1.41	0.9207	1.91	0.9719	2.82	0.9976		
0.41	0.6591	0.92	0.8212	1.42	0.9222	1.92	0.9726	2.84	0.9977		
0.42	0.6628	0.93	0.8238	1.43	0.9236	1.93	0.9732	2.86	0.9979		
0.43	0.6664	0.94	0.8264	1.44	0.9251	1.94	0.9738	2.88	0.9980		
0.44	0.6700	0.95	0.8289	1.45	0.9265	1.95	0.9744	2.90	0.9981		
0.45	0.6736	0.96	0.8315	1.46	0.9279	1.96	0.9750	2.92	0.9982		
0.46	0.6772	0.97	0.8340	1.47	0.9292	1.97	0.9756	2.94	0.9984		
0.47	0.6808	0.98	0.8365	1.48	0.9306	1.98	0.9761	2.96	0.9985		
0.48	0.6844	0.99	0.8389	1.49	0.9319	1.99	0.9767	2.98	0.9986		
0.49	0.6879	1.00	0.8413	1.50	0.9332	2.00	0.9772	3.00	0.9986		
0.50	0.6915										

Reprinted, with permission of the publisher, from *Introduction to Scientific Computing* by G. A. Pall (New York: Appleton-Century-Crofts/Plenum Publishing, 1971), p. 205.

APPENDIX C

INTRODUCTION TO CONTROL CHARTS

Control Charts for Variables Data

1. General

Control charts for *variables data* are used when these represent continuous measurements of the process output, such as time, dimensions (as the diameter of a shaft or survey measurements), electrical resistance, and the like.

Variables control charts help the interpretation of process data in terms of both *location* (average) and *spread* (measurement-to-measurement variability). Accordingly, control charts for variables are almost always prepared and analyzed in pairs: one chart for location and the other for spread.

The most commonly used corresponding pair are the $\overline{X}$ and R-charts, where $\overline{X}$ is the *average* of the data values in the sample representing a measure of location, and R is the *range* of values within each sample, representing a measure of spread—the two statistics being observed.

In some cases, the sample standard deviation s is used as a measure of spread; the corresponding control chart is known as an S-chart, and it is used in place of the R-chart in conjunction with $\overline{X}$.

Range charts are developed as measures of process variation because range is easy to calculate and is relatively efficient for small samples. The sample standard deviation s is a somewhat more effective indicator of process variability, especially for larger sample sizes. However, it requires more complex calculations and it is less sensitive in detecting special causes of variation that affect only a single value in a sample. Typically, *S*-charts are used when the recording and calculation of *s* can be automated, or when large sample sizes are available and the more effective measure of variation is appropriate.

In other cases, the median is substituted for the average of the sample, and the corresponding chart is known as a *median chart*. Median charts are alternatives to $\overline{X}$-charts and are sometimes also used as alternatives to the paired use of $\overline{X}$ and *R*-charts. While they lead to similar conclusions, median charts have the following specific advantages over $\overline{X}$ and *R*-charts:

- Ease of use: No requirement for frequent calculations; this can increase work station acceptance of the control chart approach.
- With individual values as well as medians plotted, the median chart shows the spread of process output and thereby gives an ongoing picture of process variation.
- Since both the median and the spread can be shown on a single chart, this can be used to compare the output of several processes, or of the same process at successive intervals.

When only individual readings or measurements are available and process control decisions must be made on these, rather than sample parameters (such as averages and ranges), control charts are constructed on the basis of individual measurements (*x*). While this is done similarly to $\overline{X}$ and *R* charts, it should be noted that charts for individual measurements are not as sensitive to process changes as are $\overline{X}$ and *R*-charts, nor do they isolate the measurement-to-measurement repeatability of the process. Since there is only one individual data item (measurement) per sample, values of the measured process average $(\overline{\overline{X}})$ and the estimate of the standard deviation of the process $(\hat{\sigma})$ can have a substantial variability, even if the process is stable.

2. Control Charts for $\overline{X}$ and R

The most common forms of variables charts are the $\overline{X}$ and *R*-charts. They represent the classic application of control charting to quality control, and they will serve as an example for the use of this powerful technique.

The construction and use of control charts typically comprise these six steps:

(A) Preparations
(B) Data collection
(C) Calculation of control limits
(D) Evaluation for process control
(E) Evaluation for process capability
(F) Process actions

A. PREPARATIONS[1]

A.1. Choose the *parameter* to be charted, with focus on the key factors that are the main contributors to occurring variations. (Priorities can be established by using Pareto analysis.)

A.2. Choose the *type* of control chart. (Table 3-2 provides a comparison of basic forms of control charts: $\overline{X}$, R, p, c, and so on.)

A.3. Provide the system for collecting, and even more importantly, *recording* the data. The methods of measurement and recording, as well as the working environment in which the control chart is used, will determine how data can best be entered on the chart.

B. DATA COLLECTION[2]

The $\overline{X}$ and R-charts are developed, as a pair, from measurements of the particular parameter of the process output chosen under A.1. Measurement data are collected in small samples of constant size, with samples taken at time intervals so as to detect changes in the process over time.

B.1. Choose the *rational sample*. Each point on a control chart represents a sample, consisting of several observations (or other units of data). For best results, samples should be chosen so that units *within a sample* have the greatest likelihood of being alike and units *between samples* are most likely to be different. Sample size should be kept small, approximately five individual units or measurements. The total number of samples should satisfy two criteria: (1) from a process standpoint, the number of samples should be sufficiently large to allow major sources of variation to appear; (2) from a statistical viewpoint, 20 or more samples (100 or more individual measurements) will provide a satisfactory test for stability and, for a stable process, good estimates of process capability.

B.2. Construct the *control charts*. The $\overline{X}$ and R-charts are arranged with the former above the latter (Figure C-1). In the data section, successive samples are recorded in consecutive vertical columns, with the computed values of $\overline{X}$ and R for each sample entered last. In the respective charts, the values of $\overline{X}$ and R are plotted along a vertical scale. These two characteristics are calculated for each sample:

$$\overline{X} = \frac{X_1 + X_2 + \ldots X_n}{n}$$

$$(C.1)$$

where X_1, X_2, . . . are individual measurements in each sample and n is the number of measurements in the sample.

---

[1]Adapted, with permission of the publisher, from *Quality Planning and Analysis* by J. M. Juran and F. M. Gryna, Jr. (New York: McGraw-Hill Book Co., 1980).

[2]Adapted, with permission of the publisher, from *Quality Planning and Analysis* by J. M. Juran and F. M. Gryna, Jr. (New York: McGraw-Hill Book Co., 1980).

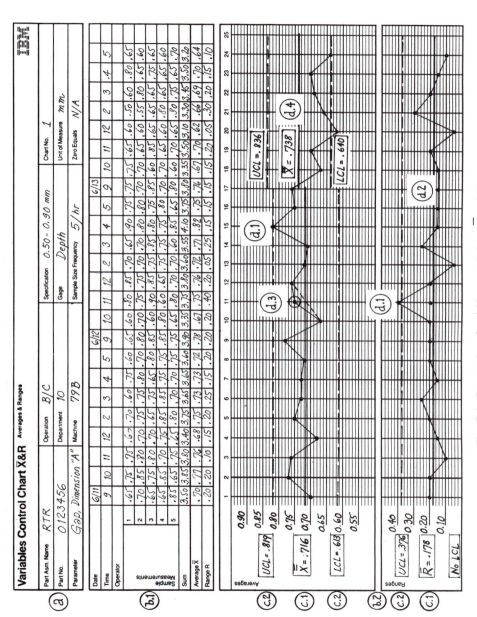

Fig. C-1. Construction of variables control chart ($\bar{X}$ and R).

Step a. Preparations. **Step b.** Data collection. **Step c.** Calculation of control limits. **Step d.** Evaluation for process control.

The sample averages $\overline{X}$ and ranges R are plotted, as individual points, on their respective charts.

C. CALCULATION OF CONTROL LIMITS[3]

C.1. Establish the *center line* to be used and the statistical basis for calculating the *control limits*. The center line may be the average of all measurement data—the process average $\overline{\overline{X}}$—or the process range, $\overline{R}$, for the study period, calculated as

$$\overline{\overline{X}} = \frac{\overline{X}_1 + \overline{X}_2 + \ldots + \overline{X}_k}{k} \qquad (C.2)$$

$$\overline{R} = \frac{R_1 + R_2 + \ldots + R_k}{k} \qquad (C.3)$$

where $\overline{X}_i$ and R_i are the average and the range of the ith sample, respectively, and k is the number of samples taken during the study period.

C.2. Calculate the *control limits*. These limits are usually set at $\pm 3\sigma$ (where σ is the standard deviation of the process), but other multiples may be chosen for different statistical risks.

Since computing the process standard deviation can be quite cumbersome, shortcut methods have been developed to avoid the need for its calculation. (Control limit formulas for the basic types of control charts are given in Table 3-2 and in the material following. For values of a and d, see Table C-1. The corresponding, generalized control chart layout for averages—$\overline{X}$—is given in Figure C-2.)

Upper and lower control limits for the *range chart*:

$$UCL = d_4 \overline{R} \qquad (C.4)$$

$$LCL = d_3 \overline{R} \qquad (C.5)$$

Table C-1. CONSTANTS FOR CONTROL LIMIT FORMULAS

					n				
	2	3	4	5	6	7	8	9	10
d_4	3.27	2.57	2.28	2.11	2.00	1.92	1.86	1.82	1.78
d_3						0.08	0.14	0.18	0.22
d_2	1.13	1.69	2.06	2.33	2.53	2.70	2.85	2.97	3.08
a_2	1.88	1.02	0.73	0.58	0.48	0.42	0.37	0.34	0.31

[3]Adapted, with permission of the publisher, from *Quality Planning and Analysis* by J. M. Juran and F. M. Gryna, Jr. (New York: McGraw-Hill Book Co., 1980).

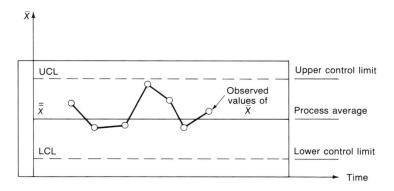

Fig. C-2. Generalized layout of control chart for averages $(\overline{X})$.

Source: Adapted, with permission of the publisher, from *Quality Planning and Analysis* by J. M. Juran and F. M. Gryna, Jr. (New York: McGraw-Hill Book Co., 1980).

Upper and lower control limits for the *averages chart*:

$$UCL = \overline{\overline{X}} + a_2\overline{R} \qquad (C.6)$$

$$LCL = \overline{\overline{X}} - a_2\overline{R} \qquad (C.7)$$

where d_4, d_3, and a_2 are constants which depend on the sample size n (Table C-1).

D. EVALUATION FOR PROCESS CONTROL

The objective of control chart analysis is to establish whether the process variability (ranges), the process average, or both are out of statistical control (not operating at a constant level), and to cause appropriate corrective action. The R and $\overline{X}$-charts are analyzed separately, but both analyses follow essentially the same pattern:

D.1 *Points beyond control limits.* Since points beyond either control limit would be rare if only variations from common causes were present, the presence of one or more points beyond the control limits signals an out-of-control situation at that point—for example, the appearance of a special cause. This in turn calls for an immediate analysis of the operation to identify and then eliminate that cause.

D.2 *Patterns or trends.* The presence of unusual trends or patterns can signal an out-of-control situation or a change in the process, even when both process variability and averages are within control limits. On the other hand, certain patterns or trends can be evidence of favorable process conditions, which could provide a basis for permanent improvement to the process. Of the many possible patterns and trends, *runs* usually signal the appearance of special causes of variation.

A simple method for the evaluation of runs on control charts[4] is:

Divide each of the two areas between the center line and the respective control limits into three equal zones (Figure C-3). Since the control limits are at $\pm 3\sigma$ from the center line, each zone will be *one* standard deviation wide. Instability in the process is indicated by any one of the following conditions:

a. A single point falls outside the $\pm 3\sigma$ limit (beyond Zone A).

b. Two out of three successive points fall in Zone A or beyond.

c. Four out of five successive points fall in Zone B or beyond.

d. Eight successive points fall in Zone C or beyond.

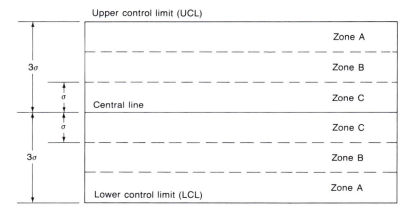

Fig. C-3. Layout of control chart zones for run evaluation.

Source: Adapted, with permission of the publisher, from *Quality Planning and Analysis* by J. M. Juran and F. M. Gryna, Jr. (New York: McGraw-Hill Book Co., 1980).

D.3 *Correction of special causes.* For each evidence of a special cause an analysis of the process is conducted (defect elimination cycle) to determine the cause of variation. Corrective action is taken as appropriate.

D.4. *Recalculation and extension of control limits.* Since correction of special causes may mean the dropping of samples representing unstable conditions, the control limits should be recalculated once all special causes have been eliminated.

When moving to cover future process operations, or to adjust central lines and control limits for a new sample size, control limits are extended for ongoing control as follows:

---

[4]Adapted, with permission of the publisher, from *Quality Planning and Analysis* by J. M. Juran and F. M. Gryna, Jr. (New York: McGraw-Hill Book Co., 1980), pp. 340–341.

(a) Using the existing sample size, the process standard deviation, $\hat{\sigma}$, is estimated by the formula

$$\hat{\sigma} = \frac{\overline{R}}{d_2}$$

(C.8)

where $\overline{R}$ is the average of sample ranges (for cases of statistical control) and d_2 is a constant varying with sample size (Table C-1).

(b) Using the constants d_2, d_3, d_4 and a_2, we calculate the new process range $\overline{R}$ and new control limits, based on the new sample size.
(c) The new control limits are plotted on both charts as the basis for ongoing process control.

The key steps of control chart analysis, as we have just summarized, are illustrated in Figure C-1.

E. EVALUATION FOR PROCESS CAPABILITY

Once the process is brought under statistical control, the question still remains whether it is *capable*—that is, does the process produce conforming output? Process capability reflects variation from common causes, and management action on the process is almost always required for process capability improvement.

The estimate of the process standard deviation $\hat{\sigma}$, calculated for the stable process, can be used for evaluating process capability.

F. PROCESS ACTIONS

They provide specific instructions on (a) the interpretation of results and (b) actions to be taken, based on those results, and by whom.

Control Charts for Attribute Data

Attribute-type data (also known as binary data) can assume only two values: conforming/nonconforming, go/no-go, pass/fail, present/absent, on/off, true/false, and the like. They are countable for recording and further analysis. Other examples can be of measurable characteristics, where the results are recorded in a binary fashion, such as the conformance of a dimension when measured on a go/no-go gauge, conformance of a measurement to tolerance limits, on-time delivery performance, and the like.

Control charts for attribute data are valuable in process management for the following reasons:

- Attribute-type situations exist universally in any type of process and their use can, in fact, help the development of consistent process management practices across the board.[5]

---

[5]The "zero defect" movement is conceptually based on converting all observations and measurements into attributes-type data and conformance/nonconformance decisions.

- The gathering and recording of attribute data are relatively simple and inexpensive procedures, requiring few or no specialized skills.
- Data gathered and compiled for management reporting and decision making are in most cases presented in attribute form. Further benefits can be derived from the application of control chart analysis to these data. Because control chart analysis offers the ability to distinguish variation from special and common causes, attributes control charts are especially helpful in supporting recommendations for management action.
- The efficient use of control charts calls for their application to high-priority problem areas where they can provide most of the leverage. The use of attributes control charts, along with other prioritization tools (such as Pareto analysis), can often point to the specific subprocesses that will need further examination and analysis—including the potential use of variables control charts and other statistical tools.

The four major types of attributes control charts are:

(1) The p-chart for proportion (percentage) of units not conforming, from samples of variable size.

(2) The np-chart for number of units not conforming, from samples of constant size.

(3) The c-chart for number of nonconformances (defects), from samples of constant size.

(4) The u-chart for number of nonconformances per unit, from samples of variable size.

It should be noted again that any statistical method will fail unless management has created a controllable and responsive process environment. Accordingly, unless properly analyzed by appropriately trained, knowledgeable personnel in a timely manner, the value of control charts can be nullified.

BIBLIOGRAPHY

1. AMERICAN NATIONAL STANDARDS INSTITUTE. *Guide for Quality Control and Control Chart Method for Analyzing Data* (ASQC Standards B1-1958 and B2-1958/ANSI Z1.1-195) snd Z1.2-1958, revised 1975). Milwaukee, WI: American Society for Quality Control.

2. AMERICAN NATIONAL STANDARDS INSTITUTE. *Control Chart Method of Controlling Quality During Production* (ASQC Standard B3-1958/ANSI Z1.3-1958, revised 1975). Milwaukee, WI: American Society for Quality Control.

3. AMERICAN SOCIETY FOR QUALITY CONTROL. *Glossary and Tables for Statistical Quality Control*. Milwaukee, WI: American Society for Quality Control, 1983.

4. AMERICAN SOCIETY FOR TESTING MATERIALS. *Manual on Presentation of Data and Control Chart Analysis* (STP-15D). Philadelphia, PA: American Society for Testing Materials, 1976.

5. BARRA, RALPH. *Putting Quality Circles to Work*. New York, NY: McGraw-Hill Book Co., 1983.

6. BURRILL, CLAUDE W., and LEON L. ELLSWORTH. *Quality Data Processing*. Tenafly, NJ: Burrill-Ellsworth Associates, Inc., 1982.

7. CHARBONNEAU, HARVEY C., and GORDON L. WEBSTER. *Industrial Quality Control*. Englewood Cliffs, NJ: Prentice-Hall, Inc., 1978.

8. CROSBY, PHILIP B. *Quality is Free*. New York, NY: The New American Library, Inc., 1979.

9. ———. *Quality Without Tears*. New York, NY: McGraw-Hill Book Co., 1984.

10. DEMING, W. EDWARDS. *Quality, Productivity, and Competitive Position*. Massachusetts Institute of Technology, Center for Advanced Engineering Study, 1982.

11. DUNCAN, ACHESON J. *Quality Control and Industrial Statistics*, 4th ed. Homewood, IL: Richard D. Irwin, Inc., 1974.

12. EDOSOMWAN, JOHNSON A. *Integrating Productivity and Quality Management*. New York, NY: Marcel Dekker, 1987.

13. FEIGENBAUM, ARMAND V. *Total Quality Control*, 3rd ed. New York, NY: McGraw-Hill Book Co., 1983.

14. GRANT, EUGENE L., and RICHARD S. LEAVENWORTH, *Statistical Quality Control*, 5th ed. New York, NY: McGraw-Hill Book Co., 1980.

15. GROOCOCK, JOHN B. *The Chain of Quality: Market Dominance Through Product Superiority*. New York, NY: John Wiley and Sons, 1986.

16. HARRINGTON, H. JAMES. *The Improvement Process*. New York, NY: McGraw-Hill Book Co., 1987.

17. INGLE, S. *Quality Circles Master Guide*. Englewood Cliffs, NJ: Prentice-Hall, Inc., 1982.

18. ISHIKAWA, KAORU. *Guide to Quality Control*, rev. ed. Tokyo: Asian Productivity Organization, 1976.

19. JURAN, J. M., and FRANK M. GRYNA, Jr. *Quality Planning and Analysis*, 2nd ed. New York, NY: McGraw-Hill Book Co., 1980.

20. ———, FRANK M. GRYNA, Jr., and R. S. BINGHAM, Jr. *Quality Control Handbook*, 3rd ed. New York, NY: McGraw-Hill Book Co., 1979.

21. ———. *Planning for Quality*. Wilton, CT: Juran Institute, Inc., 1986.

22. MONTGOMERY, DOUGLAS C. *Introduction to Statistical Quality Control*. New York, NY: John Wiley & Sons, Inc., 1985.

23. OTT, ELLIS R. *Process Quality Control*. New York, NY: McGraw-Hill Book Co., 1975.

24. OUCHI, WILLIAM G. *Theory Z*. Reading, MA: Addison-Wesley Publishing Company, Inc., 1981.

25. PALL, GABRIEL A. *Introduction to Scientific Computing*. New York, NY: Appleton-Century-Crofts, 1971.

26. PETERS, THOMAS J., and ROBERT H. WATERMAN, Jr. *In Search of Excellence*. New York, NY: Warner Books, Inc., 1982.

27. ———, and NANCY K. AUSTIN. *A Passion for Excellence*. New York, NY: Random House, Inc., 1985.

28. ROBSON, MICHAEL. *Quality Circles, A Practical Guide*. Aldershot, Hunts, England: Gower Publishing, 1984.

29. ROSS, JOEL E., and WILLIAM ROSS. *Japanese Quality Circles and Productivity*. Reston, VA: Reston Publishing, Inc., 1982.

30. SCHULTZ, WILLIAM J. *Process Control, Capability and Improvement*. Southbury, CT: The Quality Institute, IBM Corporation, 1984.

31. SHEWHART, W. A. *The Economics of Control of Quality of Manufactured Product.* New York, NY: D. Van Nostrand Company, Inc., 1931.

32. SQUIRE, FRANK H. *Successful Quality Management.* Wheaton, IL: Hitchcock Publishing, Inc., 1980.

33. THUROW, LESTER C. *The Zero-Sum Solution.* New York, NY: Simon and Schuster, Inc., 1985.

34. TOWNSEND, PATRICK, L., and JOHN E. GEBHARDT. *Commit to Quality.* New York, NY: John Wiley & Sons, Inc., 1986.

35. WESTERN ELECTRIC COMPANY. *Statistical Quality Control Handbook.* Indianapolis, IN: Western Electric Co., Inc., 1956.

INDEX

The references are to pages in the text. Page numbers for formal definitions are in *italics* references to illustrations (figures or tables) are printed in **boldface** type.